WAKING FROM THE DUST

WAKING FROM THE DUST

Daniel 12:2 and

Resurrection Hope

in Biblical Theology

MITCHELL L. CHASE

STUDIES IN
**SCRIPTURE
& BIBLICAL**
THEOLOGY

Waking from the Dust: Daniel 12:2 and Resurrection Hope in Biblical Theology
Studies in Scripture and Biblical Theology

Copyright 2026 Mitchell L. Chase

Lexham Academic, an imprint of Lexham Press
1331 Commercial St., Bellingham, WA 98225
LexhamPress.com

You may use brief quotations from this resource in presentations, articles, and books. For all other uses, please write Lexham Press for permission. Email us at permissions@lexhampress.com.

Unless otherwise noted, Scripture quotations are the author's own translation. Scripture quotations marked (ESV) are from ESV® Bible (The Holy Bible, English Standard Version®), copyright © 2001 by Crossway Bibles, a publishing ministry of Good News Publishers. Used by permission. All rights reserved.

Print ISBN 9781683598787
Digital ISBN 9781683598794
Library of Congress Control Number 2025945600

Lexham Editorial: Derek Brown, Elliot Ritzema, Robert Hand, Katy Smith,
    Kelley Mathews, Lynsey Stepan, Mandi Newell
Cover Design: Fanny Palacios
Typesetting: Abigail Stocker

25 26 27 28 29 30 31 / US / 12 11 10 9 8 7 6 5 4 3 2 1

*I dedicate this book to Stephen Dempster,
whose writings have helped me hope in the Lord of life*

Contents

List of Abbreviations xi
Acknowledgments xv
Preface xvii

1. Laying a Foundation 1
   Thesis 1
   Methodology 2
   Preliminary Issues 10
   Conclusion 23

2. Reading Daniel 12:2 in Context 24
   Introduction 24
   The Structure of Daniel 24
   Stories of Rescue and Judgment in the Book of Daniel Before 12:2 26
   The Meaning of Daniel 12:2 32
   Conclusion 48

3. Resurrection Hope before Daniel 12:2 50
   The Law 51
   The Prophets 82
   The Writings 106
   Conclusion 124

4. The Influence of Daniel 12:2 on Intertestamental Literature 127
   Daniel 12:2 in the Psuedepigrapha 128
   Daniel 12:2 in the Apocrypha 143
   Conclusion 147

5. The Use of Daniel 12:2 in the New Testament 148
   The Gospels and Acts 149
   The Epistles and Revelation 167
   Conclusion 187

Conclusion 189
Bibliography 193
Subject & Author Index 207
Scripture Index 221

List of Abbreviations

AB	Anchor Bible Commentary
ANE	Ancient Near East
AOTC	Apollos Old Testament Commentary
Apoc. Mos.	Apocalypse of Moses
AusBR	*Australian Biblical Review*
BAGD	*A Greek-English Lexicon of the New Testament and Other Early Christian Literature*
BCOT	Baker Commentary on the Old Testament
BECNT	Baker Exegetical Commentary on the New Testament
Bib	*Biblica*
BNTC	Black's New Testament Commentary
BSac	*Bibliotheca Sacra*
CBQ	*Catholic Biblical Quarterly*
CEJL	Commentaries on Early Jewish Literature
DJG	*Dictionary of Jesus and the Gospels*
DOTP	*Dictionary of the Old Testament: Pentateuch*
EBTC	Evangelical Biblical Theology Commentary
1 En.	1 Enoch
ExAud	*Ex Auditu*
HALOT	*The Hebrew and Aramaic Lexicon of the Old Testament*
HervTS	*Hervormde Teologiese Studies*
ICC	International Critical Commentary
Int	*Interpretation*
JBL	*Journal of Biblical Literature*

JBQ	*Jewish Bible Quarterly*
JETS	*Journal of the Evangelical Theological Society*
JR	*The Journal of Religion*
JSNT	*Journal for the Study of the New Testament*
JSOT	*Journal for the Study of the Old Testament*
JSOTSup	*Journal for the Study of the Old Testament-Supplement Series*
JSP	*Journal for the Study of the Pseudepigrapha*
JTS	*Journal of Theological Studies*
Jub.	Jubilees
KJV	King James Version
LQ	*Lutheran Quarterly*
LXX	Septuagint
m. Sanh.	Mishnah Sanhedrin
2 Macc.	2 Maccabees
MBC	The Mellen Biblical Commentary
MT	Masoretic Text
NAC	The New American Commentary
NASB	New American Standard Bible
NDBT	*New Dictionary of Biblical Theology*
NIBC	New International Biblical Commentary
NICNT	New International Commentary on the New Testament
NICOT	New International Commentary on the Old Testament
NIGTC	The New International Greek Testament Commentary
NIVAC	The NIV Application Commentary
NovTSup	Novum Testamentum, Supplements
NSBT	New Studies in Biblical Theology
NT	New Testament
NTL	New Testament Library
OG	Old Greek Version of the Book of Daniel
OT	Old Testament
OTL	Old Testament Library

OTS	*Oudtestamentische Studiën*
PNTC	The Pillar New Testament Commentary
Pss. Sol.	Psalms of Solomon
PTW	Preaching the Word
RB	*Revue biblique*
SBJT	The Southern Baptist Journal of Theology
Sib. Or.	Sibylline Oracles
ST	*Studia Theologica*
T. Benj.	Testament of Benjamin
T. Jud.	Testament of Judah
T. Mos.	Testament of Moses
T. Zeb.	Testament of Zebulun
TDNT	*Theological Dictionary of the New Testament*
Th	Theodotion Translation of the Book of Daniel
TOTC	Tyndale Old Testament Commentaries
TynBul	*Tyndale Bulletin*
VT	*Vetus Testamentum*
VTSup	Vetus Testamentum, Supplements
WBC	Word Biblical Commentary
Wis.	Wisdom of Solomon
WTJ	*Westminster Theological Journal*
ZAW	*Zeitschrift für die Alttestamentliche Wissenschaft*
ZECNT	Zondervan Exegetical Commentary on the New Testament

Acknowledgments

A writing project flourishes most in the context of a community because support, encouragement, and feedback lead to the best results on a printed page. The book you are holding is a revised and updated version of my dissertation, and the marks of community are all over it. I completed my PhD in Biblical Studies at The Southern Baptist Theological Seminary in 2013 under the supervision of James M. Hamilton Jr. He was an enthusiastic supporter of the project, and I value his mentorship and influence in my life to this day.

In addition to Jim Hamilton, my doctoral committee consisted of Peter Gentry, Robert Plummer, and Stephen Dempster—all men I hold in high esteem and whose scholarship has deeply blessed me. I appreciated their feedback, and it strengthened the arguments of this work. During my time as a doctoral student, my classmates in the program engaged the topic of resurrection hope with me in both formal and informal settings, and these conversations stimulated, challenged, and clarified the direction of my research and writing.

I completed my dissertation in 2013 while serving as the Preaching Pastor of Kosmosdale Baptist Church in Louisville, and I am blessed to be with these dear saints to this very day. Their support of my writing is something I do not take for granted. As with my preaching, so with my publications: I want to faithfully handle the Word of God for the edification of his people.

My wife, Stacie, and I have been married twenty years, and throughout these years she has been a private and public encourager of my work. Writing takes hours, and rewriting takes hours more, so I am thankful to God for his great kindness in bringing Stacie into my life. She truly makes the writing task easier because she makes life joyful.

I'm honored for this book to be part of Lexham's Studies in Scripture & Biblical Theology series. They are a publisher doing excellent work to serve the church, and I'm grateful for their interest in my project. Derek Brown, in particular, has blessed me with his support.

Preface

The aim of this project is to understand not only what Daniel 12:2 means but also to answer two major questions: how did the resurrection conviction in Daniel 12:2 arise, and what influence did Daniel 12:2 have on later writings?

In order to bring my arguments up to date, I have revised my 2013 dissertation to include recent publications on the topic. And to make this project as accessible as possible, I have made structural and organizational changes that I hope will serve readers well.

I remain convinced of my arguments from 2013, and I hope you will consider them carefully as, Lord willing, we press onward to worship and delight in the risen Jesus, who shall return in power and glory to empty the graves. With the cloud of witnesses who have gone before us, we "look for the resurrection of the dead, and the life of the world to come. Amen."

1

Laying a Foundation

THESIS

The final vision in the book of Daniel (10:1–12:3) concludes with a promise of vindication and judgment: "And many of those who sleep in the dust of the earth shall awake, some to everlasting life, and some to shame and everlasting contempt" (12:2).[1] Scholars dispute the dual promise in Daniel 12:2 with regard to its date, author, meaning, and connection to other literature, but most agree that the verse is about bodily resurrection and that it influences subsequent nonbiblical and biblical literature.

Some scholars consider Daniel 12:2 to be the first Old Testament prediction of individual bodily resurrection in Scripture and deny that such hope appears any earlier.[2] If the teaching of bodily resurrection occurs first in that verse, without significant precursors, then such hope is a radical innovation in the biblical worldview.

The future resurrection unto everlasting life for some and everlasting contempt for others in Daniel 12:2 is a promise unique in the Old Testament, for no earlier biblical text makes such an explicit statement about the respective resurrected fates of the righteous and the wicked.[3] But instead of seeing Daniel 12:2 as a sudden intrusion into the theology of the Old Testament, what if earlier biblical authors had been cultivating and (in their own way) asserting the concept of resurrection hope?

According to N. T. Wright, "Nobody doubts that the Old Testament speaks of the resurrection of the dead, but nobody can agree on what it

---

1. Translations are from the English Standard Version, unless otherwise indicated.
2. See, e.g., John J. Collins, *Encounters with Biblical Theology* (Minneapolis: Fortress, 2005), 28, 32; Lloyd Bailey, *Biblical Perspectives on Death* (Philadelphia: Fortress, 1979), 73.
3. This sentence is true whether scholars date the book of Daniel in the sixth or second century BC.

means, where the idea came from, or how it relates to the other things the scriptures say about the dead."[4] What if the author of Daniel 12:2 relied on earlier biblical material to express, in the clearest sense to that point in the works of the biblical authors, the future bodily resurrection of all people?

This project seeks to show that Daniel relied on earlier Old Testament texts and theological convictions when he expressed the hope of bodily resurrection, and his expression informed and shaped subsequent nonbiblical and biblical authors. I will now unpack the methodology used in subsequent chapters to demonstrate this thesis.

METHODOLOGY

This investigation will show the importance of Daniel 12:2 as the culminating expression of bodily resurrection in the Law, Prophets, and Writings. Authors in the intertestamental and New Testament eras show its influence on them. During these periods "there was a growing emphasis on the resurrection of the dead,"[5] and the effect of Daniel 12:2 on subsequent literature is acknowledged by scholars well versed in the intertestamental and New Testament books.[6] The use of this verse in such literature—especially the New Testament—will be explored with an aim for comprehensiveness.

The exploration of relevant texts takes into account four methodological issues: (1) the practice of later biblical authors using earlier ones, (2) the incorporation of nonbiblical literature into a project of biblical theology, (3) the observation of particular textual features that suggest the presence of resurrection hope, and (4) the use of the tripartite division as the preferred Old Testament order for exploring the passages therein.

LATER BIBLICAL AUTHORS USING EARLIER BIBLICAL AUTHORS

How the New Testament uses the Old Testament is a subject of vast debate. Add to this the question of how later Old Testament documents used earlier ones, and the complexities increase. The literature and

---

4. N. T. Wright, *The Resurrection of the Son of God*, Christian Origins and the Question of God, vol. 3 (Philadelphia: Fortress, 2003), 108.
5. Edwin Yamauchi, "Life, Death, and the Afterlife in the Ancient Near East," in *Life in the Face of Death: The Resurrection Message of the New Testament*, ed. Richard N. Longenecker (Grand Rapids: Eerdmans, 1998), 46.
6. See chaps. 4 and 5.

perspectives on this subject are varied and extend beyond the scope of this project,[7] but I will unpack my conclusions that serve as presuppositions for the later chapters.

The debate is not centered on whether later Scripture uses earlier Scripture but whether the later Scripture interprets the earlier in line with the original meaning.[8] Beginning with the New Testament use of the Old Testament, I believe the New Testament does not violate or contradict the original meaning of the texts it uses. In light of progressive revelation—moving from the Old Testament to the New Testament— the Old Testament passages undergo an organic expansion,[9] a development best pictured like the growth of an "acorn to an oak tree, a bud to a flower, or a seed to an apple."[10] This development means that the Old Testament meaning is enhanced and clarified by its use in subsequent Old Testament and New Testament texts.

What the Old Testament authors understood was true, though not exhaustive. Progressive and canonical revelation unfolds, builds on, and unravels the layers of compacted meaning in earlier texts.[11] The implications of this process are significant because the worldview of the biblical authors is the result of earlier texts wielding profound influence. They saw their lives in light of, and they interpreted events through a lens shaped by, the Scriptures they knew.[12] As Dempster observes, "There is an exceedingly rich intertextuality in which there are many *linguistic* and *conceptual* echoes throughout Scripture. Later

---

7. See the bibliographies in G. K. Beale, *Handbook on the New Testament Use of the Old Testament: Exegesis and Interpretation* (Grand Rapids: Baker Academic, 2012), 149–62; Beale, ed., *The Right Doctrine from the Wrong Texts: Essays on the Use of the Old Testament in the New* (Grand Rapids: Baker Books, 1994), 405–14. Also G. K. Beale and D. A. Carson, *Commentary on the New Testament Use of the Old Testament*, ed. G. K. Beale and D. A. Carson (Grand Rapids: Baker Academic, 2007); Stanley E. Porter, ed., *Hearing the Old Testament in the New Testament* (Grand Rapids: Eerdmans, 2006); Richard B. Hays, *Echoes of Scripture in the Letters of Paul* (New Haven, CT: Yale University Press, 1989); Thomas R. Schreiner, *New Testament Theology: Magnifying God in Christ* (Grand Rapids: Baker Academic, 2008).
8. Beale, *Handbook on the New Testament Use of the Old Testament*, 1.
9. Beale, *Handbook on the New Testament Use of the Old Testament*, 27.
10. J. M. Compton, "Shared Intentions? Reflections on Inspiration and Interpretation in Light of Scripture's Dual Authorship," *Themelios* 33 (2008): 30–31.
11. Beale, *Handbook on the New Testament Use of the Old Testament*, 27.
12. James M. Hamilton Jr., *God's Glory in Salvation through Judgment: A Biblical Theology* (Wheaton, IL: Crossway, 2010), 42.

biblical books consciously echo and imitate events, concepts and language found in earlier books."[13]

The task of biblical theology is of chief significance to this project because I will explore how Daniel 12:2 is built on earlier Scripture and how it influenced later authors. Biblical theology is concerned with understanding a passage of Scripture by paying attention to the literary, redemptive, and canonical contours of Scripture. Interpreters are doing biblical theology when they seek to follow the textual path of the biblical authors. That path extends from Genesis to Revelation, and Scripture's overarching story sheds light on particular passages along the way.

In this project I will show how the biblical authors transferred a hope of resurrection from the Torah through the Prophets down to the book of Daniel. And the transference went further still. "The purpose, structure and content of OT theology lie behind the major theological themes of the NT,"[14] and, being immersed in the worldview of the Old Testament authors, the New Testament authors knew, relied on, and used the Danielic appropriation of resurrection hope.

An indispensable assumption in understanding biblical theology this way—later biblical authors using earlier ones—is the unity and continuity of Scripture's story (though this does not exclude the presence of diversity as well).[15] The biblical text sustains a metanarrative from Genesis to Revelation.[16] This metanarrative consists of different books written by various authors, all of whom a divine author guided to tell the purposes of God from creation to consummation.[17] One such purpose of God is to accomplish the death of death.

THE INCORPORATION OF NONBIBLICAL LITERATURE

In order to thoroughly explore the influence of Daniel 12:2 on later literature, it is important to address works written prior to the New

---

13. Stephen G. Dempster, *Dominion and Dynasty: A Theology of the Hebrew Bible*, NSBT, vol. 15 (Downers Grove, IL: InterVarsity Press, 2003), 31-32, emphasis mine.
14. C. A. Evans, "New Testament use of the Old Testament," in *NDBT* (Downers Grove, IL: InterVarsity Press, 2000), 79.
15. For a brief reflection on the unity and diversity of Scripture, see C. L. Blomberg, "The Unity and Diversity of Scripture," in *NDBT*, 64-72.
16. For a brief summary of the Bible in terms of *creation, fall, redemption,* and *restoration*, see Hamilton, *God's Glory in Salvation through Judgment*, 49-51.
17. Hamilton, *God's Glory in Salvation through Judgment*, 64.

Testament. During the intertestamental era, there are works that used Daniel 12:2 both to warn the wicked and to encourage the righteous.[18]

We will analyze the influence of our key text on Jubilees, the Psalms of Solomon, the Sibylline Oracles, the Apocalypse of Moses, the Testament of Moses, 1 Enoch, the Testaments of the Twelve Patriarchs, the Wisdom of Solomon, and 2 Maccabees—writings that allude to Daniel 12 in order to hold out hope for Israel's liberation from pagan oppression, for the righteous to have a newly embodied existence, and for the wicked to be judged by Israel's God.[19] While not every Jewish group (e.g., the Sadducees) or extant Jewish text articulated a resurrection hope, many texts attest to a clear and strong belief in individual resurrection.[20]

Since intertestamental literature forms a historical bridge from the Old Testament to the New, an analysis of certain works will reveal that Daniel 12:2 wielded influence long before the first-century New Testament writings. While I do not grant divine inspiration or divine authority to the intertestamental works, they will help establish the importance of Daniel 12:2 prior to the New Testament era.

According to Beale and Carson, intertestamental sources help us see (1) how Old Testament texts were understood by sources roughly coterminous with the New, (2) how Jewish authorities were sometimes divided in their interpretation of certain Old Testament passages, (3) how some readings in early Judaism provide a foil for early Christian readings, (4) how the language of early Judaism may closely parallel the language of the New Testament because of chronological and cultural proximity and not necessarily because of direct literary dependence, and (5) how New Testament writers sometimes display direct dependence on intertestamental sources.[21]

Therefore, incorporating nonbiblical sources in a biblical-theological project will be useful insofar as it serves my thesis. I will only address the intertestamental works that show influence from Daniel 12:2.

---

18. Important for seeing many of these connections is George W. Nickelsburg, *Resurrection, Immortality, and Eternal Life in Intertestamental Judaism*, Harvard Theological Studies 26 (Cambridge, MA: Harvard University Press; London: Oxford University Press, 1972), 28; Steve Delamarter, *A Scripture Index to Charlesworth's* The Old Testament Pseudepigrapha (New York: Sheffield Academic Press, 2002), 35, 89.
19. Wright, *The Resurrection of the Son of God*, 150–62.
20. Wright, *The Resurrection of the Son of God*, 201.
21. G. K. Beale and D. A. Carson, "Introduction," in *Commentary on the New Testament Use of the Old Testament*, xxiv.

Verbal connections or clear conceptual links will be the criteria in determining such influence.

CRITERIA OF VERBAL LINKS, IMAGERY, AND THEOLOGICAL CONVICTIONS

Since part of this project's goal is to show the dependence of Daniel 12:2 on earlier Old Testament writings, three kinds of criteria will illuminate the presence of resurrection hope prior to Daniel 12:2: (1) verbal links between Daniel 12:2 and earlier texts, (2) imagery of resurrection in passages preceding Daniel 12:2, and (3) theological convictions shared by Daniel and earlier biblical authors. Elaboration is needed for each criterion.

Verbal links, or linguistic connections, involve verbs or nouns that tie Daniel 12:2 lexically to earlier biblical texts. Certain words or phrases appear repeatedly in resurrection passages, and their use will prove instrumental in identifying passages of resurrection hope, especially in connecting later passages with earlier ones.[22] Later authors may *quote*, *allude to*, or *echo* earlier ones.[23] If lexical links are present between

---

22. In "Hebrew Words for Resurrection," *VT* 23 (1973): 220, J. F. A. Sawyer lists eight Hebrew words that in some contexts denote bodily resurrection. About such verbs Leonard Greenspoon says, "It is essentially through verbs that Biblical writers expressed this concept, and an exploration of these verbs and associated lexical items should go far in advancing our understanding of what 'resurrection' meant in the context of the Hebrew Bible" ("The Origin of the Idea of Resurrection," in *Traditions in Transformation: Turning Points in Biblical Faith*, ed. Baruch Halpern and Jon D. Levenson [Winona Lake, IN: Eisenbrauns, 1981], 253).

23. I follow Beale's definition of quotation: "A direct citation of an OT passage that is easily recognizable by its clear and unique verbal parallelism" (*Handbook on the New Testament Use of the Old Testament*, 29). I assume Hays's definitions of *allusion* and *echo*: "The concept of allusion depends both on the notion of authorial intention and on the assumption that the reader will share with the author the requisite 'portable library' to recognize the source of the allusion; the notion of echo, however, finesses such questions: 'echo is a metaphor of, and for, alluding, and does not depend on conscious intention.' ... In general, throughout the following pages, *allusion* is used of obvious intertextual references, *echo* of subtler ones" (*Echoes of Scripture in the Letters of Paul*, 29, citing John Hollander, *The Figure of Echo: A Mode of Allusion in Milton and After* [Berkeley: University of California Press, 1981], ix). Beale says that some interpreters think "an allusion must consist of a reproduction from the OT passage of a unique combination of at least three words. Though this may be a good rule of thumb, it remains possible that fewer than three words or even an idea may be an allusion" (*Handbook on the New Testament Use of the Old Testament*, 31).

Daniel 12:2 and earlier Scripture, it will be fruitful to explore whether that earlier Scripture is linguistically related to even earlier texts. My investigation will lead us into the Torah. Scholars may concede the sparse presence of resurrection hope in the Prophets or Writings, but my insistence on its roots in the Torah will require careful argumentation and exegesis.

The presence of certain verbs is not the only indicator of resurrection hope. Sometimes images or pictures of resurrection appear in Old Testament passages but do not receive the attention they deserve from scholars. Greenspoon rightly acknowledges that the biblical authors could have communicated belief in resurrection by using language and imagery not corresponding to modern, scientific approaches to the text, so that during certain periods of textual composition there may be an interest in resurrection even when it was largely or entirely unexpressed.[24]

Biblical authors used multiple genres to convey theological truth. As Kevin Vanhoozer observes, "Narratives communicate ways of seeing and thinking about God's involvement with the world that cannot be reduced to a set of concepts. ... The main point here is that the Bible is made up of a variety of texts that need to be described not only at the linguistic but also at the literary level."[25] Do the linguistic connections still matter? Of course, but as Rosner points out, "In most cases the concept is in fact far bigger than the words normally used to refer to it, even when the words in question appear frequently."[26]

The teaching in Daniel 12:2 is not only built on lexical links and concepts of resurrection hope in earlier OT passages; the author shares theological convictions that precede him as well. After reading a verse about some rising to life and others rising to judgment, there are relevant questions to pose: *what* beliefs are behind such a verse, *who* held these beliefs previously, and *when* did these convictions arise? The biblical authors shape their narratives according to, and in order to convey and reinforce, certain theological beliefs.[27] I agree with Richard

---

24. Greenspoon, "The Origin of the Idea of Resurrection," 320–21.
25. K. J. Vanhoozer, "Exegesis and Hermeneutics," in *NDBT* (Downers Grove, IL: InterVarsity Press, 2000), 59.
26. B. S. Rosner, "Biblical Theology," in *NDBT* (Downers Grove, IL: InterVarsity Press, 2000), 6.
27. Greenspoon gives an example of a deeply held conviction integral to resurrection hope: "There is one and only one God who created the world and all that is in it; who was, is, and will always be; and whom alone it is proper to worship."

Bauckham that "hope for a resurrection stands in strong continuity with the Old Testament's portrayal of God. ... It cannot be over-emphasized that when Jews came to believe in life after death the ground for their belief was God."[28]

By using the criteria of verbal links, conceptual connections, and theological convictions, I will argue *against* the conclusions of most scholars who find belief in resurrection "only in the very latest portions of the Hebrew Bible."[29] It is true that passages composed later in Israel's history contain more overt expressions of resurrection hope, but the momentum of such hope began in the earliest chapters of Scripture. A belief in resurrection was a development "whose roots lay deep within ancient Israel itself."[30] My interest is in what the biblical authors communicated in the final form of their work and in the context of the Old Testament canon.

The interpretive criteria will not expire once we leave the Old Testament, for lexical connections, resurrection pictures, and theological convictions were appropriated by subsequent authors through the New Testament period. My focus will be on how the verbal and conceptual elements of Daniel 12:2 influenced the intertestamental and New Testament writers. After examining the relevant literature before and after Daniel 12:2, both biblical and nonbiblical, it will be clear what a watershed verse Daniel 12:2 was for the theology of the biblical authors.

THE USE OF THE TRIPARTITE DIVISION OF THE OLD TESTAMENT

When I explore the influence of Daniel 12:2 on the intertestamental literature, those works will be addressed according to their probable dates of composition (where such knowledge is possible), and I will examine the New Testament documents according to the categories of Gospels, Acts, Epistles, and Apocalypse. An explanation is needed, however, for addressing the Old Testament books according to their tripartite division.

For the Hebrew no conception of his own existence, from life through death to whatever follows, is possible apart from their belief in the Lord, God of Israel" ("The Origin of the Idea of Resurrection," 256).

28. Richard Bauckham, "Life, Death, and the Afterlife in Second Temple Judaism," in *Life in the Face of Death: The Resurrection Message of the New Testament*, ed. Richard N. Longenecker (Grand Rapids: Eerdmans, 1998), 84, 86.
29. Greenspoon, "The Origin of the Idea of Resurrection," 247. This observation by Greenspoon does not represent his personal position on dating resurrection hope.
30. Wright, *The Resurrection of the Son of God*, 125.

Christian theologians rarely treat the Old Testament in its final Jewish form—Law, Prophets, and Writings—even though this was the order known to Jesus and the early church.[31] The design of the Tanak[32] provides a hermeneutical lens through which its content can be viewed, a macro literary text for all the texts.[33] For example, the placement of Chronicles after Ezra-Nehemiah creates canonical cohesion with an eschatological ending, and the position of the Writing Prophets after the Former Prophets affects the way the Former Prophets are to be understood.[34]

The Tanak has a discernible structure: a beginning, middle, and end, with sections of narrative interrupted by substantial blocks of poetic commentary.[35] An essay by David Freedman explains how major sections of the Old Testament have a balanced Hebrew word count, a fact that further confirms the significance of the Tanak order,[36] and Stephen Dempster has appropriated Freedman's analysis in two essays titled "An 'Extraordinary Fact.'"[37] As Hamilton points out, approaching the Old Testament according to its tripartite division follows ancient tradition regarding its arrangement (see the prologue to Sirach, lines 8–10; 4QMMT, line 10; *Baba Bathra* 14b).[38] When I explore resurrection hope in the Old Testament, the sections will proceed according to the Tanak arrangement.

---

31. R. Rendtorff, *Canon and Theology: Overtures to an Old Testament Theology*, trans. M. Kohl (Minneapolis: Fortress, 1993), 55–56. See Luke 24:44 where Jesus refers to the "Law of Moses and the Prophets and the Psalms," with the Psalms representing the Writings. Michael Shepherd argues that Jesus's statement about "the blood of innocent Abel" and "the blood of Zechariah the son of Barachiah" (Matt 23:35) is a reference to the Scriptures from Genesis to 2 Chronicles, which presupposes a structure of Law, Prophets, and Writings (*Daniel in the Context of the Hebrew Bible*, Studies in Biblical Literature 123 [New York: Peter Lang, 2009], 3).
32. The consonants in TaNaK refer to the Torah (Law), Neviim (Prophets), and Ketuvim (Writings).
33. Dempster, *Dominion and Dynasty*, 42–43.
34. Dempster, *Dominion and Dynasty*, 42.
35. Dempster, *Dominion and Dynasty*, 46.
36. David N. Freedman, "The Symmetry of the Hebrew Bible," *ST* 46 (1992): 83–108. See also Freedman, *The Unity of the Hebrew Bible* (Ann Arbor: University of Michigan Press, 1991).
37. See Stephen G. Dempster, "An 'Extraordinary Fact': *Torah* and *Temple* and the Contours of the Hebrew Canons: Parts 1 and 2," *TynBul* 48 (1997): 23–56, 191–218.
38. Hamilton, *God's Glory in Salvation through Judgment*, 61. See also Shepherd, *Daniel in the Context of the Hebrew Bible*, 2.

PRELIMINARY ISSUES

Four preliminary issues are relevant to this project. First, what does the Old Testament say about the afterlife? Second, more specifically, what does the Old Testament concept of Sheol mean? Third, when was the book of Daniel written? Fourth, what have scholars said about the emergence of resurrection hope in the Old Testament?

THE AFTERLIFE IN THE OLD TESTAMENT

The hope for bodily resurrection is, in the words of N. T. Wright, hope for life *after* life after death.[39] Before I can get to that subject, the question of whether there is an afterlife in the Old Testament at all must be answered first. After the judgments administered in Genesis 3, life outside the garden ended in death, indicated by the genealogy of Genesis 5. God kept his word to Adam—and to all who came after him—that transgression brings death (cf. 2:17). As early as this portion of Scripture, the theme of exile (cf. 3:23–24) and death are linked, and this link will be important for later Scripture.

Since death is a reality seen throughout the Old Testament, is there any indication of an afterlife in these books? Alexander rightly sums up much critical scholarship when he says, "It is not uncommon to encounter statements which suggest that the Old Testament has almost nothing to say on the subject of life after death; and what little it does report is usually assessed in quite negative terms."[40] Meitzen is unabashed in his claim: "The Old Testament teaches virtually nothing about resurrection or life after death."[41] Such negative assessment is unfortunate because the biblical authors, even amid pessimistic statements about what happens after death, do use positive phrases about the afterlife.

In Genesis, when the patriarchs die, they are "gathered" to their "people" (Abraham in 25:8; Isaac in 35:29; Jacob in 49:33). While it may seem plausible to suggest that this means no more than joining ancestors' bodies in a family tomb, the first time "gathered to his people" occurs is with Abraham who did not join a family tomb of ancestors (Gen 12:1; 25:8–10; cf. 15:15). In the case of Jacob, he was gathered to his people

---

39. Wright, *The Resurrection of the Son of God*, 108–9.
40. T. D. Alexander, "The Old Testament View of Life After Death," *Themelios* 11, no. 2 (1986): 41.
41. Manfred O. Meitzen, "Some Reflections on the Resurrection and Eternal Life," *LQ* 24 (1972): 254.

(49:33) and then buried later (50:12-14), indicating that being "gathered" and being "buried" are not synonymous events.

The cases of Abraham and Jacob being "gathered" to their people is most likely an afterlife reference.[42] In Genesis, then, we see the inevitability of death as punishment for sin, but in this same book we also see that death is not the end of God's image bearers.

Outside Genesis, the narrator speaks of Aaron as gathered to his people (Num 27:13), and the same is true for Moses (Num 31:2; Deut 32:50). Also in their cases, being "gathered" cannot refer to interment with ancestors because they were not reunited with their fathers in the grave.[43] The exceptional stories of Enoch (Gen 5:24) and Elijah (2 Kgs 2:1-18)—men who did not die but were caught up by the power of God—reinforce the biblical teaching that death is not the end of a person because those men went on to something beyond earthly life.

How early in Scripture can we recognize some kind of afterlife? Genesis. And subsequent revelation does not deny what this foundational book indicates.[44]

THE MEANING OF SHEOL

Connected to the concept of the afterlife in the Old Testament is the term Sheol (שְׁאוֹל). The term occurs sixty-five times in the Old Testament and designates the place of the dead.[45] Disagreement exists, however, whether this place of the dead is anything more than the grave, and—if Sheol does denote something like the underworld—whether both the righteous and wicked go there, or only the wicked.[46]

---

42. Paul R. Williamson, *Death and the Afterlife: Biblical Perspectives on Ultimate Questions*, NSBT (Downers Grove, IL: IVP Academic, 2018), 39-40.
43. Alexander, "The Old Testament View of Life After Death," 45.
44. For an exploration of what the Old Testament teaches about life after death, see Eun-Jung Kim, "Reconsidering Eternal Life in the Old Testament: The Idea of Resurrection Rooted in the Torah," Ph.D. diss., The Southern Baptist Theological Seminary, 2015.
45. Walter C. Kaiser Jr., *Preaching and Teaching the Last Things: Old Testament Eschatology for the Life of the Church* (Grand Rapids: Baker Academic, 2011), 4; E. C. Lucas, "Cosmology," in *DOTP* (Downers Grove, IL: InterVarsity Press, 2003), 138.
46. See Matthew Y. Emerson, *"He Descended to the Dead": An Evangelical Theology of Holy Saturday* (Downers Grove, IL: IVP Academic, 2019), 127-33; Samuel D. Renihan, *Crux, Mors, Inferi: A Primer and Reader on the Descent of Christ* (Kindle Direct Publishing, 2021), 34-50.

Walton says Sheol "has no known antecedent in other cultures or religions of the ancient world, and the etymology of the word is uncertain and therefore unable to contribute to the discussion."[47] The contexts where the word occurs clarify what the biblical authors thought of it, and those contexts frame it *negatively*.

Sheol is personified as being hungry with a large appetite and as never being satisfied with the number of its prey (Hab 2:5). People do not praise God in Sheol (Ps 30:3, 9), nor do they mention him (Ps 6:5). Sheol is a place of darkness, a realm of dust, the habitation of the devouring worm where all hope is lost (Job 17:13–16). Its cords of death aim to surround, trap, and destroy people (Ps 18:4–5). It is a place of inactivity, void of knowledge or wisdom (Eccl 9:10).

While some regard Sheol as parallel only with the grave,[48] Walton points to Psalm 55:15 ("Let death steal over them; let them go down to Sheol alive; for evil is in their dwelling place and in their heart") and Psalm 139:8 ("If I ascend to heaven, you are there! If I make my bed in Sheol, you are there!") as examples that undermine this view.[49] If Sheol is just the burial place, then think about the implications from the psalmist's words: hoping people are buried alive, or having confidence that God is there in a literal grave, dilutes the impact of David's claims.

The concept of Sheol is equivalent to the underworld.[50] The term also occurs in every instance without the definite article, which suggests it is a proper name.[51] In Proverbs 15:11, Sheol is paired with another underworld term, Abaddon, reinforcing the idea that Sheol means more than the grave.

The use of the term Sheol was not limited to a particular time in Israel's history; it occurs throughout the Law, Prophets, and Writings.[52]

---

47. John H. Walton, *Ancient Near Eastern Thought and the Old Testament: Introducing the Conceptual World of the Hebrew Bible* (Grand Rapids: Baker Academic, 2006), 320. For confirmation see also Philip Johnston, *Shades of Sheol: Death and Afterlife in the Old Testament* (Downers Grove, IL: InterVarsity Press, 2002), 78; Nicholas J. Tromp, *Primitive Conceptions of Death and the Nether World in the Old Testament* (Rome: Pontifical Biblical Institute, 1969), 21–23.
48. See R. L. Harris, "The Meaning of the Word Sheol as Shown by Parallels in Poetic Texts," *JETS* 4 (1961): 129–35; Bruce K. Waltke, *An Old Testament Theology: An Exegetical, Canonical, and Thematic Approach* (Grand Rapids: Zondervan, 2007), 965; Kaiser, *Preaching and Teaching the Last Things*, 5.
49. Walton, *Ancient Near Eastern Thought and the Old Testament*, 320.
50. Walton, *Ancient Near Eastern Thought and the Old Testament*, 320.
51. Johnston, *Shades of Sheol*, 71.
52. Johnston, *Shades of Sheol*, 72.

The negative portrayal of its location is impressively uniform, indicating that what Sheol means early in the Torah is still its meaning after the exile ends. Sheol may have different nuances in different contexts, but these nuances are still of the single basic and negative concept of the underworld.[53]

Do both the righteous and the wicked descend to Sheol upon death? Walton says yes, for "Sheol is never referred to as the abode of the wicked alone."[54] However, Johnston represents those who say Sheol is the abode of the wicked alone. He says, first, that the righteous who speak about going to Sheol never actually go there,[55] while the wicked *are* reported as going there after death (e.g., Num 16:30-33;[56] 1 Kgs 2:6; Ezek 31:15-16; Isa 14:9). Second, when the righteous invoke Sheol language and descriptions, it is during circumstances and distress viewed as divine punishment or judgment, such as an untimely death or a death in an undesirable way (cf. Jacob in Gen 37:35; Job in Job 14:13; the psalmist in Ps 18:4-5; Hezekiah in Isa 38:10). Third, when the righteous speak of deliverance from Sheol, they are using the well-known term metaphorically in order to communicate that God spared them from the judgment they feared (cf. Ps 18:4-5; 30:3). So, in this view, the peril of the righteous would justify the graphic Sheol language (cf. Jonah 2:2).

Walton does concede that being sent to Sheol is an act of God's judgment. This admission is significant, for while most scholars believe everyone was destined for Sheol, in the Old Testament Sheol is predominantly the fate of the wicked, a clarification made explicit in Psalm 49:14-15:[57] "Like sheep they are appointed for Sheol; death shall be their shepherd, and the upright shall rule over them in the morning. Their

---

53. Johnston, *Shades of Sheol*, 74-75.
54. Walton, *Ancient Near Eastern Thought and the Old Testament*, 321.
55. According to Johnston, "Psalmists describe their experiences of distress and despair as an underworld experience, in direct and indirect terms. However, this language can hardly be taken literally, since they are still able to pray to Yahweh and to hope for his deliverance. ... And to insist that reference to the underworld in the laments and thanksgivings cannot be metaphorical or figurative is to impose a constraint out of keeping with their literary context" (*Shades of Sheol*, 97).
56. "This is the only occurrence of Sheol in OT narrative—otherwise it is only used in direct speech" (Philip Johnston, "Life, Disease and Death," in *DOTP*, ed. T. Desmond Alexander and David W. Barker [Downers Grove, IL: InterVarsity Press, 2003], 535).
57. Philip Johnston, "Death and Resurrection," in *NDBT* (Downers Grove, IL: InterVarsity Press, 2000), 444.

form shall be consumed in Sheol, with no place to dwell. But God will ransom my soul from the power of Sheol, for he will receive me."

In Psalm 49:14-15, Sheol seems to be for the wicked, and death is their shepherd. But the language still associates the righteous dead with Sheol. The psalmist believes that the righteous will be redeemed from its power. The upright are delivered from Sheol because God receives them; *he* is their shepherd (cf. Ps 23:1). When David said, "If I make my bed in Sheol, you are there!" (Ps 139:8), he is envisioning the help of God that brings comfort beyond death.

Johnston rightly argues that Sheol is part of a primarily negative pattern when it appears in the Old Testament, but he fails to adequately address the specific texts that speak of the righteous in Sheol's power. In fact, Johnston dismisses these uses of the term by saying the righteous psalmists were only speaking figuratively about going there.[58] Rather than dismissing these uses as being only figurative, the more compelling explanation is that the righteous *and* unrighteous have a future in Sheol but with a different experience. There is a compartment for the righteous and one for the wicked, and the righteous will be delivered from Sheol's power because of God's plan to clothe them with bodily glory and immortality.

Add to our discussion two other Old Testament texts, both of which seem to teach that everyone goes to Sheol at death. First, Psalm 89:48: "What man can live and never see death? Who can deliver his soul from the power of Sheol?" Second, Ecclesiastes 9:10: "Whatever your hand finds to do, do it with your might, for there is no work or thought or knowledge or wisdom in Sheol, to which you are going."

A survey of passages where Sheol is used reveals that it is where the ungodly go—also identified as the wicked (Isa 5:14; Pss 9:17; 31:17; 141:7), the sinners (Job 24:19), the foolish rich (Ps 49:14), the scoffers (Isa 28:15, 18), and the immoral (Prov 5:5; 7:27; 9:18).[59] But Sheol is not *only* the place of the ungodly. The righteous—like all people—will go to the grave and beyond. For the righteous, however, Sheol is not a place of their judgment. God will deliver his people from the power of Sheol.

---

58. Johnston, *Shades of Sheol*, 97.
59. Johnston, *Shades of Sheol*, 81.

DATING THE BOOK OF DANIEL

Since understanding Daniel 12:2 is central to this project, one's position on the composition of the book itself has implications as to how early (or late) the statement of resurrection hope in 12:2 appears. While a thorough defense of an early date for the book of Daniel is beyond the scope of this project, several remarks about the issue are in order.[60]

Regarding the discussion of the book's composition, Steinmann says, "Perhaps no other OT prophetic book has been dissected and denied as the work of its putative author as Daniel has been."[61] A conservative position dates the work in the sixth century BC, and a critical approach puts the book in the second century BC. The former view believes the events therein are historical, and the prophecies therein were given ahead of the events that fulfill them. The latter view rejects the historicity of the events in the book of Daniel, and it dates the composition of the prophecies after the events in question, or *ex eventu*.[62]

A critical approach to the book of Daniel assumes that genuine predictive prophecy, especially at the level of detail in the book, is impossible. Such doubts extend back to Porphyry, an anti-Christian philosopher from the third century AD, who argued that Daniel's prophecies were written after the events themselves but were written *as if* they were predictive.[63] Since scholars of this persuasion believe the final vision of Daniel refers to the Maccabean events in the second century BC, the book of Daniel must have been composed in that century too.[64] Though critical scholars date the book late, there is not widespread agreement as to how the stories and visions were composed and by whom.[65] Shepherd

---

60. For defenses of an early date for the book of Daniel, see Bruce K. Waltke, "The Date of the Book of Daniel," *BSac* 133, no. 532 (1976): 319–29; James M. Hamilton Jr., *With the Clouds of Heaven: The Book of Daniel in Biblical Theology*, NSBT (Downers Grove, IL: InterVarsity Press, 2014), 30–40. For an overview of evidence that is offered for an early date and for a late date, see Joe M. Sprinkle, *Daniel*, EBTC (Bellingham, WA: Lexham, 2020), 6–40.
61. Andrew E. Steinmann, *Daniel*, Concordia Commentary (St. Louis: Concordia, 2008), 1.
62. See Gordon Wenham's breakdown of the conservative and critical approaches to dating the book of Daniel in his article "Daniel: The Basic Issues," *Themelios* 2, no. 2 (1977): 49–52.
63. Steinmann, *Daniel*, 3.
64. Steinmann, *Daniel*, 3.
65. Steinmann, *Daniel*, 6. See the incredible claim in Hartman and Di Lella's work that as many as ten distinct authors contributed to the book of Daniel (Louis F.

is right, though, that insisting on Daniel's prophecies as *ex eventu* "is not scholarship but dogmatism."[66]

Sometimes lexical features in the book of Daniel lead scholars to propose a late composition date, but W. J. Martin contends, "There is nothing about the Hebrew of Daniel that could be considered extraordinary for a bilingual or, perhaps in this case, a trilingual speaker of the language in the sixth century BC."[67] In fact, Daniel's Hebrew is more like that of other exilic books in the OT, making a second-century BC composition unlikely.[68] Regarding the Aramaic in the book, Kitchen insists that it accords with "full-blooded Imperial Aramaic," which contrasts with the "post-Imperial Aramaic of the second and first centuries BC as illustrated by the Dead Sea Scrolls."[69] What about the presence of Persian loanwords? Since Daniel was still alive after the Persians conquered the Babylonians, the use of Persian words in the book is not improbable.[70] As Wilson puts it, "Persian words occur where one would expect them to occur—in works from Persian times—and Daniel is one of these works."[71] There are only three Greek loanwords in the book of Daniel, all of which are musical instruments in its third chapter, and even some critical scholars admit that the presence of these words is too sparse to prove anything about the date of composition.[72] A late date for the book of Daniel cannot be established on lexical grounds.

Treating the stories of Daniel as fictional and its prophecies as *ex eventu* has devastating consequences. As Steinmann rightly observes, the theology in the book is integrally tied to the historicity of the events it describes, as well as to the accuracy of genuine predictive prophecy.[73]

Hartman and A. Alexander Di Lella, *The Book of Daniel*, AB, vol. 23 [Garden City, NY: Doubleday, 1978], 13–14).

66. Shepherd, *Daniel in the Context of the Hebrew Bible*, 65.
67. W. J. Martin, "The Hebrew of Daniel," in *Notes on Some Problems in the Book of Daniel*, ed. D. J. Wiseman (London: Tyndale, 1965), 30.
68. Steinmann, *Daniel*, 8.
69. K. A. Kitchen, "The Aramaic of Daniel," in *Notes on Some Problems in the Book of Daniel*, ed. D. J. Wiseman (London: Tyndale, 1965), 78.
70. As Kitchen notes, "Such a person in the position of close contact with Persian administration that is accorded to him in the book would have to acquire—and use in his Aramaic—many terms and words from his new Persian colleagues (just like the Elamite scribes of Persepolis), from the conquest by Cyrus onwards" ("The Aramaic of Daniel," 41–42).
71. Robert Dick Wilson, *Studies in the Book of Daniel* (New York: 1938), 217.
72. Steinmann, *Daniel*, 11. See John J. Collins, *Daniel: A Commentary on the Book of Daniel*, Hermeneia (Minneapolis: Fortress, 1993), 20.
73. Steinmann, *Daniel*, 18.

If the book is not historically accurate in what it relates, then it is nothing more than a series of human documents manufactured with the attempt to bring hope and confidence to its readers.[74] As Wilson explains, "It is absurd to suppose that men who were willingly giving up their lives for the preservation of their holy writings from destruction would have been participants in a fraud to perpetuate the Book of Daniel as one of their holy writings."[75]

Since the four visions in Daniel 7–12 are disclosed to the prophet himself (7:1; 8:1; 9:2; 10:1), a natural reading of the book (a reading open to supernatural disclosure from God to a human) would grant that Daniel himself communicated the content of these prophecies. Furthermore, if we give the benefit of the doubt to the claims in the book itself, there are places where the prophet narrates the account with the first-person "I" (cf. Dan 8–10; 12:5–8). Even if Daniel is not the sole contributor to the book (in other words, if there was a final redactor), he can still rightly be considered its author.

Shepherd says, "The fact that Daniel appears as the first-person narrator in the second half of the book does not prove his authorship."[76] Perhaps, then, someone else incorporated Daniel's memoirs into a final product. If Daniel did not write those accounts, then someone wrote them in his name, someone who did not actually experience or see what was reported. Pseudonymous authorship of Daniel is not something Jesus considered, for he said the abomination of desolation was "spoken of by the prophet Daniel" (Matt 24:15).

The burden of proof rests on those who deny what Jesus said, those who say someone else crafted Daniel's prophecies and did so much later than the lifetime of the prophet. Wilson's observation is compelling: "The New Testament in its references to Daniel the prophet and to the fiery

---

74. Steinmann, *Daniel*, 18–19. Beckwith observes that the book of Daniel influenced the intertestamental works of the Book of Tobit, 1 Enoch, and Ecclesiasticus, and this influence is significant because these works are typically dated before the second century BC, when critical scholars suggest the book of Daniel was composed (Roger Beckwith, "Early Traces of the Book of Daniel," *TynBul* 53 [2002]: 75–82). The implication of Beckwith's article is that if the book of Daniel influenced the works he listed, then the book must have been composed before the second century BC.
75. Wilson, *Studies in the Book of Daniel*, 279.
76. Shepherd, *Daniel in the Context of the Hebrew Bible*, 65.

furnace and the den of lions implies at least that Daniel is what it appears to be, a record of historic facts enacted in the sixth century B.C."[77]

There is not sufficient lexical, theological, or historical reason to question the composition of the book of Daniel in the sixth century BC. Wilson summarizes the skepticism:

> It is not till the third century A.D. in the writings of a heathen assailant of Christianity that we find the first expression of the *opinion* that the book may have been a fabrication, full of pseudo-predictions written *post eventum*. This opinion was never accepted by Origen or any of the scholars claiming to be of the Jewish or Christian faith, till the beginning of the nineteenth century. ... [Such critical scholars] preferred the opinion of the neo-Platonist Porphyry in his virulent and prejudiced assault on Christianity, and especially on the Book of Daniel, to the opinions of Eusebius of Caesarea, Origen, and Jerome.[78]

This project will proceed on the ancient and well-established assumption that the prophet, his prophecies, and the events therein are historical. Since the book of Daniel was written during the lifetime of the prophet, composition was probably no later than 530 BC.[79] Daniel 1:21 says that the prophet served the Babylonian court until the first official year of Cyrus, so the book's final form was composed after the Persian conquest of Babylon, which took place in 539 BC.[80] If Daniel went to Babylon in 605 BC somewhere between the age of ten and twenty, he would have penned the book in his late eighties.[81]

POSITIONS ON THE EMERGENCE OF RESURRECTION HOPE

In scholarly approaches to the emergence of resurrection hope in the Old Testament, four positions are discernable. First, there are those who see resurrection hope present early in biblical history, as early as the Torah. Second, there are those who are confident that resurrection hope emerged sometime between the conquest of the promised land and its division (a division occurring in 930 BC). Third, there are those who see resurrection hope taught between the division of the land and the exile

---

77. Wilson, *Studies in the Book of Daniel*, 235.
78. Wilson, *Studies in the Book of Daniel*, 235.
79. Steinmann, *Daniel*, 3.
80. Steinmann, *Daniel*, 3.
81. Steinmann, *Daniel*, 3n5.

from the land (an exile occurring in 586 BC). Fourth, there are those who insist that resurrection hope is a postexilic teaching and does not clearly appear any earlier in Scripture.[82] For some of those holding this fourth position, the book of Daniel may not even be written by a historical prophet and so may be regarded as a second-century BC composition.

Let's consider the first position. Contending that resurrection hope arises early in Israel's history is a minority view, especially the notion that the Torah teaches resurrection. Those who contend for its early emergence will acknowledge many texts that teach resurrection before Daniel 12:2. They will suggest passages from Genesis, Exodus, Samuel, Kings, Job, Psalms, Isaiah, Jeremiah, and Ezekiel.

Planting himself in the minority group, Greg Beale says the "first possible hint of resurrection life may be discernible in Gen 1–3. ... The promise in Gen. 3:15 of the seed of the woman who would decisively defeat the serpent likely entails also an implicit reversal of his work that introduced death."[83] Stephen Dempster, looking at verses earlier than the punishments issued in Genesis 3, sees God depicted as the great life giver in Genesis 1 and 2.[84] Dempster holds that when God creates Eve, Adam must first "die" in a deep sleep and then return from it.[85] Even in Adam's creation, God shapes him from the dust and then brings him to life by divine breath—"a type of resurrection."[86]

Deuteronomy 32:39 is also important for those of the first position: "See now that I, even I, am he, and there is no god beside me; I kill and I make alive; I wound and I heal; and there is none that can deliver out of my hand." Beale says this verse may be the earliest *explicit* Old Testament reference to bodily resurrection.[87] Greenspoon also emphasizes this verse, saying, "This one passage, together with the other evidence already accumulated, may well be sufficient to establish the *certainty* of

---

82. According to Williamson, "Most scholars consider the doctrine of personal resurrection a late development in Old Testament thought, not really appearing before the post-exilic or Hellenistic era" (*Death and the Afterlife*, 74).
83. Beale, *A New Testament Biblical Theology*, 228.
84. Stephen G. Dempster, "The Resurrection of Christ on 'The Third Day' According to the Scriptures" (paper presented at the annual meeting of the Evangelical Theological Society, Milwaukee, WI, November 14, 2012), 4.
85. Dempster, "The Resurrection of Christ on 'The Third Day' According to the Scriptures," 4.
86. Dempster, "The Resurrection of Christ on 'The Third Day' According to the Scriptures," 4.
87. Beale, *A New Testament Biblical Theology: The Unfolding of the Old Testament in the New* (Grand Rapids: Baker Academic, 2011), 231.

an early date for the Biblical belief" in resurrection, for the word order is death followed by life, just as wounding is followed by healing.[88] The "life" in this case would be bodily life after death.

For those of the second position, who see resurrection hope emerging between the land's conquest and its division, the Psalms constitute the dominant evidence. In Psalm 16:9–10, King David writes, "Therefore my heart is glad, and my whole being rejoices; my flesh also dwells secure. For you will not abandon my soul to Sheol, or let your holy one see corruption." The apostle Peter believed that these words prophesied Jesus's resurrection from the dead (Acts 2:25–31).

In Psalm 49:16 (Eng. 49:15), we read, "But God will ransom my soul from the power of Sheol, for he will receive me." Also Psalm 73:24: "You guide me with your counsel, and afterward you will receive me to glory." According to Richard Bauckham, resurrection hope is found in these two psalms because the psalmists envision that God "will receive them" after death, language that probably echoes the stories of Enoch and Elijah being received by God (Gen 5:24; 2 Kgs 2:3).[89]

The "breakthrough" in these psalms is that God's justice and love triumph even beyond death.[90] According to Bauckham, the faith of God's people is being taken "to a newly radical conclusion," and what is new is that this faith implies God's faithfulness to love his people beyond death.[91] If God could be trusted to eventually vindicate his people and maintain his love for them, and if these purposes could be fully attained only beyond death, then a belief in resurrection was "a virtually necessary implication,"[92] and the psalmists expressed it.[93]

According to the third position, resurrection hope developed between the division of the land and the exile from the land. Crucial during this period were the ministries of the writing prophets. Hosea said, "After two days he will revive us; on the third day he will raise us up, that we

---

88. Greenspoon, "The Origin of the Idea of Resurrection," 310, emphasis mine.
89. Bauckham, "Life, Death, and the Afterlife," 85.
90. Bauckham, "Life, Death, and the Afterlife," 86.
91. Bauckham, "Life, Death, and the Afterlife," 86.
92. Bauckham, "Life, Death, and the Afterlife," 86.
93. These two psalms "cannot be dated with any degree of certainty" (Bauckham, "Life, Death, and the Afterlife," 81). But the superscription of Ps 49 ascribes the psalm to the sons of Korah, and the superscription of Ps 73 ascribes the psalm to Asaph. According to 1 Chr 6:31–32, 37, 39, the sons of Korah and Asaph all ministered before the temple was built, which logically implies that their psalms preceded the division of Israel.

may live before him" (Hos 6:2).[94] N. T. Wright says this passage is "firmly located chronologically in the eighth century BC" and can "claim to be the earliest explicit statement that YHWH will give his people a new bodily life the other side of death."[95] Moreover, Hosea appears to have influenced the wording of Daniel 12 via Isaiah 26.[96]

According to Isaiah 26:19, "Your dead shall live; their bodies shall rise. You who dwell in the dust, awake and sing for joy! For your dew is a dew of light, and the earth will give birth to the dead." Nickelsburg sees that Daniel 12:2 uses language related to this verse and that the latter predicts the hope of bodily resurrection.[97] "For Isaiah the resurrection of the righteous is *in itself* vindication for the righteous,"[98] and Daniel 12:2 builds on this notion.

Nickelsburg says the context in Isaiah 26 is about national restoration and revival, so the resurrection imagery applies to the nation, but Johnston says more than national restoration is meant.[99] Both Isaiah 26:14 and 26:19 refer to dead individuals, the former verse asserting that foreign oppressors will not rise, and the latter verse presupposing a concept of individual resurrection.[100] Isaiah 26:19 was the response to people yearning for continued communion with God, though the details of "how, where and when this resurrection would take place" are unexplored.[101]

The fourth position on the emergence of resurrection hope is minimalist indeed. As John Collins puts it, "There can be no suggestion that belief in resurrection was implicit in the Old Testament before Daniel."[102] This means that resurrection hope in the Old Testament is exclusively

---

94. I am listing Hosea before Isaiah because the former preceded the latter chronologically, even though the canonical order is different.
95. Wright, *The Resurrection of the Son of God*, 118–19.
96. Wright, *The Resurrection of the Son of God*, 119. For a compelling argument that Isa 26 depends on Hosea, see John Day, "A Case of Inner Scriptural Interpretation: The Dependence of Isaiah xxvi.13–xxvii.11 on Hosea xiii.4–xiv.10 (Eng. 9) and Its Relevance to Some Theories of the Redaction of the 'Isaiah Apocalypse,'" *JTS* 31 (1980): 309–19.
97. Nickelsburg, *Resurrection, Immortality, and Eternal Life*, 18, 41. For other scholars who believe that Isa 26:19 is the first occurrence of a belief in bodily resurrection, see Yamauchi, "Life, Death, and the Afterlife in the Ancient Near East," 46; Ladd, *I Believe in the Resurrection of Jesus* (Grand Rapids: Eerdmans, 1975), 48.
98. Nickelsburg, *Resurrection, Immortality, and Eternal Life*, 19, emphasis original.
99. Johnston, *Shades of Sheol*, 225; Johnston, "Death and Resurrection," 446.
100. Johnston, *Shades of Sheol*, 225.
101. Johnston, *Shades of Sheol*, 239.
102. Collins, *Encounters with Biblical Theology*, 32.

located in Daniel 12:2.[103] Furthermore, Collins approaches the book of Daniel with higher-critical assumptions, so its date must be in the second century BC.[104] Having ruled out implicit resurrection hope prior to Daniel 12:2, Collins's position on when the book was written means that the Old Testament had no such hope until a couple of hundred years before Christ. Bailey holds the same position as Collins regarding the first appearance of resurrection in the Old Testament.[105]

What is the response of Collins to scholars who see resurrection hope in prophets like Ezekiel or Hosea or Isaiah? In those books there is language of dry bones coming alive (Ezek 37), people being raised on the third day (Hos 6), and dust-dwellers rising from the dead (Isa 26). But Collins says these passages—often thought to precede Daniel 12 with a resurrection hope of their own—are not about individual bodily resurrection but instead concern the restoration of Israel after the exile.[106] Israel was dead in the exile, and "its restoration is as miraculous as resurrection."[107] The pre-Daniel (or pre-second century BC) resurrection language, therefore, is only metaphorical and should not be pressed into a literal and individual hope.

Collins considers the possibility that the metaphorical use of resurrection "may have been prompted indirectly by acquaintance with the Persian belief," for resurrection "was an integral part of Zoroastrianism."[108] This contention is also asserted by James Charlesworth: "The major development of resurrection belief and most likely the stimulus for Jewish resurrection belief is Iran and

---

103. See H. C. C. Cavallin, *Life after Death: Paul's Argument for the Resurrection of the Dead in 1 Cor 15* (Lund: Gleerup, 1974); Robert Martin-Achard, *From Death to Life: A Study of the Development of the Doctrine of the Resurrection in the Old Testament* (London: Oliver and Boyd, 1960), 189–91. Hartman and Di Lella say, "Our author [of the book of Daniel] must be credited with giving the first sure teaching on life beyond the grave" (*The Book of Daniel*, 309).
104. Collins, *Encounters with Biblical Theology*, 28.
105. Bailey, *Biblical Perspectives on Death*, 73.
106. Collins, *Daniel*, 395. Lucas concurs with this interpretation: "What is being promised here is the return of the exiles from Babylon and the re-establishment of the nation in its homeland" (Ernest Lucas, *Daniel*, AOTC, vol. 20 [Downers Grove, IL: InterVarsity Press, 2002], 302). See also Edmund F. Sutcliffe, *The Old Testament and the Future Life* (London: Burns, Oates & Washbourne, 1946), 125–31.
107. Collins, *Daniel*, 395.
108. Collins, *Daniel*, 396.

Zoroastrianism."[109] Still, Collins says that "the hope expressed in Daniel 12 was exceptional" because no pre-Daniel text spoke of a *double* resurrection of the righteous and the wicked.[110] Whence came the language of Daniel 12:2? The source, says Collins, was probably an earlier document. He suggests that the phraseology of Daniel 12:2 gives the impression of continuity with tradition, but this tradition was not limited to Old Testament books.[111] Indeed, "Daniel was not ... the first Jewish author to speak of a judgment of the dead," because 1 Enoch (which Collins dates prior to the book of Daniel) contains both themes of resurrection and judgment, and the author of Daniel was probably acquainted with the Enoch traditions.[112]

Among the four positions regarding the emergence of resurrection hope, only the fourth denies any resurrection precursors to Daniel 12:2 in the Old Testament. Bronner's words resonate with many scholars: belief in bodily resurrection as described in Daniel "could not have emerged spontaneously without significant precursors."[113]

CONCLUSION

Having discussed presuppositions about the afterlife in the Old Testament, the meaning of Sheol, the dating of the book of Daniel, and the four positions as to when resurrection hope emerged in the Old Testament, we have a foundation for the discussion of relevant evidence in subsequent chapters. Using the threefold criteria of linguistic connections, resurrection imagery, and theological convictions of the biblical authors, I will examine and identify resurrection hope in biblical and nonbiblical material. The cumulative evidence will demonstrate that Daniel relied on earlier Old Testament texts and theological convictions when he expressed the hope of bodily resurrection, and his expression informed and shaped subsequent nonbiblical and biblical authors. We turn now to examine Daniel 12:2 in its context.

---

109. James H. Charlesworth, "Conclusion: The Origin and Development of Resurrection Beliefs," in *Resurrection: The Origin and Future of a Biblical Doctrine*, ed. James H. Charlesworth (New York: T&T Clark, 2006), 221. Yamauchi disputes the assertion that Zoroastrianism influenced Judaism ("Life, Death, and the Afterlife," 47-49).
110. Collins, *Daniel*, 395. See also Sprinkle, *Daniel*, 329: "12:2 is the first text that unambiguously affirms the general resurrection of the dead."
111. Collins, *Daniel*, 395.
112. Collins, *Daniel*, 395-96.
113. Leila Bronner, "The Resurrection Motif in the Hebrew Bible: Allusions or Illusions?" *JBQ* 30, no. 3 (2002): 143.

2

Reading Daniel 12:2 in Context

INTRODUCTION

Before we examine what preceded and what followed Daniel 12:2 in both biblical and nonbiblical literature, we must establish the context and meaning of the verse. Then earlier Old Testament passages can be viewed in light of the conclusions drawn here. I agree with N. T. Wright's reasons for looking first to the details of Daniel 12:2: (1) it is the fullest Old Testament expression of bodily resurrection, (2) it draws on older, relevant Old Testament texts, and (3) it served as a lens through which subsequent writers viewed earlier material.[1]

The following sections will approach Daniel 12:2 the way a camera can magnify its object of interest. First, where does Daniel 12:2 fit in the outline of the whole book? Second, what precursors in Daniel 1–11 prepare the reader for the prediction in 12:2? Third, and most important, what is the meaning of the verse itself? These three questions comprise the outline of this chapter.

THE STRUCTURE OF DANIEL

Peter Leithart suggests that the complexity of the biblical authors is evident in the way they arrange their texts, arrangements that may have more than one legitimate outline: "Like intertextuality, multiple structure is virtually inescapable, especially in narratives and poetry."[2]

---

1. Wright, *The Resurrection of the Son of God*, 109.
2. Peter Leithart, *Deep Exegesis: The Mystery of Reading Scripture* (Waco, TX: Baylor University Press, 2009), 143. Of course, Leithart's point does not imply that readers can arrange a passage or book any way they want.

Regarding the structure of the book of Daniel, I propose the following divisions.[3]

> Prologue (1:1-21)
>> Four Earthly Kingdoms and a Heavenly Kingdom (2:1-49)
>>> Deliverance of the Faithful (3:1-30)
>>>> Judgment on an Arrogant King (4:1-37)
>>>> Judgment on an Arrogant King (5:1-31)
>>> Deliverance of the Faithful (6:1-28)
>> Four Earthly Kingdoms and a Heavenly Kingdom (7:1-28)
>> A Visionary Expansion on Specific Kingdoms (8:1-27)
>>> Daniel's Prayer and God's Answer (9:1-27)
>> A Visionary Expansion on Specific Kingdoms (10:1-12:3)
> Epilogue (12:4-13)

I favor this outline of Daniel for at least four reasons. First, the widely acknowledged chiasm in the Aramaic section (Dan 2-7) is preserved.[4] Second, 8:1-12:3 is structured in a way that shows the corresponding visionary expansions on specific kingdoms (Dan 8 and 10:1-12:3).[5] Third,

---

3. I have adapted my outline from those found in Peter J. Gentry and Stephen J. Wellum, *Kingdom through Covenant: A Biblical-Theological Understanding of the Covenants*, 2nd ed. (Wheaton, IL: Crossway, 2018), 600-602; Steinmann, *Daniel*, 22-25.
4. The first publication of this chiastic structure can be found in A. Lenglet, "La Structure Litteraire de Daniel 2-7," *Bib* 53 (1972): 169-90. For subsequent acknowledgment of the chiastic arrangement, see Hamilton, *God's Glory in Salvation through Judgment*, 325; John J. Collins, *The Apocalyptic Vision of the Book of Daniel* (Missoula, MT: Scholars Press, 1977), 11; Joyce G. Baldwin, *Daniel*, TOTC (Downers Grove, IL: IVP Academic, 1978), 59-60; Sidney Greidanus, *Preaching Christ from Daniel: Foundations for Expository Sermons* (Grand Rapids: Eerdmans, 2012), 20. Steinmann says, "The chiasm, therefore, is not simply happenstance, nor something perceived by scholars without any intent on the part of the author. Instead, Daniel left unambiguous clues as to his method of choosing and organizing the Aramaic chiasm" (*Daniel*, 24-25).
5. The kingdom visions of Dan 2 and 7 include four earthly kingdoms, but the visions in Dan 8 and 10:1-12:3 do not span that scope. Dan 8 and 10:1-12:3 expand on specific kingdoms. Greidanus confirms the chiastic structure of the three Hebrew visions in Dan 8-12 (*Preaching Christ from Daniel*, 20). Steinmann explains five parallels between Dan 8 and 10:1-12:3 that confirm the formation of a chiasm, with Dan 9 occupying the center (*Daniel*, 25). And van Deventer says the chiastic structure of Dan 8-12 is supported by Hebrew terms used in both Dan 8 and 10-12 ("Struktuur en Boodskap(pe) in die Boek Daniel," *HervTS* 59, no. 1 [2003]: 209). In Goldingay's judgment, "It is with chapter 8 that chapters

the centers of the two chiasms highlight the truth of God's sovereignty over judgment and salvation (Dan 4–5; 9). Fourth, this outline shows that the book has a section of material (an introduction or prologue; Dan 1) before the Aramaic section begins, and there is a section of material (an epilogue; Dan 12:4–13) after the fourth and final vision.[6]

Where does Daniel 12:2 fit in the scheme of the whole book? The verse belongs in the final vision the prophet receives. This fourth vision is also the longest, more than doubling the content in each of three previous visions (in Dan 7, 8, and 9).

The end of the book of Daniel forms an inclusio with the beginning, which narrates the exile to Babylon. This captivity is resolved in Daniel 12:2 with resurrection, which delivers God's people from death, a plight worse than Babylonian servitude. Daniel goes to Babylon in 1:1–7, and the heavenly being (who gives the final vision of the book) promises him a resurrection in 12:13. Daniel's return from death's exile will be more glorious than a geographical return to the promised land.

STORIES OF RESCUE AND JUDGMENT IN THE BOOK OF DANIEL BEFORE 12:2

While the promise of resurrection in Daniel 12:2 is the only expression of that kind in the book, it is not the first deliverance. Stories in the book of Daniel recount both divine rescue and retribution,[7] and in a lesser to greater way, these episodes form the mold of deliverance from destruction that anticipates the kind of intervention only resurrection can bring.

Again and again the book tells of pagan rulers attacking YHWH's people, trying to make them conform to new pagan ways, boasting arrogantly against the true god and his people, and of the faithful

---

10–12 have most detailed points of contact. Reminiscences of almost every verse of chapter 8 reappear here" (*Daniel*, WBC, vol. 30 [Nashville: Thomas Nelson, 1989], 283).

6. The heavenly being continues speaking to Daniel in 12:9–13 in order to answer the question in 12:8, but the sustained vision about future kings that began in 11:2 ended in 12:3. Daniel is then told to "shut up the words and seal the book" (12:4). I consider the instruction and interactions in 12:4–13 as distinguishable from 10:1–12:3.

7. In the words of Longman, "The wicked will get their due, and, though suffering in the present, the godly will get their reward. God will see to it. We have seen these themes from the beginning of the book [of Daniel]" (Tremper Longman III, *Daniel*, NIVAC [Grand Rapids: Zondervan, 1999], 292).

and wise Israelites holding on, retaining their loyalty and integrity, and being vindicated in the end as their god acts dramatically to rescue them and condemn or overthrow their oppressors. ... This encourages us to see the prediction of resurrection as the final and most explicit promise in a much longer line. ... This is how Israel's long exile will reach its climax, how the arrogant pagans will be judged, how the righteous will be delivered. ... Any second-Temple Jew who pondered the book would find in 12:2–3 not a new and outlandish idea, unanticipated and unforeseen, but the crown of all that had gone before.[8]

The following instances will picture the theme of death and resurrection in the book of Daniel.[9] This theme will be evident as death and resurrection are viewed as a wider concept, "applying to nations and to individuals in ways that are analogous to actual physical death and resurrection."[10]

STORIES OF RESCUE

In Daniel 1 the prophet and his friends requested a special diet of vegetables and water (1:12), a request putting them at odds with the king's clear instruction to eat food from his table (1:5, 8). Not only did Daniel and his friends survive the time of testing, they also thrived and exceeded the other youths who had eaten the king's food (1:10, 13, 15). When the king evaluated Daniel and his friends, he deemed them superior in wisdom and understanding (1:20). While the chief eunuch had been concerned that the change in diet could provoke the king's grave displeasure (1:10), God kept them all from royal rage.

In Daniel 2 the king became angry when none of his advisers could interpret his dream (2:5, 8–9), so he decreed the death of all wise men (2:12), which put Daniel and his friends in jeopardy (2:13). When Daniel sought mercy from God that he might not be destroyed (2:17), God revealed to Daniel the interpretation (2:19). Daniel conveyed both the dream and the interpretation to the king (2:31–45) and thus avoided the

---

8. Wright, *The Resurrection of the Son of God*, 114–15.
9. James B. Jordan, *The Handwriting on the Wall: A Commentary on the Book of Daniel* (Powder Springs, GA: American Vision, 2007), 80.
10. Jordan, *The Handwriting on the Wall*, 80. This means the stories referenced in this section do not literally describe an individual bodily resurrection from actual death. Rather the pattern of deliverance from destruction or difficulty is matched and exceeded by the prophesied resurrection in Dan 12:2.

decree of death hanging over him, his friends, and the rest of the wise men of Babylon.

In Daniel 3 the prophet's three friends—Shadrach, Meshach, and Abednego—disobeyed the king by refusing to worship the golden statue (3:5-12). When King Nebuchadnezzar confronted them about this refusal, he asked, "And who is the god who will deliver you out of my hands?" (3:15). The three Hebrews trusted that God was able to rescue them (3:17-18). Into the fiery furnace they went (3:19-23), yet none of them perished in the flames (3:25-26). God delivered his servants from the threat of death (3:28), just as they said he could.

In Daniel 6 the prophet continued his prayerful devotion to God even though King Darius had signed a document demanding that for thirty days any prayer must be made exclusively to him (6:7, 9-10). When Darius became aware of Daniel's persistence of prayer to Yahweh (6:13), he reluctantly sentenced him to the lions' den (6:16). But the next morning the king rushed to the den and, much to his relief, found that God had delivered Daniel from certain death (6:19-23).

The stories in the first half of the book demonstrate without a doubt that God delivers from the *threat* of death, and they prepare for the prophecy in the final vision that predicts deliverance from the *fact* of death. The God who will raise the dead is "the living God, enduring forever" (Dan 6:26), and he "delivers and rescues" (6:27)—from rulers, flames, lions, and even the grave. Steinmann is right: "The preservation of his faithful followers from physical harm and temporal death affords a glimpse of the salvation from eternal death and resurrection to eternal life that all God's people have through faith (12:2-3)."[11] Ultimate vindication is promised in 12:2-3, and it is preceded by episodes that display God's vindicating power.

PICTURES OF RESURRECTION

As an analogy of the greater life that resurrection will mean for the individual, the deliverances in the book of Daniel resulted in a greater state for each person God rescued.[12] In Daniel 1 the obedient prophet and his friends were better in appearance than the youths who ate the

---

11. Steinmann, *Daniel*, 322.
12. Longman confirms this pattern: "Daniel and the three friends, though put through extremely difficult times, were raised higher and higher in glory, while their enemies often were humiliated or even died" (*Daniel*, 292).

king's food (1:15) and possessed greater wisdom and understanding than all Babylonian contenders (1:20). In Daniel 2 the king gave Daniel honors, gifts, and a high position of authority (2:48). In Daniel 3 the king promoted Shadrach, Meshach, and Abednego (3:30). In Daniel 6 the prophet prospered during the reign of Darius (6:28).

Going into exile is a kind of death, and returning from exile is like a resurrection.[13] Significantly, the book of Daniel begins with the report of exile and ends with the hope of resurrection. The text reports that Daniel went into exile (Dan 1:2, 6–7), and his final vision ended with the promise that "many of those who sleep in the dust of the earth shall awake, some to everlasting life, and some to shame and everlasting contempt" (12:2). Babylonian captivity was not the worst kind of captivity to face, and a return to Jerusalem would one day be superseded by a greater vindication.

In Daniel 1 and 2 the threat of death could have materialized but did not. However, the stories in Daniel 3 and 6 told of events where Daniel's friends and Daniel himself went into the very throes of death and came out alive. In both cases God sent "his angel" (3:28; 6:22) to rescue the righteous. Against human expectation, Daniel 3 and 6 tell of deliverances through death, and the survival of the respective parties is tantamount to coming out of the grave. Lacocque believes Daniel 3 is a resurrection preview of the announcement in 12:2,[14] and Hamilton sees a resurrection picture in Daniel 6: "When the stone is rolled away, it is almost as though Daniel has been raised from the dead."[15]

---

13. See Ezek 37. I will substantiate this claim in chap. 3, which examines resurrection hope in the Law, Prophets, and Writings.
14. André Lacocque, *Le Livre de Daniel*, Commentaire de L'Ancien Testament XVb (Paris: Delachaux et Niestlé, 1976), 55. See Lacocque, *The Book of Daniel*, trans. David Pellauer (Atlanta: John Knox, 1979), 58, 70.
15. Hamilton, *God's Glory in Salvation through Judgment*, 329–30. See also Jordan, *The Handwriting on the Wall*, 80. Jordan's chapter on Daniel in the lions' den is actually called "Death and Resurrection" (309–26). W. Sibley Towner explains multiple parallels between the "passion" of Daniel and the passion of Jesus, and "of course the denouement of both accounts is the same: the person presumed dead reappears from the tomb, vindicated by God's saving power" (*Daniel*, Interpretation [Atlanta: John Knox, 1984], 84). Longman says, "Daniel's emergence from the lion's den is typological of Jesus' death and resurrection" (*Daniel*, 172). And Lacocque: "Here, as in chapter 3, we find the essence of the resurrection, that is, less a phenomenon of a life after death as the triumph of life over death, of hope over despair" (*The Book of Daniel*, 108).

In Daniel 8 and 10, could the prophet's deep sleep and return to consciousness be a picture of something greater? In Daniel 8, after the angel Gabriel spoke, Daniel says, "I fell into a deep sleep with my face to the ground. But he touched me and made me stand up" (8:18). This event, says James Jordan, pictured "a death and resurrection experience."[16] The same language and parallel experience occur again in Daniel 10. There the prophet received the final vision, and his encounter with the heavenly being was a type of resurrection: when Daniel saw the being (10:5-6), he lost his strength (10:8) and fell into a deep sleep on the ground (10:9); a hand then raised him to his hands and knees (10:10), and a voice commanded him to stand up (10:11).

At the cue of the hands and voice of the heavenly being, Daniel's return to consciousness was like returning to life. This descent and ascent echoed Adam's experience since he too went into a deep sleep and woke again (cf. Gen 2:21).[17] Abraham also fell into a deep sleep as Yahweh prepared to make a covenant with him (cf. 15:12-21). In both Adam and Abraham's situations, they woke to an important revelation. In Daniel 8 and 10, the prophet's deep sleeps are followed by important revelations as well (cf. 8:18-27; 11:2—12:3).

Unique to Daniel's experience of "deep sleep" (when compared with Adam or Abraham) is the promise at the end of the final vision that the sleepers will awake, some to life and others to shame (cf. Dan 12:2). Could it be that the prophet's pre-vision experience prefigured the vision's promise of resurrection?[18] Daniel slept and was raised (cf. 10:9-11), and in the end everyone who sleeps will rise (cf. 12:2).

STORIES OF JUDGMENT

As will be argued later in this chapter, Daniel 12:2 promises a climactic judgment for unbelievers, and this prophecy is also presaged by acts of judgment earlier in the book. Moreover, these acts affect the objects of judgment *physically*, and in a lesser to greater way the end-time

---

16. Jordan, *The Handwriting on the Wall*, 79. He is not saying Daniel physically died here.
17. Both Adam and Daniel also slept in a place associated with the river Tigris (cf. Gen 2:14, 21; Dan 10:4). And when their deep sleep occurred, they were both alone (cf. Gen 2:18, 21; Dan 10:8). In neither case did an actual death occur.
18. Jordan, *The Handwriting on the Wall*, 84. Jordan interprets Dan 12:2 differently than I will, but he still sees the prophet's experience in Dan 10 as a foreshadowing of 12:2. Jordan's chapter title for Dan 10 is "The Death and Resurrection of Daniel" (515-39).

resurrection of the wicked will affect their bodies too. In these stories God judges a disobedient people (Dan 1), complicit guards (Dan 3 and 6), and arrogant rulers (Dan 4 and 5).

In the opening verses of the book, the king of Babylon came to Jerusalem's doorstep (Dan 1:1): "And the Lord gave Jehoiakim king of Judah into his hand, with some of the vessels of the house of God. And he brought them to the land of Shinar to the house of his god, and placed the vessels in the treasury of his god. Then the king commanded Ashpenaz ... to bring some of the people of Israel" (1:2–3). Under God's judgment, Jerusalem and the temple were besieged, and the Babylonians physically displaced people from the promised land.

In Daniel 3, the prophet's three friends escaped the fiery furnace, but the bodies of the men who cast them in were not spared. "Because the king's order was urgent and the furnace overheated, the flame of the fire killed those men who took up Shadrach, Meshach, and Abednego" (3:22). Those men from Nebuchadnezzar's army received the punishment for which they had bound the three Hebrews. The fiery furnace episode demonstrated both God's judgment and deliverance.

In Daniel 4 the Lord humbled King Nebuchadnezzar. The king had boasted of the great city Babylon and said it was built "by my mighty power ... and for the glory of my majesty" (4:30). In response to this haughty proclamation, God punished the king for a season of time (4:31–32). He became like an animal, staying outside ungroomed and eating the food of beasts (4:32–33).

In Daniel 5 a king named Belshazzar held a feast and used the vessels that Nebuchadnezzar had taken from the temple in Jerusalem, praising idols with these sacred things (5:1–4). In response to this blasphemous act, God literally wrote judgment on the wall (5:5, 25–28). In fulfillment of the prophecy, "that very night Belshazzar the Chaldean king was killed" (5:30).

In Daniel 6 the lions did not eat the prophet who stayed a night in their den (6:17, 22–23). Instead, those who had accused Daniel were thrown into the den, along with their families, and the lions crushed their bodies (6:24). As in the fiery furnace story, this episode illustrates both deliverance and punishment. It foreshadows "the resurrection to eternal death, 'contempt,' and 'everlasting abhorrence' awaiting all who die as unbelievers (12:2)."[19]

---

19. Steinmann, *Daniel*, 323.

PROPHECIES OF JUDGMENT

Daniel 12:2 prophesies judgment for unbelievers at their resurrection, but it is not the first prophecy against God's opponents in the book. In addition to stories of God's punishment preceding Daniel 12, prophecies against his opponents appear before it too. Decrees of destruction prime the pump for the most condemning announcement of all.

After Nebuchadnezzar's first dream recorded in the book, the king hears the prophet's interpretation that God's kingdom will bring an end to all other kingdoms, which implies Babylon's demise (Dan 2:37-44). Daniel 7 promises the destruction of the beast (7:11), and God will remove all dominion from other rulers as his everlasting dominion comes to pass (7:12-14). In Daniel 8 the vision foretells the destruction of kingdoms (8:20-25). Such passages illustrate Daniel's declaration earlier in the book, "[God] changes times and seasons; he removes kings and sets up kings" (2:21).

SUMMARY

The words of Daniel 12:2 predict that some will rise "to everlasting life" and others "to shame and everlasting contempt." The chapters before those words contain precursors—in the form of stories and prophecies—of deliverance and judgment that prepare the way for 12:2. The rescues throughout the book pale in comparison to the resurrection of eternal bodily life, and the judgments before 12:2 are but shadows of the everlasting contempt in store for God's enemies. When we see 12:2 in the context of the whole book, the momentum of rescue and retribution finds climactic manifestation in resurrection to reward or condemnation. The book that begins with Daniel taken into captivity ends with a vision of the greatest release from the greatest captivity, death.

THE MEANING OF DANIEL 12:2

In order to establish the meaning of Daniel 12:2, this section will (1) compare the verse in the extant Masoretic Text, Old Greek, and Theodotion versions, (2) exegete the phrases of Daniel 12:2, and (3) evaluate alternative interpretations of the verse.

THE MASORETIC, OLD GREEK, AND THEODOTION VERSIONS

To exegete a text, the wording of a text must first be established.[20] The Masoretic Text (MT) of the book of Daniel is composed of Hebrew (1:1–2:4a; 8:1–12:13) and Aramaic (2:4b–7:28), which means 12:2 is in the book's second Hebrew section. Among Qumran texts, there are eight Danielic manuscripts, and they verify the trustworthiness of the MT.[21] None of those manuscripts preserve Daniel 12:2, however, so they will not be considered below.

Two Greek versions of the book of Daniel exist, known as the Old Greek (OG) and Theodotion (Th) versions. There are only three major witnesses to the OG: Codex Chisianus (a copy of Origen's Greek Hexapla) and two pre-Hexaplaric manuscripts.[22] The Th became the early church's version of the book of Daniel,[23] though the New Testament cites from the OG as well.[24]

What is the value of the OG and Th translations? They can be used in the textual criticism of the book of Daniel, and they provide insight into how Jews in antiquity understood particular Danielic passages.[25] Below is a table comparing the phrases of Daniel 12:2 in the order of the MT, the OG, and the Th.[26]

---

20. See Douglas Stuart, *Old Testament Exegesis: A Handbook for Students and Pastors*, 3rd ed. (Louisville: Westminster John Knox, 2001), 5–7; Craig L. Blomberg, with Jennifer Foutz Markley, *A Handbook of New Testament Exegesis* (Grand Rapids: Baker Academic, 2010), 63, 273.
21. Steinmann, *Daniel*, 63. Also Collins, *Daniel*, 3.
22. Steinmann, *Daniel*, 63–64.
23. Steinmann, *Daniel*, 65–66. Collins says, "Unlike the OG, the translation attributed to Theodotion is amply attested in the manuscripts and early citations. The earliest attestations are found in the NT and in the book of Baruch" (*Daniel*, 9). Steinmann says that since the NT occasionally quotes Theodotion readings, and since Josephus seems to have known it, the Theodotion translation is probably to be dated no later than the first century AD (*Daniel*, 65). For more information on this subject, see R. Timothy McLay, *The OG and Th Versions of Daniel*, Septuagint and Cognate Studies 43 (Atlanta: Scholars Press, 1996); Joseph Ziegler and Olivier Munnich, eds., *Susanna, Daniel, Bel et Draco*, 2nd ed., Septuaginta: Vetus Testamentum Graecum 16.2 (Göttingen: Vandenhoeck & Ruprecht, 1999).
24. See Alexander A. Di Lella, "The Textual History of Septuagint-Daniel and Theodotion-Daniel," in *The Book of Daniel: Composition and Reception*, ed. John J. Collins and Peter W. Flint, with Cameron VanEpps, VTSup 83 (Leiden: Brill, 2001), 2:592–93.
25. Steinmann, *Daniel*, 66.
26. This table is a modified form of the columns displayed in McLay, *The OG and Th Versions of Daniel*, 176–78.

Row	MT	OG	Th
1	וְרַבִּים	καὶ πολλοὶ	καὶ πολλοὶ
2	מִיְּשֵׁנֵי	τῶν καθευδόντων	τῶν καθευδόντων
3	אַדְמַת־עָפָר	ἐν τῷ πλάτει τῆς γῆς	ἐν γῆς χώματι
4	יָקִיצוּ	ἀναστήσονται	ἐξεγερθήσονται
5	אֵלֶּה לְחַיֵּי	οἱ μὲν εἰς ζωὴν	οὗτοι εἰς ζωὴν
6	עוֹלָם	αἰώνιον	αἰώνιον
7	וְאֵלֶּה	οἱ δὲ	καὶ οὗτοι
8	לַחֲרָפוֹת	εἰς ὀνειδισμόν	εἰς ὀνειδισμόν
9	לְדִרְאוֹן	οἱ δὲ εἰς διασπορὰν	καὶ εἰς αἰσχύνην
10	עוֹלָם	[καὶ αἰσχύνην] αἰώνιον	αἰώνιον

From this table we can draw eight conclusions. First, for rows 1, 2, 6, and 8, the OG and Th render the MT identically. Second, the difference in wording in rows 3, 4, 5, 7, and 9 does not affect the meaning at all. Third, the bracketed OG words in row 10 are probably a later gloss from Th.[27] Fourth, in rows 5 and 7, the OG renders אֵלֶּה idiomatically by using οἱ μὲν and οἱ δὲ, whereas the Th corresponds to the MT by using οὗτοι both times.[28] Fifth, the OG adds an extra δὲ in row 9, which indicates that a third group will be raised—a deviation from the MT.[29] Sixth, in row 9 the Th adds a καὶ in order to smooth out the syntax.[30] Seventh, for the most part the OG follows the MT's word order, and other than textual differences, the OG interrupts that word order with the postpositive δὲ in row 7 and with the additional δὲ in row 9.[31] Eighth, the Th of Daniel 12:2 gives a formally equivalent translation of the MT,[32] even with the extra καὶ in row 9.

---

27. McLay, *The OG and Th Versions of Daniel*, 186.
28. McLay, *The OG and Th Versions of Daniel*, 188.
29. McLay, *The OG and Th Versions of Daniel*, 188. See also F. F. Bruce, "The Oldest Greek Version of Daniel," *OTS* 20 (1975): 25–26.
30. McLay, *The OG and Th Versions of Daniel*, 188.
31. McLay, *The OG and Th Versions of Daniel*, 205–6.
32. McLay, *The OG and Th Versions of Daniel*, 206. In Bruce's judgment, "The Theodotionic version is a straightforward translation whereas the Septuagint is a targumic-style paraphrase" ("The Oldest Greek Version of Daniel," 38).

Based on these observations, we can conclude that the sense of Daniel 12:2 was preserved in the OG and Th versions. The relevance of these detailed comparisons shows that the Greek versions conveyed the notion of resurrection either to life or to judgment, though the OG speaks of a third group as well (see line 9). When we examine the influence of Daniel 12:2 on the New Testament in chapter 5, attention will be given as to whether those New Testament passages reflect (when discernment is possible) the MT, OG, or Th. As a whole, the Greek versions of Daniel 12 contain many textual differences and additions when compared to the MT, but the difficulties and differences in 12:2 are, thankfully, fewer in number.[33]

AN EXEGESIS OF DANIEL 12:2

According to John Collins, "There is virtually unanimous agreement among modern scholars that Daniel is referring to the actual resurrection of individuals from the dead,"[34] and the exegesis offered below will confirm this consensus. During the analysis of Daniel 12:2, important features will be noted, such as the use of Isaiah, connections to Genesis, and the sole occurrences (in the Old Testament) both of "eternal life" and a resurrection to judgment.

"And many" (וְרַבִּים). The conjunctive וְ connects Daniel 12:2 to 12:1, where God promises deliverance for everyone whose name is written in "the book." The context is one of persecution and martyrdom. The book of Daniel was written to motivate its readers to endurance and obedience during times of fierce testing and temptations to capitulate under mounting persecution.[35] The people of God will stand firm (11:32), though many of the wise will die by flame and sword (11:33). Not all will be faithful, however. Some will violate the covenant and be easily seduced by ungodly authority (11:32, 34b).

In a context of faithfulness unto death, God promises vindication, but for whom? The "many" are divided into two groups, some who awake to life and some who awake to shame. An issue remains, however, as to

---

33. McLay, *The OG and Th Versions of Daniel*, 175, 177–78, 186–210.
34. Collins, *Daniel*, 391–92. See Werner H. Schmidt, *The Faith of the Old Testament: A History*, trans. John Sturdy (Philadelphia: Westminster, 1983), 276.
35. The stories in Dan 1, 2, 3, and 6 tell of God's faithfulness to and deliverance of his people. Readers of the book of Daniel would hopefully trust the God of those stories and thus endure their own fiery trials and persecutions.

how wide or inclusive this "many" is. To twenty-first century ears—and perhaps to ancient ones too—"many" seems different in content than, and not as comprehensive as, a word like "all." "Many" sounds like a great amount, if not a majority, of something.

To identify the scope of רַבִּים, Old Testament scholars have offered three interpretive options. First, the word is restrictive because the resurrection is not a general promise to all people; only the martyred Jews will rise to life, and their opponents will be judged.[36] Baldwin rightly observes that this view is especially taken by interpreters who date the setting of Daniel 12:2 to the Maccabean period.[37] Nickelsburg argues the verse is not about a general resurrection of all but of those whose unjust treatment presented a theological problem for the writer.[38] And grammatically speaking, Collins believes the preposition מִן requires that רַבִּים be taken in a partitive sense.[39]

Second, the verse "is not attempting to offer a global theory of the ultimate destination of the whole human race, but simply to affirm that, in a renewed bodily life, God will give everlasting life to some and everlasting contempt to others."[40] The majority of people are simply not mentioned, but not because they do not matter or will not be raised; the prediction is "a specific promise addressed to a specific situation."[41] According to Johnston, "The resurrection ... focuses on Daniel's people. This does not preclude a wider, universal resurrection, but nor does it envisage it."[42]

---

36. Lucas, *Daniel*, 295. According to Lindenberger, "Apparently the 'many' who are awakened from death are the Jews who have died in the Seleucid persecutions. Neither the Gentiles nor those Jews who died earlier seem to be within the author's purview" (James M. Lindenberger, "Daniel 12:1–4," *Int* 39 [1985]: 184). Another variation of the "restricted resurrection" view is that those who rise to life are faithful Jews, and those who rise to shame are unfaithful Jews (C. L. Seow, *Daniel*, Westminster Bible Companion [Louisville: Westminster John Knox, 2003], 188).
37. Baldwin, *Daniel*, 225. For example, Collins says, "The primary purpose of Daniel 7–12 is to interpret the crisis of the Maccabean period" (*Encounters with Biblical Theology*, 28).
38. Nickelsburg, *Resurrection, Immortality, and Eternal Life*, 23.
39. Collins, *Daniel*, 392.
40. Wright, *The Resurrection of the Son of God*, 110.
41. Wright, *The Resurrection of the Son of God*, 110, 113.
42. Johnston, *Shades of Sheol*, 226. According to Hasel, the resurrection in Dan 12:2 has broader contours than the one in Isa 26:19 (Gerhard F. Hasel, "Resurrection in the Theology of Old Testament Apocalyptic," *ZAW* 92 [1980]: 279).

Third, רַבִּים can occasionally mean "all" and probably does in Daniel 12:2. In Isaiah 2:2-3, for instance, "all the nations" is paralleled by "many peoples," which indicates the comprehensive potential of רַבִּים.[43] The word, it seems, can have an inclusive sense like "all."[44] Jeremias argues that with or without the article, רַבִּים can mean "the many (who cannot be counted)" or "all" or "the great multitude."[45] According to this line of thinking, Daniel 12:2 would read, "And multitudes who sleep ... " The speaker of 12:2, then, is emphasizing the *great number* of those who will be raised without denying that all the dead will be raised.[46]

The third view on רַבִּים has the most to commend it, though the second view is correct in that the promise also addressed a specific circumstance. Since the book has a sixth-century BC date of composition, the context of Daniel 12 was not Maccabean persecution (as is assumed for those who hold a second-century BC date for the book). Nor is the promise only for martyrs, since in the final verse Daniel is told that he "shall rest and shall stand" (12:13), which is a reference to his own death and resurrection. Not being one of the martyrs, Daniel is an old man and is reckoned among the wise who will rise from the dead to receive an inheritance.[47] "The promise of resurrection set forth in 12:2 is now specifically applied to Daniel."[48] If this reading of 12:13 is correct, then the promise of resurrection in 12:2 is true for the faithful and wise—the people of God.

In summary, רַבִּים functions like "all," which is then divided into two groups by the construction אֵלֶּה ... וְאֵלֶּה.

"Of those who sleep in the dust of the earth" (מִיְּשֵׁנֵי אַדְמַת־עָפָר). Literally the phrase is "from sleepers of earth of dust." Sleeping in the

---

43. Steinmann contends that "what cases such as Is 2:2-3 demonstrate is that 'many' does not exclude 'all' as a possibility" (*Daniel*, 560).
44. Ludwig Koehler, and Walter Baumgartner, *HALOT*, rev. ed. (Leiden: Brill, 2001), s.v. "רַב." See Sprinkle, *Daniel*, 329. Sprinkle cites Ps 109:30; Prov 19:6; Isa 53:11-12; and Dan 9:27 as other places were "many" means "all."
45. J. Jeremias, "πολλοί," in *TDNT*, ed. Gerhard Kittel, trans. Geoffrey W. Bromiley (Grand Rapids: Eerdmans, 1964-1976), 6:536-7. According to John Calvin, "The word 'many' seems here clearly put for all" (*Commentaries on the Book of the Prophet of Daniel*, trans. Thomas Myers [Grand Rapids: Eerdmans, 1948], 2:374).
46. Steinmann, *Daniel*, 561. See also Greidanus, *Preaching Christ from Daniel*, 388.
47. Baldwin, *Daniel*, 232.
48. Stephen R. Miller, *Daniel*, NAC, vol. 18 (Nashville: B&H, 1994), 326. See also Wright, *The Resurrection of the Son of God*, 113; Steinmann, *Daniel*, 577.

dust is a metaphor for death.[49] After Genesis 3:19, a return to dust (עָפָר) meant the end of bodily life, and Daniel 12:2 shows just how long the metaphor has been in use and, by implication, how influential Genesis 3 was.[50] The temporal nature of death is probably suggested by the picture of "sleep." When people lie down to rest, they do so expecting to rise refreshed. "Sleep, in short, is a mini-death. ... In the Hebrew Bible, however, it would be more precise to say that sleep is a death that is—or one devoutly hopes will be—temporary."[51]

Why the use of the double nouns אֲדָמָה and עָפָר? Scholars have different answers. Collins says it is probably "a double reading, conflating two synonyms."[52] However, the literary artistry of the author suggests a different conclusion. Steinmann holds that the construct phrase has an adjectival genitive, meaning "dusty earth," not "the dust of the earth,"[53] but in my view the significance still lies elsewhere.

The grouping of אֲדָמָה and עָפָר occurs only four other times in the Old Testament,[54] so Daniel's use of both terms in 12:2 may be an allusion to an earlier text.[55] He is likely alluding to Genesis 2:7 and 3:19, the former being man's creation "from the dust of the ground" (מִן־הָאֲדָמָה עָפָר), and the latter being the judgment that man will return "to the ground" (אֶל־הָאֲדָמָה) and "to the dust" (אֶל־עָפָר). Probably Genesis 3:19 is foremost in mind because the context there is *death*, just as the "sleep" in Daniel 12:2 is about death. Since those who dwell in the dust will "awake," the resurrection will be a curse-reversing display of God's (re)creative power.[56] In Genesis 3 God decrees the judgment of death, and in Daniel 12 he

---

49. See Nickelsburg, *Resurrection, Immortality, and Eternal Life*, 17. For "sleep" as the equivalent of "death," see 2 Kgs 4:31; 13:21; Job 3:13; 14:12; Jer 51:39; Ps 13:3. For a book showing the connection between sleep and death in the ancient world, see Thomas H. McAlpine, *Sleep, Divine and Human in the Old Testament*, JSOTSup 38 (Sheffield: JSOT, 1987), 135–49.
50. "Dust" is the place of the dead in a number of texts, e.g., Job 7:21; 21:26; 34:15; Ps 104:29; Isa 26:19. To dwell or sleep in the "dust" is to be dead. See Tromp, *Primitive Conceptions of Death*, 85–91.
51. Jon D. Levenson, *Resurrection and the Restoration of Israel: The Ultimate Victory of the God of Life* (New Haven, CT: Yale University Press, 2006), 186.
52. Collins, *Daniel*, 392. See Shemaryahu Talmon, "Double Readings in the Massoretic Text," *Textus* 1 (1960): 167–68.
53. Steinmann, *Daniel*, 557.
54. Gen 2:7; 3:19; 28:14; and Job 5:6.
55. The contexts of Gen 28 and Job 5 are not relevant to Dan 12:2, so neither passage is the source of the author's allusion.
56. After reaching this conclusion independently, I found confirmation of it in Anne E. Gardner, "The Way to Eternal Life in Dan 12:1e–2 or How to Reverse the

promises to undo it. In Zimmerli's words, "The event of resurrection ... breaks open the world of death."[57]

"Shall awake" (יָקִיצוּ). In Daniel 12:2, if sleeping in the "dust of the earth" refers to death, then waking from that dust refers to resurrection. The verb is the Hiphil form of קיץ and thus means to "awake" from sleep or from the sleep of death[58]—a figurative use. Greenspoon is correct that an exploration of resurrection words is not a neutral task, since sometimes one must first determine whether a passage is dealing with resurrection before its vocabulary can be introduced into the discussion, and at other times the vocabulary and its interpretation enables a reader to conclude that a passage refers to resurrection.[59] In his judgment, הֵקִיץ (in the stative sense) is the verb that "best sums up what is especially characteristic of Biblical resurrection."[60]

Not only does the biblical author allude to Genesis 3:19 in Daniel 12:2, but he also uses language from Isaiah 26:19.[61] Isaiah said, "Your

---

Death Curse of Genesis 3," *AusBR* 40 (1992): 5-6. She says, "Dan 12:2 then posits a reversal of the pronouncement of Gen 3:19 where death was decreed for Adam because he disobeyed God" (9). See also Steinmann, *Daniel*, 561; Lucas, *Daniel*, 294.

57. Walther Zimmerli, *Man and His Hope in the Old Testament*, Studies in Biblical Theology (Naperville, IL: Alec R. Allenson, 1968), 148.
58. Koehler and Baumgartner, *HALOT*, s.v. "קיץ."
59. Greenspoon, "The Origin of the Idea of Resurrection," 253. In his famous study of Hebrew words for resurrection, Sawyer concludes that eight verbs can carry the weight of resurrection: (1) הֵקִיץ, (2) חָיָה, (3) עָלָה, (4) שׁוּב, (5) עָמַד, (6) צִיץ, (7) קוּם, and (8) נֵעוֹר (Sawyer, "Hebrew Words for the Resurrection of the Dead," 230n1). The appearance of these various verbs will be considered more in chap. 3 when I examine the OT resurrection passages leading up to the declaration of Dan 12:2.
60. Greenspoon, "The Origin of the Idea of Resurrection," 254. This is confirmed by Goldingay: "The OT's standard way of envisaging dying and coming back to life is by speaking of lying down and sleeping, then of waking and getting up. The former is an extreme form of the latter, which thus provides the metaphor for it" (John Goldingay, *Daniel*, WBC, vol. 30 [Nashville: Thomas Nelson, 1989], 307).
61. This latter point—the use of Isa 26:19 in Dan 12:2—is widely acknowledged by scholars. See, e.g., Collins, *Daniel*, 392; Daniel P. Bailey, "The Intertextual Relationship of Daniel 12:2 and Isaiah 26:19: Evidence from Qumran and the Greek Versions," *TynBul* 51, no. 2 (2000): 305; Steinmann, *Daniel*, 556; Wright, *The Resurrection of the Son of God*, 115; Sprinkle, *Daniel*, 329. According to Schnittjer, "Notable exegetical interventions with several of Isaiah's oracles appear in the beginning of Daniel 12, in addition to many lesser echoes elsewhere in Daniel's visions. The exegetical advancements of revelation concern resurrection and deliverance for some of those resurrected. ... Fully

dead shall live; their bodies shall rise. You who dwell in the dust, awake and sing for joy! For your dew is a dew of light, and the earth will give birth to the dead" (Isa 26:19).[62] "Awake" in both Isaiah 26 and Daniel 12 is the Hiphil of קיץ.[63] Also parallel is the word "dust" (עָפָר) in both verses. When Daniel expressed resurrection hope, he used language from the books of Genesis and Isaiah.[64]

"Some ... and some" (אֵלֶּה ... וְאֵלֶּה). A division occurs in the resurrection promise here. If רַבִּים functions as "all," then the demonstrative pronouns refer to two respective groups and can be translated as "some ... others/some" or "these ... those." These two groups will experience different realities when raised from the dust. Not every scholar, however, is convinced that two different groups will awake; rather, "some" awake and "some" do not.[65] But considering the contrasts of "to everlasting life" and "to shame and everlasting contempt," and if רַבִּים should be understood comprehensively, then Collins is right: "It is surely more natural, with most commentators, to see two groups here who awake to contrasting

---

appreciating the advances of revelation in Dan 12 requires investigating it in relation to its several Isaiah donor contexts. The revelation of resurrection in Daniel's vision does not come out of thin air. The vision interpretively enhances and expands upon Isaiah's oracles" (Gary Edward Schnittjer, *Old Testament Use of Old Testament: A Book-by-Book Guide* [Grand Rapids: Zondervan, 2021], 618).

62. I will analyze Isa 26:19 more thoroughly in chap. 3, but for now it is sufficient to note that three of Sawyer's "resurrection" verbs occur in this one verse: חָיָה, קוּם, and הֵקִיץ.

63. Bailey rightly observes that Dan 12:2 uses the Hiphil imperfect (יָקִיצוּ), whereas Isa 26:19 uses the Hiphil imperative (הָקִיצוּ) ("The Intertextual Relationship of Daniel 12:2 and Isaiah 26:19," 305).

64. John Collins counters, "It would be too simple to attribute the origin of the belief in Daniel simply to reflection on Scripture. Such reflection played a part. ... Yet it now appears that the idea of resurrection was first developed in Judaism in the Enoch tradition (1 Enoch 22), where it is presented in the context of mythical geography and is indebted to Babylonian and Greek traditions. ... It is very probable that Daniel was influenced by the noncanonical Enoch material" (*Encounters with Biblical Theology*, 32). Such statements are nullified when a higher-critical approach to the dating of the book is rejected. See Waltke, "The Date of the Book of Daniel," 319–29. If Daniel wrote the book in the sixth century BC, the pseudonymous writings of Enoch did not influence him.

65. See, e.g., B. J. Alfrink, "L'Idée de résurrection d'après Dn XII, 1, 2," *Bib* 40 (1959): 362–71; Hartman and Di Lella, *The Book of Daniel*, 308.

destinies."⁶⁶ The construction אֵלֶּה ... וְאֵלֶּה divides the רַבִּים into the groups of righteous and wicked, faithful and disobedient.

Since Daniel 12:2 speaks of two different groups rising from the dead, it is important to note that nowhere before this verse is this combination found.⁶⁷ Greenspoon calls this double resurrection an "innovation."⁶⁸ According to Hasel, the brevity of Daniel 12:2 suggests that the idea of resurrection was not novel, but the resurrection of *both* the righteous and wicked is new.⁶⁹

"To everlasting life" (לְחַיֵּי עוֹלָם). The first group of the "many" will awaken to everlasting life. The word "life" (from חַי) in Daniel 12:2 is another lexical connection to Isaiah 26:19, where the prophet says the dead "shall live" (from חָיָה). The result is what N. T. Wright has called "bodily life *after* 'life after death,' or, if you prefer, bodily life after the *state* of 'death.' "⁷⁰

The phrase "everlasting life" (לְחַיֵּי עוֹלָם) is first coined here in the Old Testament, though previous biblical authors expressed the conviction that fellowship with God would not end merely by death (Pss 16:11; 17:15; 73:23, 24; Isa 26:19).⁷¹ The concept of everlasting life is also expressed in the Old Testament (Gen 3:24; Pss 21:3; 28:9; 37:18, 27–28; 41:12; 133:3; Prov 10:25, 30).⁷²

Resurrection to life brings to pass ultimate fellowship and communion with God.⁷³ What the people of God are hoping for, and what God has held out for his people, will be achieved through bodily resurrection unto life everlasting. Any previous resuscitation stories, though supernatural and life-giving (e.g., Elisha's miracle with a woman's boy in 2 Kgs 4), still ended with the person's eventual death; the difference

---

66. Collins, *Daniel*, 393. See Lucas, *Daniel*, 295; Ben C. Ollenburger, "If Mortals Die, Will They Live Again? The Old Testament and Resurrection," *ExAud* 9 (1993): 33; Steinmann, *Daniel*, 557.
67. This point is widely acknowledged by scholars. See, e.g., Levenson, *Resurrection and the Restoration of Israel*, 197.
68. Greenspoon, "The Origin of the Idea of Resurrection," 282.
69. Hasel, "Resurrection in the Theology of Old Testament Apocalyptic," 281.
70. Wright, *The Resurrection of the Son of God*, 108–9.
71. Baldwin, *Daniel*, 226.
72. Steinmann, *Daniel*, 561. See Kim, "Reconsidering Eternal Life in the Old Testament," 110.
73. Hasel, "Resurrection in the Theology of Old Testament Apocalyptic," 284.

with the promise of Daniel 12:2 is its permanence.[74] "At long last, the periodic alternation of death and life comes to a dramatic halt."[75]

There is probably an echo of Genesis 3 in this phrase as well. Earlier I argued that the words אַדְמַת־עָפָר had Genesis 3:19 in the background, and in that same passage, only a few verses later, God exiles Adam from the garden "lest he reach out his hand and take also of the tree of life (הַחַיִּים) and eat, and live (וָחַי) forever (לְעֹלָם)" (3:22). Though Adam's exile meant that he would die and not have everlasting life, the promise of Daniel 12:2 is that God will raise his people from the sleep of death, and this resurrection will be "to everlasting life." What was lost by exile from Eden is restored by resurrection.

"To shame and everlasting contempt" (לַחֲרָפוֹת לְדִרְאוֹן עוֹלָם). When the "many" awake from their mortal slumber, some will rise to חֶרְפָּה, which means "scorn" or "disgrace."[76] The word appears in all ancient versions, though many commentators regard it as a gloss because it disturbs the parallelism between "eternal life" and "everlasting contempt."[77] Jeansonne reasons that since דִּרְאוֹן was such an infrequently used word, the explanatory gloss לַחֲרָפוֹת was added into the margin or into the text itself, and when the gloss is removed, the parallelism of the verse is restored.[78] She says the presence of a gloss best explains why those who rise from sleep in the OG are divided into three groups: once the gloss (לַחֲרָפוֹת) was added, the OG treated the words לְחַיֵּי, לַחֲרָפוֹת, and לְדִרְאוֹן as referring to three different groups and so put a οἱ δὲ in front of לַחֲרָפוֹת.[79]

It is not necessary to view the word as a gloss, however, especially since the manuscript evidence supports its inclusion. The third οἱ δὲ was no doubt added because the two words לַחֲרָפוֹת and לְדִרְאוֹן seemed to the translator(s) to refer to more than one group of people, but that text-critical explanation does not logically demand that לַחֲרָפוֹת was

---

74. Levenson, *Resurrection and the Restoration of Israel*, 187.
75. Levenson, *Resurrection and the Restoration of Israel*, 187.
76. Koehler and Baumgartner, *HALOT*, s.v. "חֶרְפָּה."
77. Gardner, "The Way to Eternal Life in Dan 12:1e-2," 11n24. For example, Nickelsburg omits it as a gloss (*Resurrection, Immortality, and Eternal Life*, 19n51), and Goldingay (*Daniel*, 281), Greenspoon ("The Origin of the Idea of Resurrection," 281), and Hartman and Di Lella (*The Book of Daniel*, 273) say it may be a gloss.
78. Sharon Pace Jeansonne, *The Old Greek Translation of Daniel 7–12*, The Catholic Biblical Quarterly Monograph Series, vol. 19 (Washington, DC: The Catholic Biblical Association of America, 1988), 101.
79. Jeansonne, *The Old Greek Translation of Daniel 7–12*, 101.

originally a gloss. True, the parallelism is not exact between "everlasting life" and "shame and everlasting contempt," but the writer may have a good reason for the inexact parallel.

The biblical author may have been influenced by Isaiah 25:8, which is a verse about resurrection: "He will swallow up death forever; and the Lord GOD will wipe away tears from all faces, and the reproach (וְחֶרְפַּת) of his people he will take away from all the earth, for the LORD has spoken." Apparently resurrection is what swallows up death (cf. 1 Cor 15:54b, which quotes Isa 25:8), and God will remove the shame from his people as they are vindicated. Furthermore, Daniel 12:2 reports that the wicked will rise to shame, the reproach that rightly belongs to them and on them.

The term חֶרְפָּה is plural in Daniel 12:2,[80] and the plural form occurs in only one other Old Testament passage, Psalm 69, in two verses. David says to God, "For zeal for your house has consumed me, and the reproaches [וְחֶרְפוֹת] of those who reproach you have fallen on me" (69:10 [69:9 Eng.]). And in the next verse we see the only other occurrence of the exact *form* from Daniel 12:2: "When I wept and humbled my soul with fasting, it became my reproach [לַחֲרָפוֹת]" (69:11 [69:10 Eng.]). The context of Psalm 69 is significant because David describes himself as being near death as he waits for divine deliverance (69:1-3). He hopes that those who hope in God will not be put to shame or dishonored (69:6). He prays for deliverance from his enemies, from the pit threatening to close its mouth over him (69:14-15). He hopes his opponents will be caught in a snare (69:22), overtaken by God's anger (69:24), and punished without a chance for acquittal (69:27).

Therefore, the context of Psalm 69 is not only relevant to Daniel 12:2 but may also be in lexical relation to it, signaled by the plural form of חֶרְפָּה. In Psalm 69, David hopes God will resurrect him from the death that is near, and he hopes God will remove the reproaches he is bearing and pour them instead upon the wicked. In Daniel 12:2, God promises that his people will be raised from the clutches of death that has swallowed them, and their end will be life, not shame. But the wicked will

---

80. The ESV, and other English translations also, translates the plural term as a singular, "contempt," instead of "contempts." Rightly Steinmann, the plural form may be intensive (as in "utter contempt"), or an abstract plural, but in either case it is appropriately rendered as a singular: "contempt" (*Daniel*, 557). See also Paul Joüon, *A Grammar of Biblical Hebrew*, trans. and rev. T. Muraoka (Rome: Editrice Pontificio Istituto Biblico, 2005), §136g.

rise to the shame that belongs on all the enemies of God. According to Daniel 12:2, God will answer David's prayer in Psalm 69, and this answer will exceed all previous deliverances and judgments.

In Daniel 12:2 the heavenly messenger heightens the horrific final state of the wicked when he tells Daniel that their resurrection to "shame" is also to "contempt" (דְּרָאוֹן), an antithetical notion to the "life" promised to the righteous. The recurrence of עוֹלָם here reinforces that the "contempt" is as lasting for the wicked as the "life" is lasting for the righteous. The outcome of this resurrection will be an unending state that cannot be reversed.

The term דְּרָאוֹן means "abhorrence"[81] and occurs in one other Old Testament text, Isaiah 66:24: "And they shall go out and look on the dead bodies of the men who have rebelled against me. For their worm shall not die, their fire shall not be quenched, and they shall be an abhorrence [דְּרָאוֹן] to all flesh." Scholars are right to see the biblical author of Daniel 12:2 using Isaiah 66:24 for his depiction of God's judgment on his enemies.[82] The occurrence of דְּרָאוֹן in two verses whose contexts both concern punishment of the wicked can hardly be a coincidence.[83] According to our passage in Daniel, God will raise the wicked to be everlasting objects of horror. Steinmann's words depict the tragedy of what this means: "Those banished away from God's gracious presence enjoy no blessing, only suffering under the wrath of the Almighty."[84]

Exegetical summary. The author of Daniel 12:2 predicted a general resurrection of the righteous and the wicked, and their respective everlasting fates will be either life or abhorrence. "A double resurrection was a conclusion drawn from these Jews' understanding of the Scriptures and from their belief that God would keep his word."[85] To express this

---

81. Koehler and Baumgartner, *HALOT*, s.v. "דְּרָאוֹן."
82. Greenspoon says, "It is probable that the writer of Daniel had in mind the divine rewards and punishments graphically portrayed in the last chapters of the book of Isaiah. ... The author of Daniel could state with certitude that exactly what Third Isaiah had foreseen as the fate of the righteous and ungodly would indeed be measured out when the dead were reawakened by God through the process of resurrection" ("The Origin of the Idea of Resurrection," 283–84). See Gardner, "The Way to Eternal Life in Dan 12:1e–2," 8.
83. Greenspoon, "The Origin of the Idea of Resurrection," 284. See also Schnittjer, *Old Testament Use of Old Testament*, 625.
84. Steinmann, *Daniel*, 561.
85. Nickelsburg, *Resurrection, Immortality, and Eternal Life*, 22. In Brueggemann's words, "Only in Daniel 12:2 is the notion of resurrection closely linked to judgment—that is, to punishment and blessing" (Walter Brueggemann,

promise the writer alluded to verses from Genesis 3:19, Isaiah 26:19, and Isaiah 66:24,[86] and verses from Genesis 3, Isaiah 25, and Psalm 69 serve as the possible background for several words as well.[87]

Gardner is on point here when she says Daniel 12:2 "evidences reflection upon passages in the Hebrew Bible which suggest that the 'death' pronouncements of Genesis 3 could be overturned."[88] And according to Wright, resurrection is about "the *reversal* of death itself. It is not about discovering that Sheol is not such a bad place after all. It is not a way of saying that the dust will learn to be happy as dust. The language of awakening is not a new, exciting way of talking about sleep. It is a way of saying that a time will come when sleepers will sleep no more."[89]

ALTERNATIVE INTERPRETATIONS OF DANIEL 12:2

Levenson may call Daniel 12:2 the "first transparent and indisputable prediction of the resurrection of the dead in the Hebrew Bible,"[90] but scholars (though not many) have still disputed this understanding of the verse. Their alternative proposals deserve a response.

Spiritual awakening only? According to Armerding, Daniel 12:2 "refers to a spiritual awakening rather than to a physical resurrection."[91] He says the word for "sleep" (יָשֵׁן) in that verse is not the usual word for the "sleep of death" in the Old Testament, so physical death cannot be in view; and if physical death is not meant, then neither is physical resurrection.[92] But the verb ישׁן *does* mean to sleep in death in several

---

Reverberations of Faith: A Theological Handbook of Old Testament Themes [Louisville: Westminster John Knox, 2002], 173).

86. See Steinmann, *Daniel*, 561 for this same conclusion.
87. Biblical allusions used by the author of Daniel validate the claim Childs makes: "The Old Testament provided the grounds on which both later Jews and Christians developed their understanding of the afterlife" (Brevard Childs, *Old Testament Theology in a Canonical Context* [Minneapolis: Fortress, 1986], 245). Collins calls Childs's statement an "oversimplification. ... It would be too simple to attribute the origin of the belief in Daniel simply to reflection on Scripture" (*Encounters with Biblical Theology*, 31–32). Though Collins criticizes Childs for oversimplification, Collins is underestimating the biblical authors. Dan 12:2 is an OT text whose background is earlier OT texts! Daniel is a biblical theologian expressing his theology with the words and concepts of previous biblical authors.
88. Gardner, "The Way to Eternal Life in Dan 12:1e-2," 19.
89. Wright, *The Resurrection of the Son of God*, 127–28.
90. Levenson, *Resurrection and the Restoration of Israel*, 181.
91. Carl Edwin Armerding, "Asleep in the Dust," *BSac* 121 (1964): 156.
92. Carl Edwin Armerding, "Asleep in the Dust," *BSac* 121 (1964): 156.

instances (cf. Job 3:13; Ps 13:4; Jer 51:39, 57),[93] so a reference to a group of dead sleepers does *not* violate the word's semantic range. In fact, the word choice may echo Genesis 2, when Adam was in a deep sleep (2:21, וַיִּישָׁן). In Daniel 12:2 the use of יָשֵׁן does not negate the physical emphasis of death.

Armerding also seeks to bolster his argument for an exclusively spiritual interpretation of Daniel 12:2 by appealing to the LXX, which renders the verb יָשֵׁן with καθεύδω. He implies that καθεύδω does not mean physical death in the LXX, and he says explicitly that it "is never used of the physically dead in the New Testament."[94] Yet in Psalm 87:6 LXX, the use of καθεύδω cannot mean anything other than physical death ("who sleep in the tomb," καθεύδοντες ἐν τάφῳ). And in 1 Thessalonians 5:10, καθεύδω certainly refers to the physically dead as well ("so that whether we are awake or asleep," ἵνα εἴτε γρηγορῶμεν εἴτε καθεύδωμεν). Armerding's claims are incorrect, and he overstates his case. The word καθεύδω can be used figuratively to mean the sleep of death,[95] so the OG and Th renderings maintain that figurative sense in Daniel 12:2.

Revival of Israelites during the Maccabean era? In the third century AD, Porphyry believed the resurrection of Daniel 12:2 was metaphorical for the family of Mattathias, who slumbered in the dust until they arose and began their revolution in the second century BC.[96] Goldingay broadens this view to encompass the Israelites: "an awakening of the dead of nations other than Israel is hardly within the concern of v. 2."[97] What does this awakening involve? "The seer could be promising a revival of the nation after the Antiochene persecution. ... But the revival is to 'lasting life,' which suggests more than that, as does the reference to the destiny of 'others.'"[98] So, in Goldingay's judgment, is the awakening communal or individual? "There is both a community and an individual

---

93. Koehler and Baumgartner, *HALOT*, s.v. "יָשֵׁן."
94. Armerding, "Asleep in the Dust," 156–57.
95. Walter Bauer, *A Greek-English Lexicon of the New Testament and Other Early Christian Literature*, ed. and trans. William F. Arndt, F. Wilber Gingrich, and Frederick W. Danker, 3rd ed. (Chicago: University of Chicago Press, 2001), s.v. "καθεύδω."
96. George Wesley Buchanan, *The Book of Daniel*, MBC, vol. 25 (Lewiston, NY: Mellen Biblical Press, 1999), 379. See M. Casey, "Porphyry and Syrian Exegesis of the Book of Daniel," *ZAW* 81 (1990): 141.
97. Goldingay, *Daniel*, 307.
98. Goldingay, *Daniel*, 307. See Seow, *Daniel*, 187–88.

aspect to this awakening. ... Dan 12 promises the awakening of people individually, but with a view to their sharing a corporate destiny."[99]

Greidanus points out a glaring problem with this view: Porphyry was a pagan critic of Christianity who claimed that prophecy cannot predict events centuries in advance, which means the author of Daniel was not actually Daniel but a second-century BC writer who recorded the "prophecies" *ex eventu*.[100] Porphyry's reasoning is akin to post-Enlightenment skepticism of the miraculous.[101] Such scholars read Old Testament prophecy with a deficient view of the supernatural, and they may even be anti-supernatural.[102] This agenda obscures the natural reading of Daniel 12:2.

In the context prior to Daniel 12, the faithful Jews are vulnerable to sword and flame (11:33), and many will die (11:41). Daniel 12:2 is the divine response to the faithful who suffer. There is a death problem, and Daniel hears about a resurrection remedy. Wright is correct: "Daniel 12 is best seen ... as reflecting an awareness of *extended and continuing* exile, focused now in suffering and martyrdom."[103] When God acts in this resurrection, the results will be everlasting. The finality of the outcome poses a problem with the merely "national restoration" view.[104]

Revival of God's people after the Messiah's coming? James Jordan contends, "The resurrection of 'those who sleep in the dust of the ground' in Daniel 12:2 is *not* a prediction of the final physical resurrection, but alludes back to Daniel's own fall to the ground, and refers to the resurrection of the people of God as a community after the coming of the Messiah."[105] This means that, like Ezekiel 37, the resurrection is a national one and "is the only credible possibility."[106]

The problems with Jordan's view are manifold. First, most scholars—even higher-critical ones I have already referenced—agree that Daniel

---

99. Goldingay, *Daniel*, 307.
100. Greidanus, *Preaching Christ from Daniel*, 5.
101. Collins: "Porphyry's line of reasoning is ... similar to that of modern critics" (*Daniel*, 25).
102. See, e.g., Towner, who says that "human beings are unable accurately to predict future events centuries in advance" (*Daniel*, 115).
103. Wright, *The Resurrection of the Son of God*, 122. Wright is an example of someone who sees physical resurrection as the promise foretold in Dan 12:2 while at the same being a scholar who dates Daniel to the second century BC.
104. Lucas, *Daniel*, 294.
105. Jordan, *The Handwriting on the Wall*, 84.
106. Jordan, *The Handwriting on the Wall*, 617.

12:2 is a clear expression of physical resurrection, even if they insist it is the first emergence of its kind, so Jordan's statement that his view "is the only credible possibility" is a serious overstatement. Second, while I would grant that Daniel 12:2 may connect to the prophet's fall in 10:9, it is better to see 12:2 as escalation in the sense of physical death actually occurring, especially in light of the promise that Daniel himself would die (12:13), a promise that was not about falling to the ground again. Third, the permanence of the outcomes ("everlasting life" or "everlasting contempt" in 12:2) undermines an earthly revival. Fourth, Jordan does not grant enough significance to the idiom of "sleeping in the dust" as equivalent to death, and to the notion of "waking" as a metaphor for resurrection in previous Old Testament passages. Fifth, the author of Daniel 12:2 uses earlier Scripture (see the previous exegesis showing dependence on Genesis and Isaiah) about physical death, physical resurrection, and physical judgment, and this reuse of Old Testament passages results in the fullest statement of resurrection hope in the Old Testament.

SUMMARY

Daniel 12:2 promises a future bodily resurrection of God's people and enemies, and these respective groups will be given either everlasting life or everlasting shame. This interpretation is exegetically sound and coheres with the Old Testament texts that the biblical author used in the verse. Alternative interpretations of Daniel 12:2 that insist on a nonphysical and (to some degree) national restoration of God's people—either in the second century BC or the first century AD—are unsound exegetically and create more problems than they solve.

CONCLUSION

The resurrection hope of Daniel 12:2 was not a radical innovation in the theology of the biblical author. Rather, this verse was an explicit elaboration on already-held beliefs that God would vindicate his people and judge his enemies. The chapters in the book (before 12:2) interweaved these beliefs and preserved the momentum leading to the climactic promise in the book's final vision.

Now that we have established the context and meaning of Daniel 12:2, it will be appropriate to proceed to the Law, Prophets, and Writings. What passages, stories, and theological convictions lay behind the hope of Daniel 12:2? And how early does this hope emerge, even if only in seed form? Belief in resurrection "is sown in the same soil as the beliefs of the

Patriarchs; seed and soil, indeed, are important clues to the continuity, as well as the discontinuity, between (for instance) Genesis and Daniel."[107] It is time to move backward from the postexilic years to a much earlier stage in history.

---

107. Wright, *The Resurrection of the Son of God*, 87.

3

Resurrection Hope before Daniel 12:2

The resurrection hope of Daniel 12:2 did not emerge without Old Testament precursors.

The line of this hope is long and runs deep. The verse has linguistic, theological, and figural precursors that advance a resurrection hope. We will examine the Law, Prophets, and Writings to see where, how, and why the biblical authors cultivate this hope for the people of God.[1] Evidence will be presented in two categories: *strong* evidence and *supporting* evidence.

The first category encompasses instances that suggest resurrection hope either explicitly or implicitly, and these instances should be considered strong contenders for advancing that hope. The second category includes passages that are not as strong but still reinforce a belief in future bodily life. My case for resurrection hope existing before Daniel 12:2 does not depend on this second category, but it is certainly helped by secondary support that adds contours and details to the framework of thought. With the following evidence added to the arguments in the previous chapter, I aim to demonstrate the first part of my thesis, that Daniel relied on earlier Old Testament texts and theological convictions when he expressed the hope of bodily resurrection.[2]

---

1. I may address a passage only in its immediate context because no later Old Testament or New Testament author uses it, while at other times I will discuss both the immediate context and later use of a passage. Both OT and NT authors can clarify what an earlier passage is communicating. When a biblical author interprets an earlier verse or passage, the reader can be wholly confident about the meaning asserted, for the biblical authors are *inspired* interpreters. They read earlier biblical texts accurately, and their example should be followed by interpreters who adopt their presuppositions.
2. For a concise volume on resurrection hope in Scripture, see Mitchell L. Chase, *Resurrection Hope and the Death of Death*, Short Studies in Biblical Theology (Wheaton: Crossway, 2022).

THE LAW

INTRODUCTION

What Elmer Smick wrote over forty years ago remains true today: "The consensus of critical opinion still insists that emergent belief in the resurrection of the dead was a thing unattested in the literature of preexilic Israel."[3] Such critical opinion applies especially to the Torah. Collins is unmistakably clear with his insistence that belief in resurrection is not even *implicit* before the book of Daniel.[4] But certain biblical characters in the New Testament interpret those early books with eyes that saw resurrection hope. Either those characters are wrong, or the critical scholars are wrong.

Consider the words of the apostle Paul, and then hear the surprising claim of Jesus. When Paul spoke before Felix at Caesarea, the apostle confessed that he believed "everything laid down by the Law and written in the Prophets, having a hope in God ... that there will be a resurrection of both the just and the unjust" (Acts 24:14-15).[5] Paul's hope for resurrection was rooted in what he believed, and he does not only list the Prophets as a foundation for this hope. Paul says he believed "everything laid down by the *Law*," so somehow this section of Scripture stimulated his resurrection hope as well. Thirty years earlier, a group of Sadducees—who did not believe in a future bodily resurrection (cf. Matt 22:23; Acts 23:8)—questioned Jesus about that topic in order to trap him (Matt 22:23-28). Jesus left them speechless when he quoted from the book of Exodus to affirm the resurrection (Matt 22:31-32, 34; Exod 3:6). The significance of his citation is *where* it came from, for Sadducees only accepted the Torah as authoritative. To their surprise Jesus showed the hope of resurrection *from their Scriptures*.[6]

This project sides with Jesus and Paul against the Sadducees. Recognizing resurrection in the first five Old Testament books was serious business, for according to the Mishnah nothing less than eternal

---

3. Elmer Smick, "The Bearing of New Philological Data on the Subjects of Resurrection and Immortality in the Old Testament," *WTJ* 31 (1969): 12.
4. Collins, *Encounters with Biblical Theology*, 32.
5. This passage from Acts will be discussed in chap. 5, but for now it will serve as sufficient evidence that the Torah holds out a hope for resurrection.
6. As Wright points out, the rabbis insisted on the presence of resurrection hope in the Torah, and the main Talmudic discussion in Sanhedrin 90-92 offers many examples (Wright, *The Resurrection of the Son of God*, 197).

inheritance is on the line: "And these are the ones who do not have a share in the World-to-Come: He who says that the resurrection of the dead is not in the Torah, [he who says] that the Torah is not from Heaven, and the skeptic" (m. Sanh. 10:1).

By looking at certain passages in the Law, we will be putting our ear to the ground to hear the faint but discernible rumblings of what will arrive later and louder in the words of the prophets.[7]

STRONG EVIDENCE

Strong evidence for resurrection hope exists in Genesis, Exodus, and Deuteronomy.[8]

The God of Abraham, Isaac, and Jacob (Exod 3:6). Only in this subsection will I present a passage out of its canonical order. The first verse to be examined is from Exodus because (1) it is cited in the New Testament as an answer to people who did not believe resurrection was taught in the Pentateuch, and (2) its use by Jesus is in a context that illuminates the hermeneutic he uses, a hermeneutic crucial to identifying other instances of implicit resurrection hope. For these reasons this first piece of evidence will be treated at greater length than others that follow.

Exodus 3 narrates an encounter between Moses and God. Moses heard a voice from a burning bush call to him, "Moses, Moses!" (Exod 3:4). He followed instructions and removed his sandals because of the holy ground on which he stood (3:5). The voice identified itself: "I am the God of your father, the God of Abraham, the God of Isaac, and the God of Jacob" (3:6). Moses is face-to-fire with the God of the patriarchs, that family line of Abraham to whom God made special promises about a blessing agenda for the nations (Gen 12:2-3).[9]

What does Exodus 3 have to do with resurrection? On the surface there seems to be no such belief advocated at all. Yahweh, the promise-keeping God of Abraham, Isaac, and Jacob, commits to deliver the

---

7. For an article exploring resurrection hope in the Old Testament, see Mitchell L. Chase, "From Dust You Shall Arise: Resurrection Hope in the Old Testament," *SBJT* 18, no. 4 (2014): 9-29.
8. For an article exploring the seeds of resurrection hope in the book of Genesis, see Mitchell L. Chase, "The Genesis of Resurrection Hope: Exploring Its Early Presence and Deep Roots," *JETS* 57, no. 3 (2014): 467-80.
9. For an explanation of how God's promises of blessing in Gen 12 were answers to the curses in Gen 3, see James M. Hamilton Jr., "The Seed of the Woman and the Blessing of Abraham," *TynBul* 58, no. 2 (2007): 253-73.

captive Israelites from the Egyptians (Exod 3:6-8). There is, however, no apparent death reversed, no promise to restore life to bodies in a grave. How strange, then, that Jesus cites Exodus 3 in a conversation with Sadducees to show that their Scriptures teach resurrection hope.

In the Synoptic Gospels, the Sadducees (who do not believe in a bodily resurrection; cf. Matt 22:23; Acts 23:8) approach Jesus to trap him with a question. They articulate a hypothetical scenario in order to show that belief in resurrection is problematic: if a man dies without having children, and then his seven brothers—each of whom marries the widow after the previous sibling dies (according to the practice of levirate marriage in Deut 25:5-10)—were unable to leave their first dead brother any children either, whose wife would the widow be at the resurrection? (Matt 22:24-28).

Jesus observed that the Sadducees, first of all, wrongly conceived what the resurrection would involve, for there is no marriage in heaven (Matt 22:30). Their question commits a logical fallacy, a category mistake. Their marriage scenario does not disprove, or render impractical, a future resurrection, for it concerns something not applicable to the realization of that hope. Jesus does not end the conversation with his correction of their poor understanding. They try to trap him, so first he exposes their misunderstanding, and now he exposes their ignorance. He proceeds to quote their own Scriptures (sola Torah) to prove a future resurrection: "And as for the resurrection of the dead, have you not read what was said to you by God: 'I am the God of Abraham, and the God of Isaac, and the God of Jacob'? He is not God of the dead, but of the living" (Matt 22:31-32).[10]

The verse Jesus quotes is Exodus 3:6. He does not leave his audience to draw the implication. He states clearly what he means them to understand: "He is not God of the dead, but of the living" (Matt 22:32b). How does citing Exodus 3:6 support resurrection? How would it silence the Sadducees and astonish the crowds who heard the teaching?

---

10. Hays explains, "Presumably, in fact, their rejection of the resurrection rests precisely on appeals to the authority of Scripture: no such belief was taught by Moses, so it should not be accepted. By challenging them at this point, Jesus creates the expectation that he will produce scriptural evidence to discredit their skepticism" (Richard B. Hays, "Reading Scripture in Light of the Resurrection," in *The Art of Reading Scripture*, ed. Ellen F. Davis and Richard B. Hays [Grand Rapids: Eerdmans, 2003], 226).

Jesus's point does not seem to demand anything more than the spirit's existence after death. Commentators typically explain how Jesus relates Exodus 3:6 to a future resurrection by pointing out that the verb is *am* and not *was*: "I *am* the God."[11] This means, apparently, that the patriarchs are currently alive[12] and, by implication, will see bodily life once more.[13] But how does this understanding of Jesus's words carry the hope of bodily resurrection?

If dying physically and going to be with God were sufficient to imply that disembodied life would lead to resurrection one day, Jesus could have quoted the reports in Genesis that Abraham (Gen 25:8), Isaac (35:29),

---

11. Hays says, "Most New Testament commentators say that the argument turns on a grammatical technicality: because God says 'I *am* the God of Abraham, the God of Isaac, and the God of Jacob,' not 'I *was* the God of Abraham ... ,' it must be inferred that these three patriarchs—who had long since departed earthly life—are to be found among the living, not the dead. ... One difficulty, however, is that it is not at all clear how the argument, so construed, actually would support *resurrection*, as distinct from immortality of the soul" ("Reading Scripture in Light of the Resurrection," 227). Morris, as a representative of the typical interpretation, says, "The threefold repetition is most impressive, and presumably the Sadducees, like many others, had been so attracted by the majesty of the words and what they told them of the experiences of the patriarchs that they had never stopped to think of the implications of the saying. So Jesus points out that the present tense is important" (Leon Morris, *The Gospel According to Matthew*, PNTC [Grand Rapids: Eerdmans, 1992], 561).

12. Reflecting on the Markan parallel, Wright notes that the phrase "He is not God of the dead, but of the living" (Mark 12:27a) "can be misunderstood. Jesus is not simply saying that Abraham, Isaac and Jacob are still alive in the presence of God, and that their present afterlife is what is meant by 'resurrection.' ... The point is precisely that they are 'dead' at present, but that since God desires to be known as their God he must be intending to raise them from death in the future" (Tom Wright, *Mark for Everyone* [Louisville: Westminster John Knox, 2004], 168). Wright seems to argue that according to Jesus, the patriarchs are actually dead even as the Sadducees hear him, but God will raise the dead because he desires to be known as the God of the living. Yet according to Edwards, if the patriarchs *are* dead, then Jesus would be conceding the Sadducees' point: "If Abraham, Isaac, and Jacob are dead, as the Sadducees believe, then God's promise to them was limited to the duration of their earthly lives, which renders his promises finite and unfulfilled" (James R. Edwards, *The Gospel According to Mark*, PNTC [Grand Rapids: Eerdmans, 2002], 369).

13. Hagner comments, "If God is the God of the patriarchs, they are by implication alive after their death ... and thus the ground is prepared for the reality of the future resurrection" (Donald A. Hagner, *Matthew 14–28*, WBC, vol. 33B [Nashville: Thomas Nelson, 1995], 642). But Jesus effectively rebukes the Sadducees in Matt 22 not by bringing up a passage that only lays the *groundwork* for the reality of resurrection but by calling to mind a text that, to him, *actually suggests* resurrection hope.

and Jacob (49:33) were all gathered to their people, which is a promise of life beyond death.[14] Instead he quotes God's claim from Exodus 3:6, which pulls the names of the patriarchs together in one phrase, and somehow this assertion supports the very notion the Sadducees were denying.[15]

The key to interpreting Jesus's words is probably at the beginning of the hypothetical scenario.[16] The Sadducees posited a man who died with no seed and whose brother married the widow to raise up offspring (ἀναστήσει σπέρμα) for the deceased (Matt 22:24–25). Childlessness continued through the other brothers who, one by one after the death of the predecessor, married the widow but failed to raise up seed (22:26). After the Sadducees finished the story, Jesus told them, "You are wrong, because you know neither the Scriptures nor the power of God" (22:29). When Jesus said, "And as for the resurrection of the dead," he proceeded to recount a statement to demonstrate both "the Scriptures" they should know and "the power of God" that should be evident.

How, then, does the claim "I am the God of Abraham, and the God of Isaac, and the God of Jacob" accomplish Jesus's intent to teach the Sadducees that resurrection hope is found in the Torah? The logic is critical here. The statement mentions the patriarchs who each had their own struggles raising up seed. Jesus's citation of Exodus 3:6 is a direct response to the kind of scenario the Sadducees described, which was about the failure to raise up descendants. The Sadducees told Jesus a story permeated with sterility that ended in futile hope and death, so he evoked the story of their ancestors whose challenges of sterility were no secret.[17] God is the God of Abraham, Isaac, and Jacob (Matt 22:32a), and thus the God of the living (22:32b), because he alone preserved and raised up the lineage from Abraham. The Sadducees made up a story

---

14. For a distinction between burial and being "gathered to his people," see chap. 1.
15. For an investigation of the use of the formula "the God of Abraham, and the God of Isaac, and the God of Jacob" in the Bible and in the era of Jesus, see F. Dreyfus, "L'Argument scripturaire de Jésus en faveur de la résurrection des morts (Marc XII, vv. 26–27)," RB 66 (1959): 213–24.
16. J. Gerald Janzen, "Resurrection and Hermeneutics: On Exodus 3.6 in Mark 12.26," JSNT 23 (1985): 46–48. "What is unambiguous is the fact that the Sadducees play on two meanings of the verb 'raise up' and its noun cognate 'raising up/resurrection'" (47).
17. Janzen, "Resurrection and Hermeneutics," 50–51. "The irony will consist in the way in which the Sadducees, in attempting to debunk resurrection, are shown drawing the very analogy upon which Jesus' argument for resurrection will turn" (47).

about childlessness in order to portray resurrection as a ludicrous concept. Rather than responding with a made-up story of his own, Jesus quoted their Bible to them, showing that in fact they did *not* know the Scriptures *or* the power of God, for stories of barrenness and sterility were the very kind of situations in which God had displayed his power time and time again.[18]

The concept of God's preserving power fits the original Exodus 3 context as well. The descendants of Abraham, Isaac, and Jacob were not in the land he promised to those patriarchs. The people were multiplying under Egyptian rule (Exod 1:7–8), but the new king wanted the number of descendants to stop increasing, "lest they multiply, and, if war breaks out, they join our enemies and fight against us and escape from the land" (1:10). The Israelites were subjected to slavery (1:11–14). To keep them from growing, the pharaoh ordered the killing of newborn sons (1:16; cf. 1:22). But "God remembered his covenant with Abraham, with Isaac, and with Jacob" (2:24). He had promised them descendants, he had promised a land for them to dwell in, and he had promised to bless the nations through Abraham's line (cf. Gen 12:1–7), and no baby-killing, power-hungry ruler in Egypt was going to undermine God's bringing to pass his every promise.[19]

So when God came to Moses in the burning bush, he identified himself as the covenant-keeping God who *had* and who *would* overcome every obstacle in raising up descendants.[20] Currently the flourishing of the people was in jeopardy, so God told Moses, "I have come down

---

18. According to Hays, "When we read Scripture in light of the resurrection [of Christ], *we understand Scripture as testimony to the life-giving power of God.* The resurrection of Jesus is not an isolated miracle but a disclosure of God's purpose finally to subdue death and to embrace us within the life of the resurrection. ... The God with whom we have to do is a God who wills life and wholeness for us. If we read the biblical story rightly as a story about this God, we will learn to read it in hopeful trust, open to joyous surprises" (Richard B. Hays, *Reading with the Grain of Scripture* [Grand Rapids: Eerdmans, 2020], 64), emphasis original.
19. Witherington rightly notes, "The biblical God had made promises to these patriarchs, and since they had not all yet been fulfilled, it must be assumed they are still alive" (Ben Witherington III, *Matthew*, Smyth & Helwys Bible Commentary [Macon, GA: Smyth & Helwys, 2006], 416). But his words do not go far enough, for an implication of life in a disembodied state does not further imply their future resurrection.
20. Janzen reasons, "Such a general ancient exegetical use of the three-ancestral formula, I suggest, rests upon a hermeneutical assumption. ... For it is implicit in the scene at the burning bush that some kind of analogy exists

to deliver them out of the hand of the Egyptians and to bring them up out of that land to a good and broad land, a land flowing with milk and honey" (Exod 3:8). The stories of Abraham, Isaac, and Jacob were stories of God keeping promises and displaying his power, which was chiefly manifested in preserving the Abrahamic line. These were the things, though, that the Sadducees failed to see.

Hays writes, "God's faithfulness in securing the future of his chosen people is the sure basis on which the descendants of the patriarchs can continue to hope for the future."[21] When Jesus quoted Exodus 3:6 to his resurrection-denying listeners, it became clear that in the stories of Abraham, Isaac, and Jacob, God had been displaying his "power" and raising life from the dead.[22] Jesus's appeal to Exodus "makes more explicit what is already there for those who have eyes to see."[23] The Sadducees did not have such sight.

But how does reversing barrenness and preserving a family line relate to hope for bodily resurrection? How would quoting Exodus 3:6 silence the Sadducees and astonish the crowds? The explanation that best fits the facts is one that views personal identity in both individual and familial terms, such that the fate of the individual is wrapped up in the fate of that individual's family. Our highly individualistic culture may easily separate people from their immediate social context, but the Hebrew culture made no such fine distinction.[24] A person's identity continued in the survival and propagation of progeny. Levenson is right to note that this was the logic undergirding the practice of levirate

---

between the ancestral situations and the situation of the generation of Moses" ("Resurrection and Hermeneutics," 45).

21. Hays, "Reading Scripture in Light of the Resurrection," 227. Eugene Boring is in the right direction when he says of the Markan parallel, "In any case, there is no verb in the Hebrew text of Exodus or the Markan citation. ... [The point] is not grammar but the faithfulness and power of God, who had made a covenant with Abraham, Isaac, and Jacob, and who would not allow even death to annul it" (M. Eugene Boring, *Mark: A Commentary*, NTL [Louisville: Westminster John Knox, 2006], 340). Keener is right: "If God was still God of Abraham, Isaac and Jacob, and if his power was unlimited, then he would ultimately fulfill his promise to them—not only corporately through their descendants, but personally to them" (Craig S. Keener, *Matthew*, The IVP New Testament Commentary Series, vol. 1 [Downers Grove, IL: InterVarsity Press, 1997], 328).

22. See Janzen, "Resurrection and Hermeneutics," 55.
23. Hays, "Reading Scripture in Light of the Resurrection," 228.
24. See Levenson, *Resurrection and the Restoration of Israel*, 109.

marriage,[25] which, interestingly enough, was the very practice in the illustration the Sadducees gave to Jesus (cf. Matt 22:24; Deut 25:5).

Therefore, the experience of barrenness (Gen 11:30; 16:2; 18:11-13) or the loss of children (e.g. Gen 37:33-35; 48:11; Jer 31:15) were devastating obstacles for a couple to face.[26] Life was bound up partly in social identity, meaning that the end of a family line was the functional equivalent of death.[27] In Genesis 15 God told Abraham, "Your reward shall be very great" (15:1), but he feared childlessness and asked, "O Lord GOD, what will you give me, for I continue childless. ... Behold, you have given me no offspring" (15:2-3). To Abraham all the reward in all the world could not compensate for childlessness.[28] When Rachel faced barrenness, she told Jacob, "Give me children, or I shall die!" (30:1). Robert Alter observes that her plea can be translated, "Give me sons; if not, I am dead."[29] Different was Job's situation, for he experienced not a lack of children but the loss of them, prompting bereavement and misery.[30] And in the New Testament we see that to renounce your family was a kind of death, as in the case of the prodigal son in Luke 15, who left his home only to return later and hear his father say to the other sibling, "Your brother was dead, and is alive; he was lost, and is found" (Luke 15:32).

Going back to Matthew 22, it is noteworthy that Jesus sees resurrection in a passage where no verb would overtly suggest it. But if we grant that individuals and their familial sphere were not sharply separated in antiquity, then we can see how reversing the death of the family line can also stir hope for reversing the death of individuals who are part of that line. The arc of life propelled by God through the Abrahamic line encountered more than once the threat of sterility that put divine

---

25. Levenson, *Resurrection and the Restoration of Israel*, 120. He later says, "By a kind of legal fiction, his family brings something of their dead kinsman back to life, birth again reversing death. *Levirate marriage is a mode of redemption of the dead*" (121, emphasis mine).
26. Levenson, *Resurrection and the Restoration of Israel*, 109-10.
27. Levenson, *Resurrection and the Restoration of Israel*, 113. As Levenson later says, "In other words, given the construction of personal identity in the Hebrew Bible, infertility and the loss of children serve as the functional equivalent of death. Striking at each generation of the patriarchs of Genesis, and then at Judah in the next, childlessness in one or both of these modes threatens to terminate the family, thus evoking the terror that later generations (including our own) feel in the face of their personal deaths" (119-20).
28. Levenson, *Resurrection and the Restoration of Israel*, 115.
29. Robert Alter, *The Art of Biblical Narrative* (New York: Basic Books, 1981), 187.
30. Levenson, *Resurrection and the Restoration of Israel*, 115.

promises in jeopardy. And each time, Yahweh, being the covenant-making and promise-keeping God that he is, raised the family line from the dead.[31]

Yahweh is therefore the God of Abraham, Isaac, and Jacob, the God of the living, the God whom Jesus said the Sadducees should have known and seen from the Scriptures. Janzen distills the matter: "The issue at the heart of [the Sadducees'] story—the problem of sterility and death—is now seen to be the issue which is addressed by appeal directly to the identical ancestral and the analogous Exodus themes through the quotation of one sentence uttered by God at the bush."[32]

At this point an objection to the preceding points might be, "How is reversing barrenness a type of death and resurrection when the wives of the patriarchs never lost the ability to conceive in the first place?" We must accurately pinpoint *where* the analogy applies, and that location is *not* to an individual wife. The analogy applies to the family line itself, which goes through one patriarch's wife to the next. The line of progeny is alive, advancing on until the next case of barrenness arises, causing a functional death. God then overcomes this obstacle, which is resurrection, corporately speaking, but with individual implications because of how the Hebrews conceived of personal identity.[33] And if I have accurately discerned the original context of Exodus 3:6 as well as Jesus's use of it in Matthew 22, then his words are sufficient and inspired proof that God's power displayed in advancing the Abrahamic line should have convinced the Sadducees that the dead would one day be raised.

Exodus 3:6 reinforces two important points integral to the argument of this project. First, resurrection hope appears in the Torah, something Sadducees and critical scholars have denied. The words of

---

31. Corporate resurrection will be seen most clearly later in Israel's history when they are exiled from the promised land and return by Persian permission. Their exile and restoration are a national death and resurrection, and we will see how individual hopes are wrapped up in what happens on a larger scale (e.g., Ezek 37; Hos 6). But for now, the corporate family unit serves as something that can undergo a death and resurrection, in which individual hopes are also intricately and inseparably interwoven. Jordan says it this way: "Death and resurrection can be and often is a wider concept, applying to nations and to individuals in ways that are analogous to actual physical death and resurrection" (Jordan, *The Handwriting on the Wall*, 80).
32. Janzen, "Resurrection and Hermeneutics," 55.
33. As Dempster puts it, "The overcoming of sterility in new life with the birth of children ... [is] the renewal of life—resurrection!" (Dempster, "The Resurrection of Christ," 6).

Jesus demonstrate that this hope surfaces earlier than the Prophets and Writings. And if Jesus sees resurrection in words from the Torah, then his interpretation trumps the naysayers. Second, the logic of Jesus's quotation suggests that resurrection hope can be present even if explicit expressions are absent. As long as interpreters insist on affirming resurrection only if certain words are present, then Jesus's argument to the Sadducees will seem nonsensical. If I have accurately explained how his argument works in Matthew 22, however, then it confirms the presence of resurrection hope in the Torah, even if only implicitly.

Jesus told the Sadducees, "You are wrong, because you know neither the Scriptures nor the power of God" (Matt 22:29).[34] Janzen says, "'Knowing the scriptures' is not just a matter of *what* one reads, it is equally a matter of *how* one reads."[35] Hays states, "To know the Scriptures and the power of God is to discern in Israel's story the working of the same God who raised Jesus from the dead."[36]

The tree of life and immortal physicality (Gen 2:9; 3:22). God filled the garden of Eden with trees pleasing to the eye and good for food (Gen 2:9). Two of these trees had unusual significance and stood in the middle of the garden: the tree of the knowledge of good and evil, and the tree of life (2:9). After Adam and Eve ate of the former, God prohibited access to the latter. God sent our disobedient representative from the garden "lest he reach out his hand and take also of the tree of life and eat, and live forever" (3:22).

---

34. According to Hays, Jesus "implies that knowledge of biblical content is not the same thing as 'knowing the Scriptures' in the way that matters. The telling of this controversy story suggests that authentic knowledge of the Scriptures depends on a hermeneutic of resurrection, the ability to discern in Scripture a witness of God's life-giving power" ("Reading Scripture in Light of the Resurrection," 226).
35. Janzen, "Resurrection and Hermeneutics," 50.
36. Hays, "Reading Scripture in Light of the Resurrection," 229. Hays gives sound guidance to Bible readers: "Reading in light of the resurrection is figural reading. Because the Old Testament's pointers to the resurrection are indirect and symbolic in character, the resurrection teaches us to read for figuration and latent sense. The Sadducees were literalists, but God seems to have delighted in veiled anticipations of the gospel. ... Resurrection-informed reading sees the life-giving power of God manifested and prefigured in unexpected ways throughout Scripture. ... The Jesus who taught the disciples on the Emmaus road that *all* the scriptures bore witness to him continues to teach us to discover figural senses of Scripture that are not developed in the New Testament" (234).

Consider what the fruit of the tree of life represented: *immortal bodily existence*. This tree held out hope for something Adam and Eve did not yet have. Their mortal bodies died in the conditions outside Eden. But the teaching of the biblical author in Genesis 3:22 is that if Adam and Eve had eaten of the tree, they would have lived forever.[37] Therefore, barring them from the tree of life ensured their death, which God promised if they ate the forbidden fruit (2:17). The cherubim and flaming sword were a visible reminder that God kept his promise.

If God created the tree of life for his image bearers to eat from and thus acquire bodily immortality, but then barred access to it when they transgressed his command, would he ever reopen access? Would the cherubim someday sheathe the flaming sword? If Adam's exile meant death, what would return from exile mean?[38]

If indeed the Old Testament teaches that God will make all things new at the appointed consummation,[39] even surpassing the original quality and scope of the garden, then humanity will get the chance to feast from the tree of life. In Revelation 22:2 the "tree of life" is in the New Jerusalem. Though people were once barred from accessing it, this tree will dwell amid the nations for their healing (22:2b). The name is identical to the one in Genesis 2–3, so there is no reason to believe that what its fruit represents has changed. This tree *will* live up to its designation, bearing fruit of immortality.[40] That fruit in the garden existed to be eaten, and John says that in the New Jerusalem the tree of life will yield fruit each month (cf. Rev 22:2), probably indicating the replacement of what is eaten.

---

37. Presumably this state would have been bodily as well. This implication is reasonable because God exiled them to ensure their bodily death.
38. In Gen 3 the important themes of exile and death are linked, the former meaning the latter. This observation matters for future occasions when God's people are exiled and thus undergo a kind of death. This equation (exile = death) prepares for an even more important equation (return = resurrection). See Paul's words in Rom 11:15.
39. Defending this assertion is beyond the scope of this section. For an explanation on the purpose of the garden and God's intention to fill the world with image-bearing people, see G. K. Beale, *The Temple and the Church's Mission: A Biblical Theology of the Dwelling Place of God*, NSBT, vol. 17 (Downers Grove, IL: InterVarsity Press, 2004), 29–122; T. D. Alexander, *From Eden to the New Jerusalem: An Introduction to Biblical Theology* (Grand Rapids: Kregel, 2008), 13–73.
40. Alexander, *From Eden to the New Jerusalem*, 156.

Adam and Eve died because of the curse of sin and exile from the garden, but the very presence of the tree of life there held out hope for bodily immortality. That tree was a picture of the bodily life in store for the people of God, and the biblical author indicated with the expression in Genesis 3:22 that anyone who ate of it would have this life forever. Waltke concludes, "This highest potency of life was available in the garden and … will be experienced consummately in the resurrection of our bodies."[41]

The defeat of the serpent (Gen 3:15). Between Adam and Eve's disobedience (Gen 3:6) and exile (3:24), God promised the serpent's defeat: "I will put enmity between you and the woman, and between your offspring and her offspring; he shall bruise your head, and you shall bruise his heel" (3:15). The woman's future offspring would have victory. What would this mean for the seed of the woman?

At present the seed endured difficulty and travail (Gen 3:16-19), but the future judgment of the serpent was certain. The serpent was the deceiver in the garden and instigator of the image bearers' rebellion, so his defeat may have implications for the image bearers also. When that defeat was finally accomplished, the seed of the woman would find relief from the curse (cf. 5:29).

Beale believes that the promise in Genesis 3:15 likely implies a reversal of the serpent's work and sin's curse.[42] If this reversal is true, and since part of sin's curse involves the death of bodies, then undoing the curse will mean the reversal of death. If God will one day turn back the effects of sin, then resurrection hope is reasonable. Thus Beale states, "The first possible hint of resurrection life may be discernible in Gen 1-3."[43] The strength of this possibility increases with the next piece of evidence, for there we will see the biblical author interpreting the language in Genesis 3 to mean that someone—the anticipated seed of the woman—will reverse the curse and restore the rest previously enjoyed only in the garden.

Lamech's hope for his son Noah (Gen 5:29). Lamech, the grandson of Enoch, fathers Noah and expresses great hope for him: "Out of the

---

41. Waltke, *An Old Testament Theology*, 257. See also Waltke, *Genesis: A Commentary* (Grand Rapids: Zondervan, 2001), 86.
42. Beale, *A New Testament Biblical Theology*, 228-29.
43. Beale, *A New Testament Biblical Theology*, 228. See M. Jeff Brannon, *The Hope of Life After Death: A Biblical Theology of Resurrection*, Essential Studies in Biblical Theology (Downers Grove, IL: IVP Academic, 2022), 28-30, 35.

ground that the LORD has cursed this one shall bring us relief from our work and from the painful toil of our hands" (Gen 5:29).

Where does Lamech get the ideas of cursed ground and toilsome work? They are unmistakable references to God's words in Genesis 3:17–19.[44] There God told Adam the ground is "cursed ... because of you; in pain you shall eat of it," and "by the sweat of your face you shall eat bread, till you return to the ground, for out of it you were taken" (3:17b, 19a). The biblical author indicates that the content of the curse had been transmitted generation after generation, from Adam down to Lamech. The ground would be a source of difficulty (3:18), and in the end it would subdue the image bearers in the dust (3:19). No matter how hard or how long they worked, they would return at death to the ground God cursed.

With knowledge of this curse on the ground, why did Lamech hope Noah would bring an end to its effects? Because not only was the content of Adam's judgment passed from one generation to the next, the content of the serpent's punishment was also conveyed. In Genesis 3:15 God promised a seed of the woman who would defeat the serpent. Lamech's words in 5:29 show his knowledge of both the judgment *and* the deliverance God promised in the garden. The future son's victory would benefit image bearers ("this *one* shall bring *us* relief," Lamech said) by reversing the curse under which humanity lived ("from our work and ... toil").

Once we grant Lamech's knowledge of the judgment and hope in Genesis 3, his reasoning in 5:29 is understandable: Noah is part of Eve's offspring, so perhaps Noah would be the seed of the woman who will defeat the serpent and bring rest from the curse.[45] Lamech may not speak explicitly of Noah being the catalyst for *death's* reversal, but the allusion to 3:17–19 includes an effect on death. For just as the reference to a coming individual implies the promise of the woman's seed and serpent's defeat, so relief from the curse means more than only rest from toil.[46] The curse of toilsome work would end in death (cf. 3:19), for toil outside the garden would never bring the rest inherent to life inside it.

---

44. Hamilton, *God's Glory in Salvation through Judgment*, 88.
45. According to Walton, "It may have been Lamech's hope that Noah would somehow bring about the reversal of the curse" (John H. Walton, *Genesis*, NIVAC [Grand Rapids: Zondervan, 2001], 281).
46. Calvin says that the words "work" and "painful toil" are a synecdoche because this labor represents the "whole miserable state into which mankind had fallen" (*Genesis*, Crossway Classic Commentaries [Wheaton, IL: Crossway, 2001], 65).

If the victor's work will turn back the curse, then he will undo the power of death. After all, the work Adam initially performed was without toil and not heading toward death (2:5, 15). The rest he enjoyed was in the garden, a rest his disobedience compromised. Outside Eden, the lot of humans was toilsome until the grave. Lamech hoped for the day when rest would once more come to God's image bearers, and others clearly shared that hope.

Abraham's trust in God to preserve the seed (Gen 22:5). Genesis 22 narrates Abraham's compliance to a shocking divine command: "Take your son, your only son Isaac … and offer him there as a burnt offering" (Gen 22:2). Readers sense conflict at this point, for years earlier God promised Abraham and Sarah a son (15:4; 18:14) who would begin fulfilling the plan of blessing the nations through the family line (12:2–3). Now that the long-awaited heir of Abraham had arrived (21:2–3), God put his own promises in jeopardy when he commanded the patriarch to sacrifice the offspring. Why would God promise Abraham descendants who would outnumber the stars (15:5) and then set up the demise of that promise with a dreadful command regarding a father's son?

The Genesis account reports Abraham's response with fast-paced narration: he rose early, saddled his donkey, took two men and his son, cut wood, and went to the predetermined place (Gen 22:3). When the time came to offer the sacrifice, Abraham spoke words that warrant close reflection. He told the two men: "I and the boy will go [נֵלְכָה] over there and worship [וְנִשְׁתַּחֲוֶה] and come again [וְנָשׁוּבָה] to you" (22:5). All three verbs are plural, conveying that Abraham would be returning with Isaac.[47]

Now why did Abraham speak about *both* of them coming back? Did Abraham secretly intend to disobey God's command? Was there an unnarrated conversation between God and Abraham where God told him what would transpire on the mountain? Were Abraham's words to the two men a ruse to prevent a possible intervention on Isaac's behalf?[48]

---

47. Hamilton, *God's Glory in Salvation through Judgment*, 88. According to Schreiner, "In a narrative such as this, carefully constructed and dramatically effective, the inclusion of such words cannot be waved off as insignificant" (Thomas R. Schreiner, *The King in His Beauty: A Biblical Theology of the Old and New Testaments* [Grand Rapids: Baker Academic, 2013], 21).

48. Wenham says, "It seems likely that none of these rival interpretations need be ruled out. White lie, prophecy, hope, even disobedience, can surely coexist in the believer, especially in times of acute crisis. The enigmatic ambiguity of 'we shall return' perhaps gives an insight into the quite contrary ideas agitating

The best explanation of the plural verbs is to see the biblical author highlighting Abraham's faith that God would keep his word to preserve the seed.[49] Years earlier God had promised Abraham an heir (Gen 15:4) and kept his word with the birth of Isaac (21:1-3). God specified Isaac as the one through whom "shall your offspring be named" (21:12), so according to God's promise Isaac would be the father of other descendants. Therefore, when Abraham ascended the mountain, he intended to obey God's command to offer his son on the altar, but he did not believe the death of Isaac would nullify the promise of offspring through Isaac. Maybe Kaiser is right that "Abraham's servants ... knew that their master's mission was to sacrifice his only son on Mount Moriah," and they did not intervene because they also held (or at least were confident in) his hope in God.[50]

The writer of Hebrews gives an inspired lens through which to view Abraham's reasoning (Heb 11:19): if God said there would be offspring through Isaac but also wanted him as a sacrifice before any such offspring were born, then God must intend to raise him from the dead. What would give Abraham such confidence? Perhaps the very fact of Isaac's birth bolstered Abraham's faith. He and Sarah had experienced the miracle of procreation after they both passed the reasonable biological expiration date for it (Gen 17:17; 18:11-12). They both expressed skepticism at the notion of conceiving a child in their old age, but God said, "Is anything too hard for the LORD?" (18:14a). So even though God's command to kill Isaac seemed to simultaneously kill God's promise, perhaps on the mountain Abraham raised the knife over his son because God's question still echoed in his mind: "Is anything too hard for the LORD?" If God could bring life to a dead womb, he could bring it to a dead boy.

Hughes says, "So dramatic was the sequence of events that it was as though Isaac really had died and been raised up to life again."[51] Beale views the story of Abraham's near sacrifice of Isaac as a picture of

---

Abraham's mind at this time" (Gordon J. Wenham, *Genesis 16-50*, WBC, vol. 2 [Nashville: Thomas Nelson, 1994], 108).

49. As Waltke says, "Although he does not know how God will work it out, his faith harmonizes God's promise that in Isaac his offspring will be reckoned (21:1-13) with God's command to sacrifice Isaac. According to Heb 11:17-19, he expresses a type of 'resurrection' faith" (*Genesis*, 307).

50. Walter C. Kaiser Jr., *Toward Rediscovering the Old Testament* (Grand Rapids: Academie, 1987), 142.

51. Philip E. Hughes, *A Commentary on the Epistle to the Hebrews* (Grand Rapids: Eerdmans, 1977), 484.

resurrection,[52] an observation the author of Hebrews validates. Abraham offered his son on the altar because he "considered that God was able even to raise him from the dead, from which, figuratively speaking, he did receive him back" (Heb 11:19).

Important to distinguish in the Hebrews 11:19 explanation is *what Abraham was thinking* and *what the figurative result was*. In this unusual verse, interpreters have access to the patriarch's thoughts, but our interest is also in how the author of Hebrews interprets the outcome: Isaac's deliverance was a picture of resurrection. This interpretation is remarkable given the fact that Isaac did not actually die; he simply *neared* death and was delivered from it. Isaac's deliverance from death was a figure of resurrection. Clear also, though, is the patriarch's conviction that God had the power to reverse the death by sacrifice. This conviction is implied in the plural verbs Abraham spoke to his servants, for he said that he and Isaac would be returning from the mountain.

Does the interpretation of Genesis 22 in Hebrews 11—like that of Exodus 3 in Matthew 22—supply lenses through which an interpreter can legitimately discern a type of resurrection? If so, what criteria might be necessary for the writer of Hebrews to make such a statement, criteria that could be applied to other episodes in the Old Testament? Wheaton offers his take on what the author of Hebrews 11:19 is taking into account:

> This text provides us with several clues for reading other narratives of the OT for their allusion to the resurrection. First, the "victim" is under some sort of sentence of death. Second, the process of execution is in progress. Third, there is no human possibility of rescue; the end is imminent. Fourth, the dying process is miraculously overcome so that the victim is restored to life. Fifth, the "resurrection" issues in a new future for the victim and those associated with him.[53]

Wheaton is correct that locating a "type" of resurrection would mean finding such elements present. On occasions where a victim is delivered through divine intervention from imminent demise, the biblical

---

52. Beale calls God's preservation of Abraham's seed through the deliverance of Isaac a "type" of the future resurrection of the dead (*A New Testament Biblical Theology*, 320).
53. Byron Wheaton, "As It Is Written: Old Testament Foundations for Jesus' Expectation of Resurrection," *WTJ* 70 (2008): 248.

authors would be narrating God's power over the apparent inevitability of death.

The burial of bones in Canaan (Gen 25:9). When Abraham died, Isaac and Ishmael buried him in the cave of Machpelah, which was in Canaan (Gen 25:9). When Isaac died, Esau and Jacob buried him in the same cave (35:29; 49:31). As Jacob was dying, he instructed his twelve sons to "bury me with my fathers in the cave that is in the field of Ephron the Hittite, in the cave that is in the field at Machpelah" (49:29–30; 50:13). And near his own death, Joseph instructed that his bones be carried from Egypt to Canaan too (50:24–25; Heb 11:22).

Why did the patriarchs and Joseph want burial in the land of Canaan? Their instructions were expressions of faith, for God promised Abraham, "And I will give to you and to your offspring after you the land of your sojournings, all the land of Canaan, for an everlasting possession, and I will be their God" (Gen 17:8; cf. 12:7; 13:15; 15:18).

When Abraham died, he did not own more than a burial plot in the promised land.[54] At their respective deaths, the patriarchs and Joseph no longer dwelled in the land of Canaan,[55] but they believed burial there was important so that they would receive the land as an everlasting possession. Their conviction was that God would keep his word. Somehow not even death could stop God from fulfilling his promise that they would possess the promised land.[56] Is anything too hard for the LORD?

The God who kills and makes alive (Deut 32:39). As the descendants of the wilderness generation readied to enter the land under Joshua's leadership, Moses prepared their hearts with a reminder of what had happened before them and explained what it would look like for them to be faithful in the promised land. These reminders and

---

54. Donald E. Gowan, *Theology of the Prophetic Books: The Death and Resurrection of Israel* (Louisville: Westminster John Knox, 1998), 17.
55. At death the patriarchs were gathered to their people. The phrase "gathered to his people" (Gen 25:8, 17; 35:29; 49:33) meant more than interment in a grave, for Abraham was not united with his physical ancestors in a family tomb, and Jacob was "gathered to his people" (49:33) months before being buried in the ground (Alexander, "The Old Testament View of Life After Death," 45). See also Johnston, *Shades of Sheol*, 33–34.
56. Wright says that none of the rabbis "supposed that the patriarchs, Moses, Reuben or anyone else had yet been given this resurrection life. The point of demonstrating that there were promises yet outstanding to the patriarchs was that God must be capable of fulfilling them in the world yet to come" (*The Resurrection of the Son of God*, 199–200).

instructions comprise the book of Deuteronomy. Toward the end of this book, there is a line in Moses's song that expresses resurrection hope.

At the beginning of "the song of Moses" (Deut 32:1-43), Moses gives advance notice that he "will proclaim the name of the LORD; ascribe greatness to our God!" (32:3). He teaches that God was just, but a twisted generation forsook him (32:4-9). God showed mercy and guided them, though they provoked his jealousy with their idolatry (32:10-18). Divine anger burned against them (32:19-22), and disaster would deservedly be poured upon them (32:23-27). They lacked wisdom (32:28-33). Yahweh would have vengeance in due time (32:34-35) and prove the uselessness of the idols (32:36-38). His claim could not be rivaled: "See now that I, even I, am he, and there is no god beside me; I kill and I make alive; I wound and I heal; and there is none that can deliver out of my hand" (32:39). God would bring judgment, and his sword would spare no enemy of his (32:40-43).

The divine claim in Deuteronomy 32:39 is the focus of this section because of the language of death and life. The verbs "I kill" (אָמִית) and "I make alive" (וַאֲחַיֶּה) are parallel to the next claim, "I wound and I heal." Since the order of the second line is significant (wounding followed by healing), the order of killing and making alive is too.[57] Greenspoon argues that if the words were "simply pointing to God's role in the birth and death of each individual, then we would expect these verbs to appear in the reverse order, which would then correctly reflect the sequence in which every human experiences these two aspects of divine power."[58]

In Deuteronomy 32:39, God claims the power to raise the dead, and this is the first place in the Old Testament where he claims it. God is asserting his uniqueness compared to the idols, which can do nothing.[59] He can heal the wounded; he can raise the dead! Greenspoon posits,

---

57. Bronner says, "The arrangement of the key words ... suggests that they are dealing with a resurrection motif" ("The Resurrection Motif in the Hebrew Bible," 145).
58. Greenspoon, "The Origin of the Idea of Resurrection," 311.
59. Greenspoon again: "Since there is perhaps no other action of God's which displays the totality and uniqueness of His power more forcefully than the process by which He restores His dead to life, a reference to bodily resurrection is surely in keeping with the context at this point" ("The Origin of the Idea of Resurrection," 312).

"This one passage ... may well be sufficient to establish the *certainty of an early date* for the Biblical belief" in bodily resurrection.[60]

Prior to Deuteronomy 32:39 there is no report of God raising the dead, though some resuscitations will occur later in Israel's history. The incredible claim stands on its own for now, with no instance of literal resurrection preceding it. Here, at the end of the Law, God insists he will vindicate his people. If he has dealt wounds, he will bind them; if he has brought death, he can reverse that too. No impotent idol can do what almighty Yahweh will do. God has made "outstanding promises" to his people, and through resurrection he will keep them.[61]

SUPPORTING EVIDENCE

From Genesis, Exodus, Leviticus, Numbers, and Deuteronomy, the following supporting passages undergird a belief in resurrection, strengthening the evidence already offered.

The life-giving God who makes the world (Gen 1:9–13; 2:7). Beholding an earth without form, the Spirit of God hovered over the waters (Gen 1:2). On the third day of creation God brought forth land from the water (1:9), and then he made vegetation and fruit-bearing plants and trees from that land (1:11). God is a God of *life*, and the acts narrated in Genesis 1 make this power public.[62]

After the account of how God made the world (Gen 1:1–2:3), a more detailed record of humanity's creation begins in 2:4. The order is significant to observe: God first forms the man from the dust and then imparts the breath of life (2:7). The author is teaching the first readers of Genesis about the kind of existence for which God made humankind. The readers lived under limits imposed by God. Death ended earthly life, but that outcome did not imply that bodies were bad.[63] He designed

---

60. Greenspoon, "The Origin of the Idea of Resurrection," 310, emphasis mine. While in previous sections I have argued that resurrection hope extends back to Genesis, here Greenspoon's point is that Deut 32:39 contains the earliest *explicit* expression of God giving life to dead people, and his observation is correct. See Beale's confirmation: "Perhaps the earliest explicit OT reference to resurrection is Deut 32:39" (*A New Testament Biblical Theology*, 231).
61. Levenson, *Resurrection and the Restoration of Israel*, 200.
62. Dempster calls God "the great life-giver *par excellence* in Genesis 1 and 2" (Dempster, "The Resurrection of Christ," 4).
63. For the notion of death as punishment, see Alexander, "The Old Testament View of Life After Death," 42.

image bearers to be *embodied* beings.⁶⁴ Once God exiled the first couple from Eden, bodies died as part of sin's wage. Therefore, according to the way Moses presents the narratives in the opening chapters of Genesis, being embodied people—who were infused with breath from the God of life—was the divine design.

Crucial for a belief in resurrection is the confidence in God's power to grant life, and Genesis 1-2 lays the foundation for this conviction. While the creation of a body (which God then animated) speaks to God's good design in making embodied image bearers, that body was formed out of "dust from the ground" (2:7), and dust will become an important part of resurrection hope. Those who sleep in the dust will awake (Isa 26:19; Dan 12:2). In Wright's words, "The fresh gift of his breath will then bring the dust to life. The promise of resurrection is thus firmly linked to creation itself."⁶⁵

The death of Abel and the birth of Seth (Gen 4:1, 8, 25). God promised to defeat the serpent through a descendent of Eve (Gen 3:15). Collins rightly notes that the singular pronouns ("he," הוּא; "you shall bruise him," תְּשׁוּפֶנּוּ) point to a single descendant as the fulfillment of Genesis 3:15,⁶⁶ and the LXX renders it with masculine singular pronouns ("he," αὐτός; "his," αὐτοῦ). Since this person is the offspring of the woman, he will be human; and since he overcomes the serpent, he will have power extraordinary enough to win.⁶⁷

In light of this promise, when Eve bore Cain she said, "I have gotten a man with the help of the LORD" (Gen 4:1), which probably means she thought the defeat of the serpent would be soon. Her offspring increased when she birthed Abel (4:2). Now with two descendants, surely one would be the promised victor.

But the unexpected happened when Cain murdered Abel (Gen 4:8), an event that manifested the hostility between the serpent's seed and the woman's seed (cf. 3:15). The author shows that the respective seeds

---

64. According to Ladd, "The idea of man as an animated body, and the faith in a sovereign God whose power and promises could not be broken by death, led to the belief in the eschatological resurrection of the body" (*I Believe in the Resurrection of Jesus*, 49).
65. Wright, *The Resurrection of the Son of God*, 122.
66. C. John Collins, *Genesis 1-4: A Linguistic, Literary, and Theological Commentary* (Phillipsburg, NJ: P&R, 2006), 156.
67. Collins, *Genesis 1-4*, 157. See also James M. Hamilton, "The Skull Crushing Seed of the Woman: Inner-Biblical Interpretation of Genesis 3:15," *SBJT* 10, no. 2 (2006): 30-54.

consist (at least in part) of human beings, and the division is one of spiritual alliance. The serpent's offspring is aligned against God, and the woman's offspring is aligned with God.

After the murder of Abel, two things become clear: Cain belongs to the seed of the serpent (cf. 1 John 3:12), and the seed of the woman is now dead. The serpent's offspring seems to have prevailed, which is the reverse of what Genesis 3:15 said would happen. But Eve conceives again and names her new son Seth because "God has appointed for me another offspring instead of Abel, for Cain killed him" (4:25). She believes Seth is the replacement for the brother who perished. This belief is significant because it shows a hope based in 3:15.[68]

In Genesis 4:25 the word "appointed" is from שית, which the LXX renders as ἐξανίστημι ("raised up"). In one sense, God appointed Seth to the stage of history by bringing him into the world through the woman. In another sense, the birth of Seth is the reversal of the death that Eve endured with Abel's murder. Seth's birth is a reversal of death not because Seth is Abel reincarnate, nor because someone was raised bodily from the dead, but because the *promised seed* experienced a death when Abel was murdered, and now the family line of promise and hope can continue because God granted Eve another son.

The theme of obstacles to the line of promise is something Moses records again and again in the Pentateuch, and the earliest attestation of the pattern (birth reversing the death of the woman's line) is found here in Genesis 4.[69] As I argued in the section addressing Exodus 3—and how Jesus used Exodus 3:6 in Matthew 22:32—the notion of personal identity was both individual and familial, meaning that the fate of the individual was conceptually related to what happened to his family. Jesus's use of Exodus 3 may show interpreters that other pictures of resurrection can be detected in the pattern of birth reversing the death of the line of promise, and the line meets the functional equivalent of death in circumstances like barrenness or—as in Eve's case—the loss of a child.

In Genesis 4 life is lost, but in another sense God brings restoration. Restoration of the promised seed is analogous to resurrection because the line once dead now lives again. The biblical author shows that God keeps his promises: Eve was told that she would bear a victor, a seed

---

68. Dempster, *Dominion and Dynasty*, 71.
69. Levenson, *Resurrection and the Restoration of Israel*, 116, 133.

who would crush the serpent, and the text shows that death will not make God a promise breaker.

The unusual departure of Enoch apart from death (Gen 5:24). Genesis 5 has a predictable rhythm of someone being born, fathering sons and daughters, and dying at the end of a long life. In this ten-member genealogy the seventh name is Enoch, and he interrupts the rhythm. Compared to the other lifespans, his is the shortest (Gen 5:23). There is also a brief and exemplary report on his life: he walked with God not for a few years or decades but for *centuries* (5:22, 24; cf. Heb 11:5b).

But most unusual is Enoch's last day on earth: when he was 365 years old, "he was not, for God took him" (Gen 5:24). Unlike the other members of the genealogy, Enoch's earthly life did not end in death. The manner of Enoch's exit was fodder for much speculation about his heavenly departure and all the sights he must have beheld and information he must have learned.[70] One indisputable point for Jews, though, was this: God did not "take" Enoch *through* death but *before* death. The author of Hebrews confirms this interpretation. "By faith Enoch was taken up so that he should not see death, and he was not found, because God had taken him" (Heb 11:5a).

Kaiser contends that Enoch's removal probably started "a whole new line of thinking" about afterlife issues,[71] and that assertion is possible. The Old Testament does not directly incorporate Enoch's story into a development of afterlife theology, nor did this unusual departure become a story that Jews believed God would repeat for devoted people.[72] Wright observes, "Nobody suggested that if someone lived an exceptionally holy life, or accomplished some great deed, they might be similarly treated."[73]

Enoch's rapture did say something important, however, about death and God's power: God can close the mouth of the grave whenever he wants for whomever he wants, a truth stemming from his cosmic lordship. Death is not a power that bound God's hands, for he could overrule its apparent inevitability. And if his power could take a person before death, could God, with that same power, resurrect a person after death?

---

70. See the pseudepigraphal book of 1 Enoch.
71. Kaiser, *Preaching and Teaching the Last Things*, 1.
72. See, though, 2 Kgs 2:11, where God takes Elijah apart from death. Since this event is outside the Torah, this section on Genesis will not address it.
73. Wright, *The Resurrection of the Son of God*, 95. See also Johnston, *Shades of Sheol*, 200, 216.

It is not a great leap to hope that the same God who can close the grave's mouth can also open the grave's mouth.

Floodwaters covering and uncovering the world (Gen 7–8). In the days of Noah, God promised to flood the world to judge the wicked (Gen 6:13). The only refuge from the flood judgment would be an ark carrying Noah and seven others—Noah's wife, their three sons, and their sons' wives. This family would pass through the waters of judgment.

When the rains fell for forty days, and when the depths burst with water from below, the land and hills and mountains were covered (Gen 7:17–20). The scene was a de-creation. In Genesis 1, God caused dry land to appear (1:9–10), and during the flood he covered this land once more. In Genesis 1, God put animals and image bearers in the world (1:20–31), and during the flood he covered all the creatures and image bearers. In a world filled with life, God brought judgment and death.

The events in Genesis 7–8 were not the end of the world, however. Restoration followed the devastation. In 8:11, the waters had receded, and the land was visible again. The narrative pictured a new creation, a clean slate. Sin still affected the world, so this post-flood condition was not pristine or pre-fall, but the visibility of the land recalled God's work in Genesis 1 to fill the world and bless its creatures. In 8:18–19, the animals and image bearers left the ark and filled the land.

The arc of the ark story is death and resurrection.[74] The world was covered by watery death and then came to life again. Reading the account through this lens is confirmed by the apostle Peter when he wrote about baptism. He said that Noah and his family "were brought safely through water. Baptism, which corresponds to this, now saves you, not as a removal of dirt from the body but as an appeal to God for a good conscience, through the resurrection of Jesus Christ" (1 Pet 3:20–21). The ordinance of baptism is about the believer's union with Christ in death and resurrection, and when Peter wrote about baptism, he knew that the events of Genesis 7–8 were a picture of death and resurrection. The waters of the flood "depict in a figure a death of the old and a rising of the new. In a symbolic way, Noah and his family ... were all undergoing a resurrection to new life."[75]

---

74. See the explanation in Nicholas P. Lunn, "'Raised on the Third Day According to the Scriptures': Resurrection Typology in the Genesis Creation Narrative," *JETS* 57, no. 3 (2014): 527–28.
75. Lunn, "'Raised on the Third Day According to the Scripture,'" 529.

Life granted to a dead womb (Gen 21:1-2). God promised Abraham that all the families of the earth would be blessed through him (Gen 12:2-3), but an obvious obstacle at the giving of the promise was his barren wife (11:30). God promised land to Abraham's offspring (12:7), but how could there be offspring when Sarah could not have children? God made the incredible promise that Abraham's offspring would be more numerous than the stars (15:5), and in the fullness of time he fulfilled his word: "The LORD visited Sarah as he had said, and the LORD did to Sarah as he had promised. And Sarah conceived and bore Abraham a son in his old age at the time of which God had spoken to him" (21:1-2).

As I have established in previous passages, sterility was the functional equivalent of death.[76] Agur the sage says, "Three things are never satisfied; four never say, 'Enough': Sheol, the barren womb, the land never satisfied with water, and the fire that never says, 'Enough'" (Prov 30:15-16). Sheol is a realm of the dead, the barren womb cannot house life, parched land cannot sustain life, and unquenchable fire destroys what it touches. The four insatiable things that Agur mentions are, in one way or another, functional equivalents of death.[77] When God reverses these situations, his triumphant power is on display, and it is only the God of life who can restore and raise up.

God's reversal of Sarah's infertility brought life from death in the same way Seth's birth brought hope after Abel died. When Paul reflected on this episode, he said Abraham's body "was as good as dead," and Sarah's womb was barren (Rom 4:19). God, Paul said, "gives life to the dead and calls into existence the things that do not exist" (4:17). Out of expired reproductive organs, God did the impossible (cf. Heb 11:11-12). This pattern is repeated when God opened the wombs of Rebekah (Gen 25:21), Leah (29:31), and Rachel (30:22).

Reversals of barrenness strengthen the confidence that God has the power to reverse destruction and to overcome any obstacles impeding the advance of his promises and the seed of the woman. When it comes to death, then, the momentum established by the biblical author in these stories of reversal leads readers to expect God's power to remain uncontested. Abraham was "fully convinced that God was able to do what he had promised" (Rom 4:21).

---

76. Levenson, *Resurrection and the Restoration of Israel*, 114-15.
77. Levenson, *Resurrection and the Restoration of Israel*, 114.

The rise of Joseph (Gen 41:41). The path of Joseph's life is a narrative of descent and ascent. His brothers rejected him and cast him into a waterless pit (Gen 37:24). Then they sold him to Midianite traders who took him to Egypt (37:28). Joseph went "down" to Egypt (39:1). After being falsely accused by Potiphar's wife, Joseph went to prison (39:11–20).

These difficult circumstances in Joseph's life had indications of God's plan to elevate him. He had told his brothers about dreams in which he foresaw his own reign over them (Gen 37:5–8). In Potiphar's house, Joseph became successful and was given charge over everything in Potiphar's household (39:3–6). Even in prison, the keeper put Joseph in charge over all the other prisoners (39:22–23). These providential confirmations of Joseph's integrity and abilities prepared the way for the greatest elevation yet. When Pharaoh needed his dreams interpreted, Joseph discerned the meaning (41:25–36). This interpretation led to Pharaoh's promotion of Joseph over all of Egypt (41:41–45).

Joseph's story is a picture of descent and ascent, death and resurrection.[78] In Genesis 37 Joseph is in the pit, and in Genesis 41 he's the second in command over Egypt. His vindication is exaltation, and this exaltation points to the power of God, which can raise up his people from situations of distress, prison, and the gates of death. Figuratively speaking, Joseph entered suffering and then, through vindication, experienced the restoration of life. The words of Jacob—Joseph's father—speak about death and life. In 37:33 Jacob said, "It is my son's robe. A fierce animal has devoured him. Joseph is without doubt torn to pieces." Then, in 45:28, Jacob said, "It is enough; Joseph my son is still alive. I will go and see him before I die."[79]

The preservation of Moses in waters of death (Exod 2:3, 10). When the shrewd Pharaoh determined to avoid any future threat that the Israelite population might pose to him, he ordered the watery death

---

78. For a book-length treatment of Joseph's story depicting death and resurrection, see Jeffrey Pulse, *Figuring Resurrection: Joseph as a Death and Resurrection Figure in the Old Testament and Second Temple Judaism*, Studies in Scripture & Biblical Theology (Bellingham, WA: Lexham, 2021). According to Brannon, "Joseph's story serves as a paradigm of God working good out of evil and bringing life out of death" (*The Hope of Life After Death*, 43).
79. Samuel Emadi argues that Joseph is a type of Christ and that the themes of suffering and glory are interwoven in Joseph's life, themes that connect to figurative death and resurrection. See Samuel Emadi, *From Prisoner to Prince: The Joseph Story in Biblical Theology*, New Studies in Biblical Theology (Downers Grove, IL: IVP Academic, 2022), 95–99.

of every Hebrew firstborn son (Exod 1:10, 22). When a Levite woman gave birth to a son, however, she hid him and then put him in a basket to float along the Nile (2:1-3). This baby, later discovered and raised in Pharaoh's family, was named Moses because "I drew him out of the water" (2:5-6, 10).[80]

Moses's name speaks to the symbolic significance of what had happened, at least from the narrator's perspective. Pharaoh's daughter knew Moses was not literally drawn out of the *water*; she found Moses in a basket (Exod 2:5-6). Yet God spared Moses through this vessel of bulrushes, so the baby did not die as the others did in the Nile. Enns calls the event Moses's "'death and rebirth' on the Nile."[81] The Nile was the grave, and Moses was drawn out of the watery death that consumed the children thrown into it.

Moses's deliverance was not from a literal death but is an analogy to it. So could this event be a *type* of resurrection, of the same caliber as Isaac's figurative death and resurrection? If the author of Hebrews provides a legitimate hermeneutic, then perhaps his phrase "from the dead, from which, figuratively speaking, he did receive him back" (Heb 11:19) helps us see types of resurrection in episodes like Moses's rescue from the Nile.

Why do types of resurrection matter? In chapter 2, I presented evidence that the author of Daniel preceded his promise of resurrection with many stories of rescue, and these stories set a course of expectation for what God would do in vindicating his people, the greatest vindication being the defeat of death through resurrection, promised in Daniel 12:2. This present chapter is seeking to prove that Daniel's words were also preceded by theological convictions, pictures, and expressions that occur outside the book of Daniel. The pictures, in particular, include patterns or types of resurrection, and their frequency and momentum turn up the heat of hope for God to do something about death itself. With each divine rescue—be it of Isaac or Moses or someone else—the temperature rises.

The rescue from the tenth plague (Exod 12:23). The escalating situation of Egyptian obstinance—represented by the Pharaoh himself—involved one plague after another from God upon the land of Egypt. The

---

80. The name מֹשֶׁה sounds like the verb משה. Wheaton says, "His name attests to his being delivered/resurrected from the waters" ("As It Is Written," 250). See Dempster, "The Resurrection of Christ," 5.
81. Peter Enns, *Exodus*, NIVAC (Grand Rapids: Zondervan, 2000), 71.

tenth plague would be the death of the firstborn. If the Israelites would follow particular ritual instructions and trust the Lord's plan, they would be spared this plague, and their firstborn would live. In Exodus 12, Moses conveyed the instructions to the Israelites: take the blood of an unblemished lamb (12:5) and daub its blood on the doorposts and lintel of the Israelite households (12:7). That night, the Lord "will pass through to strike the Egyptians, and when he sees the blood on the lintel and on the two doorposts" (12:23), the judgment would pass over them and not strike the firstborn son in the home.

The Israelites followed Moses's instructions. When midnight arrived, the Lord struck down the firstborn throughout the land of Egypt (Exod 12:29). Death had come to the land, and rescue from death was a figurative resurrection. The plague had fallen, and the Israelite households testified to the mercy and power of God. According to Brannon, "The Passover account is another example of a sacrifice and substitute that brings life to God's people."[82]

The Israelites crossing the Red Sea (Exod 14:21-22). During the exodus of the Israelites, the oppressive pharaoh led his army in pursuit of them (Exod 14:6-9). As he and his legion drew closer, the Israelites expressed to Moses the sentence of death they felt: "Is it because there are no graves in Egypt that you have taken us away to die in the wilderness?" (14:11). The Israelites believed they were standing alive in their own graves. This metaphorical language is significant for what God did next.

With a wind God divided the waters into two standing walls (Exod 14:21-22). Rescued from their looming fate, the Israelites crossed through the water on dry ground (14:22, 30). They saw the power of Yahweh displayed in this event (14:31). The Egyptians sank into the depths under the judgment of God (15:5, 10, 12), and God's people were vindicated because of his triumphant might (15:11-13, 21).

The Israelites, who had been in Egyptian captivity, have life through the God who redeemed them. Since the garden of Eden, God's people have been in exile, which meant death for Adam and all who are in him. For God to lead his people to a new land is a kind of return to Eden, and such a goal was the purpose of the exodus: "I have come down to deliver them out of the hand of the Egyptians and to bring them up out of

---

82. Brannon, *The Hope of Life After Death*, 45.

that land to a good and broad land, a land flowing with milk and honey" (Exod 3:8).

In a corporate sense the Israelites dwelled in the death of their Egyptian captivity, from which God delivered them.[83] The day the Red Sea parted they saw "the salvation of the LORD" (Exod 14:13). The route of their escape would not be lined with their graves as they had feared. God promised to bring them up in Exodus 3:8 (לְהַעֲלֹתוֹ), and indeed they rose as a nation.

The exodus became a type of God's national deliverance. His redeeming power would bring to pass his promises and liberate his people from bondage. As we will see in the Prophets, the events of the nation subsume within it the hope for individual liberation as well, freedom from decay and death (cf. Hos 6; Ezek 37). The nation's future exile, captivity, and return will link inextricably to the notion of individual resurrection from death, which is the greatest captor of bodies. As Levenson explains, "The exodus has become a prototype of ultimate redemption, and historical liberation has become a partial, proleptic experience of eschatological liberation, a token, perhaps *the* token, of things to come."[84]

As the Old Testament unfolds, the biblical authors advance individual hope through the experiences of the nation. What may only be a blurry image in Exodus 14 is seen with greater clarity in hindsight: liberation from Egypt and deliverance through the Red Sea is a picture of future life from the dead, for "resurrection is the ultimate and final liberation."[85]

Approaching the tabernacle (Exod 40:35). According to instructions from God through Moses, the Israelites were to build a portable dwelling place that represented the presence of God in their camp. This portable house—the tabernacle—contained a larger room called the Holy Place and a smaller room called the Most Holy Place. Around the tabernacle was a courtyard, and outside the courtyard was the tribal arrangement of Israel's camp.

---

83. In the OT, deliverance from captivity (followed by restoration to the land) will be pictured with resurrection language, which implies that slavery can be used figuratively for death (Levenson, *Resurrection and the Restoration of Israel*, 161). See Othmar Keel, *The Symbolism of the Biblical World: Ancient Near Eastern Iconography and the Book of Psalms* (New York: Seabury, 1978).
84. Levenson, *Resurrection and the Restoration of Israel*, 27.
85. Levenson, *Resurrection and the Restoration of Israel*, 28.

After the tabernacle was set up and the glory of the Lord filled it, "Moses was not able to enter the tent of meeting because the cloud settled on it, and the glory of the Lord filled the tabernacle" (Exod 40:35). The appointed priests would eventually be able to enter the tabernacle for the tasks they were to perform, but the report in 40:35 is a theological assertion of God's deadly holiness, his resplendent glory, his unapproachable presence. Yet he welcomed the people to approach the tabernacle if they were ritually fit (or ceremonially clean), and they would come to the mediating priests with various offerings (see Lev 1–7).

Because God is a God of life, approaching the tabernacle was moving toward life, and movement away from the tabernacle was movement away from life. If an Israelite became ritually unclean, going to the tabernacle was prohibited. Ceremonial uncleanness was a kind of death, and this state was unfit for the God of life. The realm "outside the camp" designated the realm of the unclean and the dead. Outside the camp was exile, far from the God of life whose presence blessed and filled the tabernacle.

According to Morales, "There is even a sense where one could read Genesis 1 to Exodus 40 as a complete narrative, a story about being expelled from God's Presence in Eden, then, finally, being brought back into that Presence *through the tabernacle cultus*—a story about Paradise lost and regained."[86] Approaching the tabernacle was going from death to life, because the lifegiving presence of God dwelled in the camp to bless his people and receive them to himself.

Restoration of those with a skin disease (Lev 13:1–17). An effect of living in a fallen world could be acquiring a skin disease by which a person seemed to outwardly waste away.[87] If the priest confirmed the presence of a skin disease on a person, he declared that person "unclean" (Lev 13:8). As long as he has the disease, the unclean person "shall live alone. His dwelling shall be outside the camp" (13:46). When the skin disease was resolved, the priest would pronounce the person "clean" and thus restore him to the community.

---

86. L. Michael Morales, *Who Shall Ascend the Mountain of the Lord? A Biblical Theology of the Book of Leviticus*, NSBT (Downers Grove, IL: IVP Academic, 2015), 75.
87. According to Anderson, "Death's power is felt in the midst of life to the degree that one experiences any weakening of personal vitality through illness" (Bernard W. Anderson with Steven Bishop, *Contours of Old Testament Theology* [Minneapolis: Fortress, 1999], 312).

A skin disease—including what we know as modern-day leprosy, or Hansen's Disease—was bodily affliction, and it resulted in alienation from the normal family and social relationships within the Israelite camp. According to Leviticus 13, the skin-diseased person must go outside the camp, because outside the camp was the realm of the unclean. The presence of the tabernacle in the center of Israel's camp is what symbolized life and holiness. Because a skin disease was physical corruption, it was the opposite of life and holiness, and therefore the person was unclean and needed to dwell in the realm of the unclean. When Moses's sister Miriam had leprosy in Numbers 12, Aaron said, "Let her not be as one dead, whose flesh is half eaten away when he comes out of his mother's womb" (Num 12:12).

Leprosy marked the physical body with the signs of death. Restoration of the body was like resurrection of the body, because the alienated and unclean individual could be welcomed back to the life and fellowship that was temporarily lost. A skin disease was the result of the power of death at work. A reversal of the condition, then, was the victory of life.

Dying and rising in the wilderness (Num 14:31-32). Near the promised land in Numbers 13, the Israelites rebelled against the Lord when they embraced the majority—and negative—report from the twelve spies (Num 13:25-33). The Lord responded with the promise of judgment. Instead of the exodus generation inheriting the land, those Israelites would perish in the wilderness over a forty-year period while their children grew up and prepared to inherit the land.

The Lord said, "But your little ones, who you said would become a prey, I will bring in, and they shall know the land that you have rejected. But as for you, your dead bodies shall fall in this wilderness" (Num 14:31-32). During several decades, the nation of Israel would undergo a significant change, a change tantamount to death and resurrection. The nation would die and rise in the wilderness. The people who were counted in the first census of warriors (Num 1) would not be the same group who were counted in the second census of warriors (Num 26). The span of time between those two censuses was a forty-year period of wandering and judgment. During those years the Israelites experienced a corporate death and resurrection.

Think of the wilderness as a grave. It received the bodies of the rebellious generation. But the children of the rebels were delivered from this grave. They grew up with the prospect and promise of inheritance. The forty-year judgment was the time when Israel died and rose again.

Raising up a prophet like Moses (Deut 18:15). Moses learned that after his days, God would "raise up" a prophet like him from among the Israelites, a prophet whose mouth would speak the words of God (Deut 18:15, 18). At first, the notion of "raising up" such a prophet sounds like simply bringing him onto the stage of history. But could the language of "raise up" suggest something more?

The apostle Peter sees the signal of resurrection in the words of Deuteronomy 18:15. While preaching in Jerusalem in Acts 3, Peter is explaining that the coming of Christ fulfilled what God had spoken earlier in Scripture. The contemporaries had "killed the Author of life, whom God raised from the dead" (Acts 3:15). Peter turns to Deuteronomy 18:15. "Moses said, 'The Lord God will raise up for you a prophet like me from your brothers. You shall listen to him in whatever he tells you. And it shall be that every soul who does not listen to that prophet shall be destroyed from the people.' .... God, having raised up his servant, sent him to you first, to bless you by turning every one of you from your wickedness" (Acts 3:22–23, 26).

The promise of God in Deuteronomy 18:15 was about more than bringing the Messiah onto the stage of history. The promise was ultimately about a literal resurrection of this servant. The prophet like Moses came to his own, but his own received him not. The people killed the prophet like Moses. But God, just as he promised in the Torah, raised him up.

SUMMARY

Levenson maintains that seeking a single point of origin and cause for the belief in resurrection "is fruitless and misguided,"[88] and he may be correct with regard to a *single* cause. Nonetheless, it is a worthy pursuit to see how early such hope appears, even if a single point of origin eludes scholars. Contrary to the modern consensus, but in keeping with the hermeneutic of Jesus and Paul, resurrection hope exists as early as the Law of Moses.[89] Dempster is right that death and life can be viewed in more dynamic ways, ways not reducible to "biological continuity or discontinuity."[90] The stories cited above show that "God is at work to

---

88. Levenson, *Resurrection and the Restoration of Israel*, xiii.
89. See Jon D. Levenson, "Resurrection in the Torah? A Second Look" (Palmer Lecture, Center of Theological Inquiry, Princeton, NJ, March 21, 2002).
90. Dempster, "The Resurrection of Christ," 5. As Levenson puts it, "Death and life in the Hebrew Bible are often best seen as relational events and are for

reverse the forces of death that have entered the world."[91] Through the expressions, theological convictions, and pictures of resurrection, we now turn to such hope in the Prophets.

THE PROPHETS

INTRODUCTION

When Paul speaks to Governor Felix about resurrection hope, he affirms its presence in the Prophets (Acts 24:14-15). This section will explore the theological convictions, lexical connections, and pictures that advance this belief throughout the second part of the Tanak. Evidence will be presented in terms of what is *strong* and what is *supporting*, with each subsection moving through the canonical order of the Prophets.

STRONG EVIDENCE

In the Prophets, strong evidence advancing hope for resurrection can be discerned in at least thirteen passages in the books of 1 Samuel, 1-2 Kings, Isaiah, Jeremiah, Ezekiel, Hosea, and Jonah.

The God who kills and brings to life (1 Sam 2:6). Hannah took her new son, Samuel, to the temple to dedicate him to God in fulfillment of her vow. Her prayer (1 Sam 2:1-10) extolled the power of God to reverse situations.[92] For example, the hungry are satisfied (2:5), and the

---

the selfsame reason inseparable from the personal circumstances of those described as living or as dead. To be alive in this frequent biblical sense of the word inevitably entailed more than merely existing in a certain physical state. It also entailed having one's being within a flourishing and continuing kin group that dwelt in a productive and secure association with its land. Conversely, to be widowed, bereaved of children, or in exile was necessarily to experience death. Indeed, each of these states (even death) and others (notably, health or illness) could serve as a synecdoche for the condition brought about by any of the others" (*Resurrection and the Restoration of Israel*, 154-55). See Keel, *The Symbolism of the Biblical World*.

91. Dempster, "The Resurrection of Christ," 9.
92. Dempster helps to set the scene further: "The song of Hannah in 1 Samuel 2 merits consideration because it elaborates on the theme of Deuteronomy 32, which closed the Torah on a note of death and resurrection, showing how this emphasis will work itself out in the future history of Israel. This Old Testament Magnificat reveals God's power in history in elevating the humble and abasing the proud. The thanksgiving hymn is sung in honour of Yahweh's action in generating life from the womb of Hannah to produce the first kingmaker of ancient Israel" ("The Resurrection of Christ," 11).

needy inherit a seat of honor (2:8). Dempster rightly sees the reversals in Hannah's song as comprising a unit of seven, with the central bicolon being an exultation in God's power to raise the dead.[93] "The LORD kills and brings to life; he brings down to Sheol and raises up" (2:6). The final verse discussed in the Law section (Deut 32:39) conveys the same truth as this verse:

"I kill [אָמִית] and I make alive [וַאֲחַיֶּה]" (Deut 32:39)

"The LORD kills [מֵמִית] and brings to life [וּמְחַיֶּה]" (1 Sam 2:6a)

Seen parallel to each other, four contrasts between the verses are evident: (1) the first is in a song from Moses, and the second verse is in a prayer from Hannah; (2) the former is in the Law, the latter is in the Prophets; (3) the former is in first-person, the latter is in third-person; (4) the former uses finite verbs, the latter uses participles. But two similarities between the verses are also noteworthy: (1) the actions come from the same verbs (מות and חיה) and (2) are in the same order (first מות, then חיה).[94]

Did Hannah's prayer consciously incorporate that lyric from Moses's song? Her prayer has other similarities to Deuteronomy 32: reference to God as a Rock (1 Sam 2:2; cf. Deut 32:4, 15, 18), a confidence that he will judge his enemies (1 Sam 2:9-10; cf. Deut 32:23-24, 35, 41-43), a hope that he will avenge the oppressed (1 Sam 2:8-10; Deut 32:36), and a reference to Sheol (1 Sam 2:6b; cf. Deut 32:22). Hannah's prayer reflects an awareness of Moses's song.

The phrases before and after 1 Samuel 2:6a are important because the first deals with barrenness and the second with Sheol. Hannah says, "The barren has borne seven, but she who has many children is forlorn" (1 Sam 2:5b). When the next line speaks of God's power to kill and make alive, it reinforces the idea that God reversing barrenness and God giving life are not unrelated acts. Then, parallel with Yahweh killing and bringing to life is this claim:

"The LORD kills and brings to life [וּמְחַיֶּה]" (1 Sam 2:6a)

"He brings down to Sheol and raises up [וַיָּעַל]" (1 Sam 2:6b)

---

93. Dempster, "The Resurrection of Christ," 12.
94. Greenspoon says, "To us this order is significant, inasmuch as it places the life-stimulating activity of God after the reference to death" ("The Origin of the Idea of Resurrection," 311).

In the first line of 1 Samuel 2:6, the ideas of "killing" and "bringing down to Sheol" denote death, and the actions of "bringing to life" and "raising up" denote resurrection from the dead.[95] In fact both verbs for resurrection here (חיה and עלה) are listed among Sawyer's verbs that sometimes occur in the Old Testament with a meaning of resurrection.[96] Of course, the mere presence of those verbs does not mean resurrection in every case, but the verbs are preceded in both lines by a reference to death, and life that reverses death is resurrection.

Hannah's song prayerfully extols God's sovereign power to take life and then take it up again.[97] Greenspoon reasons, "An interpretation of the divine activity described in 1 Sam 2:6a in terms of the Biblical concept of bodily resurrection ... explains the choice of vocabulary and its ordering in this particular verse and, at the same time, allows for a more profound understanding of the Song as a whole."[98]

Elijah's resuscitation of the widow's son (1 Kgs 17:20–23). In 1–2 Kings there are three instances of dead people coming back to life under the ministries of Elijah and Elisha.[99] In the first instance Elijah is accused of being the reason for the death of a widow's son (1 Kgs 17:17–18). The prophet first acknowledges that God brought to pass the son's death (17:20), but he believes life could be restored again. He stretches himself over the child and cries, "O LORD my God, let this child's life come into him again [תָּשָׁב]" (17:21). God answers Elijah's prayer. "And the life of the child came into him again [וַתָּשָׁב], and he revived [וַיֶּחִי]" (17:22b). To consider this event a resurrection is justified by the language of the text

---

95. See Levenson, *Resurrection and the Restoration of Israel*, 172–73. According to Baldwin, "This, the most surprising couplet of all, envisages the Lord bringing people back to life from the realm of the dead" (Joyce G. Baldwin, *1 & 2 Samuel*, TOTC [Downers Grove, IL: InterVarsity Press, 1988], 57). Contra this notion is Klein's claim: "God's preserving of life (literally: he makes alive) probably refers to his healing of those who are desperately ill. ... The thought of resurrection was probably not in the poet's mind" (Ralph W. Klein, *1 Samuel*, WBC, vol. 10 [Waco, TX: Word, 1983], 16).
96. Sawyer, "Hebrew Words for the Resurrection of the Dead," 230n1.
97. Greenspoon rightly sees 1 Sam 2:6 as "an expression of faith that death is not to be viewed as a permanent situation any more than earthly power or wealth. By His power to effect change, God can 'reverse the fortune' of those weak from the sleep of death through the introduction of the vitality of life" ("The Origin of the Idea of Resurrection," 314).
98. Greenspoon, "The Origin of the Idea of Resurrection," 315.
99. Wright says these resuscitations "are not particularly relevant to the study of Israelite beliefs about death and life beyond" (*The Resurrection of the Son of God*, 96), but he has underestimated their importance.

itself, for the wording leaves no doubt that the child died and that he reawakened to life.[100]

There are at least five reasons why this story is significant for this project. First, before this event the Bible has not reported anyone coming back from the dead. Second, since Deuteronomy 32:39 and 1 Samuel 2:6 substantiate God's power over death and resurrection, the story in 1 Kings 17 is a display of his ability. Third, the boy's new life is not to a permanent resurrected state but is a lesser manifestation of that greater resurrection still to come on the last day.[101] Fourth, the verbs שוב and חיה are used to tell this story. Fifth, the story enforces the theme of Yahweh as a "Divine Warrior" who manifests his power.

That fifth reason needs elaboration. The Divine Warrior theme surfaces when God overcomes (or even reverses) events in nature that accord with curse and corruption rather than blessing. The title "Divine Warrior" is intended to capture the power and might displayed in divine acts, especially since he is uncontested in the reversals he accomplishes.[102]

The Divine Warrior theme is relevant to discussion about resurrection hope because the outcome of death fits with the corruption and decay evident in the natural order. When God raises the dead, he is triumphing as a Divine Warrior over chaos and restoring order, so the dead boy is raised to enjoy the full vitality of life that he previously knew before death.[103] Levenson argues compellingly that the Divine Warrior concept is where resurrection hope is deeply rooted, for God's victorious power is what transforms sterility to fertility and reverses death with life.[104]

---

100. Greenspoon is correct that "it is certainly beside the point to argue that a panicky woman of the 9th century might have mistaken a severe illness for death, since the text is not presented to us through the mother's perspective but from that of the author" ("The Origin of the Idea of Resurrection," 315). The perspective of the biblical author is what matters, and that perspective narrates a resurrection from the dead.
101. "In this context, what Elijah carried out could be termed a preliminary resurrection, but a resurrection nonetheless" (Greenspoon, "The Origin of the Idea of Resurrection," 315).
102. For scholars who use this title to describe the God who triumphs over the forces of chaos, corruption, and even death, see Frank Moore Cross, *Canaanite Myth and Hebrew Epic* (Cambridge, MA: Harvard University Press, 1973), 156; Jon Levenson, *Theology of the Program of Restoration of Ezekiel 40–48* (Missoula, MT: Scholars Press, 1976), 31.
103. Greenspoon, "The Origin of the Idea of Resurrection," 300.
104. Levenson, *Resurrection and the Restoration of Israel*, 216–17. He also says, "The notion of the Divine Warrior is *the most important influence* on the expectation

Elisha's resuscitation of the Shunammite's son (2 Kgs 4:34–35). Like his predecessor Elijah, Elisha raises a dead boy. A Shunammite's son died, and the family sent for Elisha, the man of God (2 Kgs 4:20–24). Elisha sent his staff with Gehazi and gave instructions to lay it on the face of the child, but Gehazi returned with the report of no success: "The child has not awakened" (4:31b). The verb "awakened" (הֵקִיץ) is used metaphorically here for rising from the sleep of death.[105]

> Gehazi is thus admitting his failure to bring about the child's resurrection. In other words, Elisha, however well-intentioned, cannot appoint a surrogate through whom God's power as Divine Warrior is to be made manifest. ... Elisha alone is the chosen vehicle for his generation and thus the only one through whom God acts to effect the re-awakening or restoration to life of one of His dead.[106]

The prophet arrived at the home, entered the room where the child lay dead, and shut the door for privacy (2 Kgs 4:32–33). As Elisha stretched himself over the child, the dead body became warm (4:34). When Elisha repeated this action, the child opened his eyes (4:35). The previous use of הֵקִיץ in 4:31 for the sleep of death prepares the reader for what will happen and how the event is described. When the child's body warms and his eyes open, the narrator does not tell us the child has risen from the dead, but the absence of a verb at this point does not negate the natural sense of what occurred in the room.

Levenson sees the miracle as "the triumph of the wonder-working God (and the validity of his wonder-working prophet, the 'man of God') over the cruel course of nature."[107] God displayed his power, and Elisha resuscitated a boy. The child opened his eyes as he woke up from death. Like the case of the boy in 1 Kings 17, this child would eventually die again, so Elisha's reversal of death does not accomplish what the promise of Daniel 12:2 holds out. But Levenson observes the lesson to be learned: "It is simply that long before the apocalyptic framework came

---

in question" (216, emphasis mine).

105. "The resurrection that the miracle-working prophet Elisha performs is not, of course, the general resurrection that Judaism later expected at the end-time, but it does demonstrate a firm faith in God's power over death, a key point in the later expectation that is often mistakenly thought to be an innovation in the late sources" (Levenson, *Resurrection and the Restoration of Israel*, xii).
106. Greenspoon, "The Origin of the Idea of Resurrection," 305.
107. Levenson, *Resurrection and the Restoration of Israel*, 125.

into existence, the resurrection of the dead was thought possible—not according to nature, of course, but through the miraculous intervention of the living God."[108]

The life-giving power of Elisha's bones (2 Kgs 13:20-21). Elisha was buried after his death (2 Kgs 13:20). Later, "as a man was being buried, behold, a marauding band was seen and the man was thrown into the grave of Elisha, and as soon as the man touched the bones of Elisha, he revived [וַיְחִי] and stood [וַיָּקָם] on his feet" (13:21). The two verbs depicting the man's resuscitation (חיה and קום) demonstrate that a return to life can also be pictured as standing up. The man, once lying dead on his back, is now on his feet in the grave.

Greenspoon says, "We ought to note that this story is preceded by two full accounts of the process of bodily resurrection"—see my comments on 1 Kings 17 and 2 Kings 4 above—"both of which amply demonstrate the theological and other ramifications of this Biblical concept."[109] The power displayed in Elisha's ministry, power which once raised a dead boy while the prophet was still alive, now gave life to a dead man when nothing remained of the prophet but his bones.[110]

While Elijah performed one resurrection, Elisha performed two![111] Significantly, the climactic wonder performed in association with both men was a resurrection from death.[112] The resurrections associated with these two prophets reinforce the conviction that God has the power to grant life, and since the bodies were not raised to an immortal state, they typify God's plan to raise the dead.

The promise to swallow up death forever (Isa 25:8). The book of Isaiah contains the most important material thus far regarding the topic of bodily resurrection. Isaiah's prophetic ministry during the eighth century BC promised judgment followed by the vindication and

---

108. Levenson, *Resurrection and the Restoration of Israel*, 132.
109. Greenspoon, "The Origin of the Idea of Resurrection," 306.
110. Greenspoon says, "This account illustrates that Elisha's links with God as Divine Warrior were not severed by the prophet's death; rather, God continued to work through the prophet, even through his dead and buried bones, to bring about that reawakening to life which is resurrection" ("The Origin of the Idea of Resurrection," 306).
111. Smith says, "The fact that Elijah and Elisha brought to life two different dead boys (1 Kgs 17:17-24; 2 Kgs 4:18-37) and that a dead man was brought back to life after his body touched ... Elisha's bones (2 Kgs 13:20-21) indicates that individual resurrection from the dead was known long before the days of Isaiah" (Gary V. Smith, *Isaiah 1-39*, NAC, vol. 15A [Nashville: B&H, 2007], 452).
112. Dempster, "The Resurrection of Christ," 10.

restoration of God's people. Exile would come but would not be the final word. Most significantly, "The main source for Daniel's ideas and images in 12.2-3 is undoubtedly Isaiah."[113]

Isaiah 24-27 is known as the Little Apocalypse.[114] In these four chapters the focus is eschatological, "fixed firmly on the frightening yet (for some) joyous events about to dawn."[115] As Smith outlines these four chapters, the prophet Isaiah speaks of the destruction of God's enemies (24-25) in order to motivate the people of Judah (26-27).[116] God's victory over his enemies should compel his people to place their faith in him now.[117]

Ever since Genesis 3 death has ended the earthly sojourn of God's image bearers, but one day God will bring an end to death: "He will swallow up death forever" (Isa 25:8a). In the larger context of Isaiah 25, the chapter describes the future glory of God's people and their dwelling place, and it assures readers that his enemies and their strongholds will be brought down. Isaiah 25 contrasts with the previous chapter, which narrates God's judgment and cosmic destruction (24:1, 3-6, 17, 19-20). Judgment (Isa 24) is followed by renewal (Isa 25), and God's consumption of death is part of this renewing work.[118] Death is one of God's enemies, "even the ultimate enemy," so the final victory of God "requires the elimination of his great foe, death."[119]

When Paul talks about the perishable putting on the imperishable and the mortal donning immortality, he quotes Isaiah 25:8: "Then shall come to pass the saying that is written: 'Death is swallowed up in victory'" (1 Cor 15:54-55). Paul understands the promise of Isaiah 25:8 (that death will end) to be fulfilled when "the dead will be raised imperishable" (1 Cor 15:42). Until then, death will consume people with its insatiable appetite, and the dust will have no rest.

The dead rulers who will not live (Isa 26:14). Isaiah 26 continues the Little Apocalypse and begins with the gracious dealings of God with his people. The righteous enter the restored land (26:1-2, 7) and know

---

113. Wright, *The Resurrection of the Son of God*, 115.
114. With Hasel, "Critical scholarship has been unable to reach a consensus on the dating of the Isaiah Apocalypse. For our purposes it will suffice to suggest that Isa 26:19 was composed earlier than Dan 12:1-4" (Gerhard F. Hasel, "Resurrection in the Theology of Old Testament Apocalyptic," ZAW 92 [1980]: 269).
115. Levenson, *Resurrection and the Restoration of Israel*, 198.
116. Smith, *Isaiah 1-39*, 410.
117. Smith, *Isaiah 1-39*, 439.
118. See Dempster, "The Resurrection of Christ," 15.
119. Levenson, *Resurrection and the Restoration of Israel*, 200.

God's peace (26:3, 12). The lords who once ruled the righteous are now forgotten (26:13). Those rulers "are dead, they will not live [בַּל־יִחְיוּ]; they are shades, they will not arise [בַּל־יָקֻמוּ]; to that end you have visited them with destruction and wiped out all remembrance of them" (26:14).

At first glance the words of Isaiah 26:14 seem to deny a resurrection of the wicked, but the context of the chapter offers a more nuanced conclusion. Up to that verse Isaiah 26 has been narrating the favor and peace enjoyed by the righteous in the land, and one group that will not dwell there is the wicked. While 26:14 says these wicked will not rise, the promise of Daniel 12:2 clarifies that it will not be a resurrection *to life*. Instead, the wicked have "destruction" as their end (Isa 26:14), an end manifested ultimately in their resurrection to shame and contempt (Dan 12:2). "To be sure, Isaiah 26 gives no indication that [the wicked] will 'awake' to punishment, but the notion of contrasting verdicts and a revival of the faithful is prominent there nonetheless."[120] The obvious contrast between 26:14 and 26:19 (see below) shows that more than national restoration is meant in those verses.[121] Greenspoon's reasoning is sound:

> Surely, no one anticipated a restoration, national or otherwise, for Israel's godless oppressors! On the other hand, it would certainly be valuable to fashion a clear statement about the respective post mortem fates of the righteous and the wicked, so as to dispel any misapprehension that death severed the link between the just and their God or offered an avenue of escape to a better "life" for those who opposed God while on earth.[122]

The significance of Isaiah 26:14 to the subject of resurrection hope is threefold. First, the resurrection in view is both individual and bodily. Clearly *persons*, not a nation or nations, are being discussed as to whether they will rise from the dead. Second, the final state of the righteous is different from the wicked: the former will live under the favor of God, while the latter face the destruction of divine judgment. Third, the verbs referring to rising—חיה and קוּם—have appeared earlier in the Old Testament in contexts of resurrection and so reinforce their appropriation by the biblical author for the subject of resurrection in 26:14. Moreover, the verbs are parallel to each other ("they will not live ... they

---

120. Levenson, *Resurrection and the Restoration of Israel*, 199.
121. Hasel, "Resurrection in the Theology of Old Testament Apocalyptic," 274; Nickelsburg, *Resurrection, Immortality, and Eternal Life*, 18.
122. Greenspoon, "The Origin of the Idea of Resurrection," 286.

will not arise"), and this arrangement verifies the use of either one for denoting resurrection.

The dead who live, rise, and awake (Isa 26:19). A few verses after refuting the notion that the wicked will have bodily life in God's land (Isa 26:14), God's people learn that *they* will see life again. "Your dead shall live [יִחְיוּ]; their bodies shall rise [יְקוּמוּן]. You who dwell in the dust, awake [הָקִיצוּ] and sing for joy! For your dew is a dew of light, and the earth will give birth to the dead" (26:19).

Both Isaiah 26:14 and 26:19 use the two verbs חיה and קוּם, and 26:19 adds קיץ. The meaning of 26:19 is clearly about resurrection because the action of the verbs happens to the "dead," to "bodies," and to those who "dwell in the dust."[123] But is the resurrection individual in nature? Given the immediate background and meaning of 26:14, it is probable that individual bodily resurrection is also meant in 26:19. A national focus is not necessarily excluded, but neither does it exhaust the meaning of the verse.

As Robert Martin-Achard correctly observes, "The author of Isa 26:19 is not, like Ezekiel, envisaging the political revival of the nation; he is not even speaking about an event that would concern all Israel; he is thinking only of certain members of the chosen People, of those to whom 'thy dead' refer."[124] Even the imagery drawn from nature (bodies, dust, dew) would seem to have no function if only restoration rather than actual resurrection was involved.[125] In the context of Isaiah 26:19 there is no mention of restoration of the nation, so there is no indication that the language of resurrection should be understood only at a national level.[126]

Wright's insistence should be heeded: "The either/or that has tended to drive a wedge between different interpretations of key passages (*either* 'individual resurrection' *or* 'national restoration') must be exposed as fallacious."[127] Applying Wright's words to the verse at hand, God

---

123. Hasel rightly observes, "It is difficult to accept the suggestion that the designation '(the) dwellers of (the) dust' which is employed in parallelism to the 'dead' refers to some other entity than those who have physically died" ("Resurrection in the Theology of Old Testament Apocalyptic," 272).
124. Martin-Achard, *From Death to Life*, 131. Levenson elaborates: "The implication seems to be that some (but not all) of Israel will rise. The verse can thus be profitably contrasted with Ezekiel 37" (*Resurrection and the Restoration of Israel*, 199).
125. Greenspoon, "The Origin of the Idea of Resurrection," 285.
126. Smith, *Isaiah 1-39*, 452.
127. Wright, *The Resurrection of the Son of God*, 116.

is promising an end to exile, and restoration by bodily resurrection is the end to the deepest exile of all.[128]

Isaiah 26:19 is a source for Daniel 12:2.[129] Both verses use the image of being in the "dust," and both use the Hiphil of קיץ to mean "awake." Clearly the belief in resurrection was already present before Daniel.[130] But is there a prior source for the language found in Isaiah 26:19, other than 26:14?

Bronner rightly sees that the last line in Isaiah 26:19, "For your dew is a dew of light, and the earth will give birth to the dead," is reminiscent of Hosea 6:3 and 14:5-6, which contain "a similar theme of God's control of the life-giving power of moisture to revive the dead."[131] John Day not only believes Isaiah 26 is reminiscent of verses in Hosea, he believes it was *dependent* on Hosea.[132] The following table summarizes the parallels he suggests:

John Day's Eight Parallels Between Hosea 13-14 and Isaiah 26-27

The parallel suggested by Day	From Hosea	From Isaiah
(1) Israel knows no lords/gods but Yahweh	13:4	26:13
(2) Imagery of birth pangs but child refuses to be born	13:13	26:17-18
(3) Deliverance from Sheol	13:14	26:19
(4) Imagery of destructive east wind symbolic of exile	13:15	27:8
(5) Imagery of life-giving dew	14:6 [Eng. 14:5]	26:19
(6) Israel blossoming and like a vineyard	14:6-8 [Eng. 14:5-7]	27:2-6
(7) Condemnation of idolatry, including the Asherim	14:9 [Eng. 14:8]	27:9
(8) The importance of discernment; judgment for the wicked	14:10 [Eng. 14:9]	27:11

---

128. Wright, *The Resurrection of the Son of God*, 116.
129. See Levenson, *Resurrection and the Restoration of Israel*, 197. Greenspoon: "It is hard to imagine that the author of Daniel worked with no knowledge of this passage" ("The Origin of the Idea of Resurrection," 284).
130. Bronner, "The Resurrection Motif in the Hebrew Bible," 151.
131. Bronner, "The Resurrection Motif in the Hebrew Bible," 152. See Smith, *Isaiah 1-39*, 454.
132. See Day, "A Case of Inner Scriptural Interpretation," 309-19.

Levenson rightly confirms the value of Day's insights and adds a clarifying comment for anyone who may push back against Day's claims: "Whatever the weakness of some of Day's parallels taken individually, the sheer density of them in a delimited corpus is highly curious and suggests that Hosea 13-14 has indeed had an influence to one degree or another on Isaiah 26-27."[133] Most specifically, therefore, Hosea influenced Isaiah 26:19. This influence is discernible between Hosea 6:2 and Isaiah 26:19 because the former uses the same verbs (חיה and קוּם) that appear in the latter.

In Sawyer's words, Isaiah 26:19 "is a reference to the resurrection of the dead which no-one but a Sadducee, ancient or modern, could possibly misconstrue."[134] According to Wright, it is "the most obvious 'resurrection' passage in Isaiah."[135]

The Suffering Servant who shall see and be satisfied (Isa 53:10-11). In one of the Servant songs in the book of Isaiah, the role of that Servant will include vicarious suffering and death (Isa 53:4-9). But death is not the end. It is Yahweh's will to crush him, yet the night of death will end with light: "When his soul makes an offering for guilt, he shall see his offspring; he shall prolong his days; the will of the LORD shall prosper in his hand. Out of the anguish of his soul he shall see and be satisfied" (53:10-11).

According to Isaiah, the Servant makes an offering but will prosper in prolonged days, and after anguish will come satisfaction. Not a single verb of resurrection is used in Isaiah 53:10-11, but the *picture* is of resurrection nonetheless. Death has occurred, a conclusion safely reached by the accumulation of terms like *smitten, afflicted, wounded, crushed, chastisement, stripes, oppressed, slaughter, judgment, cut off, stricken, grave,* and *death* (53:4-9). Greenspoon says, "The overall impression is that the text speaks of an individual's death and burial."[136]

Following the demise of this Servant, he once again experiences vitality of life (Isa 53:10-11). Beale is right that it is "best read to refer to

---

133. Levenson, *Resurrection and the Restoration of Israel*, 204. Schreiner confirms this relationship as well and adds, "Intertextual connections between Hosea and Isa 26-27 suggest that the former anticipated the resurrection of the dead" (*The King in His Beauty*, 410n36). The presence of resurrection hope in Hosea will be discussed in the corresponding section below.
134. Sawyer, "Hebrew Words for the Resurrection of the Dead," 234.
135. Wright, *The Resurrection of the Son of God*, 116.
136. Greenspoon, "The Origin of the Idea of Resurrection," 295.

the Servant's recovery from death," thus *resurrection*.[137] According to Dempster, the Servant is "cut off from the land of the living, but ... he is later able to see his seed and lengthen his days which suggest that he is alive to see his spiritual progeny."[138] So while the author of Isaiah 53 does not explain how the Servant reawakened from the sleep of death, "we must nevertheless insist that this passage retains its relevance in any discussion of the Biblical concept of resurrection, precisely because of what it does not say. The author of this passage *assumes* knowledge, and acceptance, of the concept of resurrection on the part of his audience."[139] In other words, the reader should supply what was clearly understood but did not need to be explicitly stated.[140]

The perpetual sleep of the wicked Babylonians (Jer 51:39, 57). In Jeremiah 51 Yahweh promises the utter destruction of Babylon. He says the Babylonians will "then sleep a perpetual sleep and not wake [יָקִיצוּ]" (51:39). "Sleep" is a metaphor for death.[141] Also, the same verb for waking is used later in that chapter about Babylon's leaders specifically: "They shall sleep a perpetual sleep and not wake (יָקִיצוּ)" (51:57).

The assertion in Jeremiah 51:39 and 51:57 is the same as Isaiah 26:14: the wicked will not experience a resurrection unto life. Judgment, pictured as a statement of "permanent aridity and sterility," is their lot.[142] In fact, Jeremiah 51 is a chapter devoted to narrating Babylon's demise. Seen through the post-Jeremiah book of Daniel (cf. Dan 9:2), the judgment on God's enemies will result in end-time bodily judgment, and his Babylonian enemies are no exception to this. In Jeremiah 51, however, the focus is on Babylon's destruction, which vindicates God's people (cf.

---

137. Beale, *A New Testament Theology*, 232. See Levenson's confirmation: "The God of life triumphs dramatically over death in this passage" (*Resurrection and the Restoration of Israel*, 188).
138. Dempster, "The Resurrection of Christ," 15.
139. Greenspoon, "The Origin of the Idea of Resurrection," 296. According to Williamson, "While resurrection is not explicit here, the Servant clearly suffers fatally (53:7–9, 12), and thus resurrection from the dead is at least implicit" (Williamson, *Death and the Afterlife*, 79).
140. Greenspoon, "The Origin of the Idea of Resurrection," 296. Greenspoon adds, "In saying nothing, he bears eloquent testimony to just how well- and widely-known the belief in bodily resurrection was." According to Johnston, "Whenever the book of Isaiah was finalized, and whoever completed it, 53:10–12 could then be understood as a post-resurrection life of the suffering servant" (*Shades of Sheol*, 228).
141. Nickelsburg, *Resurrection, Immortality, and Eternal Life*, 17n33.
142. Greenspoon, "The Origin of the Idea of Resurrection," 288.

51:48-49). The desolation God will bring is permanent (51:62-64). Thus this judgment on Babylon is a type of the final one, when God will press upon the wicked the ultimate consequences of his curse.

The resurrection of dry bones (Ezek 37:7-10). Ezekiel had a vision of a valley filled with bones (Ezek 37:1-2), and God told him to prophesy over them that they might live again (37:3-6). Ezekiel tells the reader what happened next.

> So I prophesied as I was commanded. And as I prophesied, there was a sound, and behold, a rattling, and the bones came together, bone to its bone. And I looked, and behold, there were sinews on them, and flesh had come upon them, and skin had covered them. But there was no breath in them. Then he said to me, "Prophesy to the breath; prophesy, son of man, and say to the breath, Thus says the Lord GOD: Come from the four winds, O breath, and breathe on these slain, that they may live." So I prophesied as he commanded me, and the breath came into them, and they lived and stood on their feet, an exceedingly great army. (Ezek 37:7-10)

Wright calls Ezekiel 37 the "most famous of all 'resurrection' passages in the Old Testament."[143] That this scene pictures a resurrection of the dead is not disputed. Bones come together, sinews and flesh come upon them, and skin covers it all. These bodies then receive the animating breath of God and come alive (37:10, "and they lived," וַיִּחְיוּ).[144] Now alive and breathing, these bodies stand up on their feet (37:10, "and they stood," וַיַּעַמְדוּ).

What is disputed about Ezekiel 37, however, is whether the raised bodies refer to a corporate restoration of Israel only, or whether the hope is for bodily resurrection. The verses that must be addressed in this question are 37:11-12, where God says to Ezekiel, "Son of man, these bones are the whole house of Israel. ... Therefore prophesy, and say to them, Thus says the Lord GOD: Behold, I will open your graves and raise you from your graves, O my people. And I will bring you into the land of Israel."

---

143. Wright, *The Resurrection of the Son of God*, 119.
144. Bronner rightly notes that the verb חיה, which appears six times in 37:1-14, alerts the interpreter to the motif of resurrection, and all the physical elements necessary for reconstructing the human body are present in the passage as well ("The Resurrection Motif in the Hebrew Bible," 150).

It appears that Ezekiel 37:7-10 is a promise to restore exiled Israel to the promised land, and thus the resurrection is of a corporate nature. God himself interpreted the revived bones as "the whole house of Israel." And most commentators agree to limit the application of Ezekiel's vision to national restoration.[145] But does this necessarily exclude an individual component to this resurrection hope? Greenspoon is right: "We have no doubt that those scholars are correct who see in Ezekiel's Vision a hope for national restoration addressed to his fellow exiles. We also have no doubt that they are incorrect when they limit Ezekiel's message to only this."[146] In fact, according to extant writings, many Jews understood Ezekiel 37 as a reference to bodily resurrection.[147]

The source of the language and imagery used in Ezekiel 37 is an intriguing question. The picture of God animating a body with his breath echoes the creation of man from the ground (cf. Gen 2:7).[148] And as with Adam and Eve's eviction from the garden of Eden, exile from the land meant death, whereas the return would be like resurrection. The bond between the concepts of restoration and resurrection is a close and inseparable one.

Perhaps the final miracle of (postmortem) Elisha also informed the scene in the valley of dry bones.[149] A man's corpse was thrown into Elisha's grave, and the man revived and stood up when his body touched the prophet's bones (2 Kgs 13:21). Now, in the valley that also mentions bones, bodies come alive and stand to their feet (Ezek 37:3, 10). This is the work of the Divine Warrior, whose initiative reawakens the lifeless bones,[150] and who promised in Ezekiel 36 to transform the land "like the garden of Eden" (36:35). Much earlier than Ezekiel's ministry, the Divine

---

145. Greenspoon, "The Origin of the Idea of Resurrection," 292.
146. Greenspoon, "The Origin of the Idea of Resurrection," 293.
147. N. T. Wright, *The New Testament and the People of God*, Christian Origins and the Question of God, vol. 1 (Minneapolis: Fortress, 1992), 332. See Beale, *A New Testament Biblical Theology*, 230.
148. See Wright, *The Resurrection of the Son of God*, 120; Dempster, *Dominion and Dynasty*, 170.
149. Dempster says, "Here when these bones come into contact with the prophetic word of God, they become a new humanity living and moving and having its being in God, in a remarkable escalation and multiplication of the Elisha story in which one corpse was revivified by touching the prophet's bones" ("The Resurrection of Christ," 16).
150. Greenspoon, "The Origin of the Idea of Resurrection," 292.

Warrior worked through the human instruments Elijah and Elisha, each of whom played decisive roles in events of resurrection from the dead.[151]

Even if interpreters are not convinced that Ezekiel's language can be legitimately extended to bodily resurrection, the prophet must have been aware of such a hope because of the nature of the vision's content. The choice of language—dry bones, sinews, skin, breath—would function most effectively when placed in a context provided by the concept of bodily resurrection.[152] According to Carnley, "The standard use of any term is presupposed by the metaphorical use, and we would not understand the metaphor without it."[153] Would the metaphor have been as powerful and hope-giving to Ezekiel and the readers of his prophecy if they did not already believe God could do to bodies what the vision described? Greenspoon asserts, "It is sufficiently clear that Ezekiel was working with a concept of the resurrection of the dead well enough known to his audience to allow for the simultaneous application of this belief to 'literal' resurrection and national restoration."[154]

Instead of Ezekiel 37 being a prophecy of corporate resurrection that influenced later writers (e.g., the prophet Daniel) to hope for bodily resurrection, could it be that the people already possessed a hope for bodily resurrection? If so, then this hope upheld the power of—and gave greater significance to—a metaphor like the valley of dry bones.

Raised to life on the third day (Hos 6:2). God promises judgment on rebellious Israel. He will be to them a lion, and no one will deliver them from his roaring wrath (Hos 5:11-14). Then the people say they should return to Yahweh for healing and restoration. "After two days he will revive us [יְחַיֵּנוּ]; on the third day he will raise us up [יְקִמֵנוּ], that we may live [וְנִחְיֶה] before him" (6:2).

Their confidence should not be taken as true repentance yet, for Hosea says, "What shall I do with you, O Ephraim? What shall I do with you, O Judah? Your love is like a morning cloud, like the dew that goes early away" (Hos 6:4). The sincerity of the people may be in question,

---

151. Greenspoon, "The Origin of the Idea of Resurrection," 293.
152. Greenspoon, "The Origin of the Idea of Resurrection," 293.
153. Peter Carnley, *The Structure of Resurrection Belief* (Oxford: Clarendon, 1987), 229. According to Ladd, "The very fact that the vision sees the restoration of dead bones to life suggests that the *idea* of bodily resurrection was familiar" (*I Believe in the Resurrection of Jesus*, 48).
154. Greenspoon, "The Origin of the Idea of Resurrection," 294.

but that does not mean they are wrong about God's ability and plan to raise the dead.[155]

The phrase in Hosea 6:1, "he has torn us, that he may heal us," is reminiscent of Deuteronomy 32:39, "I wound and I heal."[156] In both verses there is also the notion of being made alive ("he will revive us ... he will raise us up," Hos 6:2; "I make alive," Deut 32:39). The people believe that God can raise them—or revive them—from the dead. There is no warrant for finding a connection to pagan myths about gods rising from the dead, such as Baal in the Canaanite religion, for "the death and resurrection of the people has nothing to in common with a myth in which *a god* dies and comes back to life."[157]

Their revival as a nation will be a picture of resurrection, but the meaning is more than national restoration.[158] The next verse, Hosea 6:3, invokes the Divine Warrior motif that replenishes the land with rain: "Let us know; let us press on to know the LORD; his going out is sure as the dawn; he will come to us as the showers, as the spring rains that water the earth." Since resurrection hope existed prior to the ministry of Hosea, what the prophet did was adapt individual bodily resurrection to the experience of the nation.[159] Similar to the claim made in the

---

155. As Dempster puts it, "The prophet does not argue with the theology of this liturgy but with the nature of intended repentance. ... Thus the prophet is not disagreeing with the statement of the people which is based on Deuteronomy and God's transcendence and compassion, he is disagreeing with the use of it here where the people only produce transient repentance and devotion" ("The Resurrection of Christ," 18). And as Greenspoon observes, "Although the people who speak in Hos 6:1–3 misuse the Biblical concept of bodily resurrection, their very misuse is valuable evidence for the existence of this concept during the 8th century" ("The Origin of the Idea of Resurrection," 309).
156. See Dempster, "The Resurrection of Christ," 17: "The resonances with Deuteronomy are patent: The repentant exiles will experience ultimate vindication and there will be atonement for the land because Yahweh is sovereign not only having the ability to kill, but also to resurrect, not only the ability to wound but to heal since no one can deliver from his hand."
157. Francis I. Andersen and David Noel Freedman, *Hosea*, AB, vol. 24 (Garden City, NY: Doubleday, 1980), 420. See Bronner, "The Resurrection Motif in the Hebrew Bible," 148; Greenspoon, "The Origin of the Idea of Resurrection," 308.
158. See Bronner, "The Resurrection Motif in the Hebrew Bible," 149. Contra Bronner, Ladd says "The passage more likely refers to the restoration of the nation" (*I Believe in the Resurrection of Jesus*, 48).
159. Andersen and Freedman, *Hosea*, 420. Again, there is still application to the nation in terms of restoration, but the meaning is not exhausted by that interpretation. Hamilton is right: "The 'tearing' of the lion is probably a figurative way of saying that Yahweh will exile Israel. When he drives them from the

section above on Ezekiel 37, Andersen and Freedman insist with regard to Hosea 6 that metaphorical language "must have been grounded in a certain type of expectation about the future life."[160]

Likely backgrounds to the resurrection statements in Hosea 6:2 are the miraculous ministries of the prophets Elijah and Elisha.[161] Earlier in northern Israel these two men each raised individuals from the dead. Their stories were surely known and admired by the northern Israelites, and their respective miracles demonstrated the power of Yahweh over against impotent idols. Most significant, the two verbs for resurrection in Hosea 6:2 (חיה and קום) appear together in one earlier Old Testament resurrection text, 2 Kings 13:21. Greenspoon's conclusion is reasonable and compelling: "Thus, against the prevailing view, we would argue that these northern Israelites [of Hosea's day] derived their imagery and language from a concept of resurrection that was already known in Israel, and what is more, associated with prophets whose authority as men of God could not be questioned."[162]

The ransom of people from Sheol and death (Hos 13:14). In Hosea 13 identical notions of judgment and resurrection from Hosea 6 reappear. God will be a lion to the rebellious people and judge them (13:7–8). Then, knowing their unrepentant state, God asks, "Shall I ransom them from the power of Sheol? Shall I redeem them from Death?" (13:14a–b).[163]

Sheol and death are parallel in Hosea 13:14, so deliverance from them is resurrection. The verbs "ransom" and "redeem," which come from פָּדָה and גָּאַל, respectively, are also parallel and result in the same outcome: the objects of God's rescue are taken from the mouth of Sheol. God the Divine Warrior is able to overcome the force and power of death so that it is not an impenetrable stronghold. Furthermore, while פָּדָה and גָּאַל are not the typical verbs used in passages of resurrection, the description of God ransoming his people from death is nothing less than this hope of renewed life, so those two verbs become terms of resurrection in this passage.

---

land, they will enter the realm of the dead. They will die as a nation. Through the judgment of Yahweh's tearing like a lion comes the salvation of Yahweh raising as from the dead" (*God's Glory in Salvation through Judgment*, 238).

160. Andersen and Freedman, *Hosea*, 421.
161. Bronner, "The Resurrection Motif in the Hebrew Bible," 148.
162. Greenspoon, "The Origin of the Idea of Resurrection," 309.
163. Beale translates the first two clauses of Hos 13:14 as statements of promise instead of questions ("I will ransom them from the power of Sheol; I will redeem them from death") (*A New Testament Biblical Theology*, 231n8).

The phrase "ransom ... from the power of Sheol" (Hos 13:14) occurs only once more in the Old Testament, in Psalm 49:16 (Eng. 49:15), so the former is probably dependent on the latter. Hosea employs the language of the psalm and interprets it as resurrection. The parallels are unmistakable when viewed together in Hebrew:

יִפְדֶּה ... מִיַּד־שְׁאוֹל (Ps 49:16 [Eng. 49:15])

מִיַּד שְׁאוֹל אֶפְדֵּם (Hos 13:14)

The significant difference between these two verses is the location of the form of פדה: it is at the beginning of the phrase in Psalm 49:16 (Eng. 49:15) but is at the end of the phrase in Hosea 13:14. Again, however, since a combination of these words does not occur anywhere in the Old Testament but in these two places, Hosea 13:14 was most likely dependent on Psalm 49:16 (Eng. 49:15), for the author believed that it expressed, as well as pictured, resurrection hope.[164]

Jonah's deliverance from the deep and the fish (Jon 2:7 [Eng. 2:6]; 2:11 [Eng. 2:10]). The prophet Jonah disobeyed Yahweh's command about preaching to Ninevites and fled by boat in the opposite direction (Jonah 1:2–3). God sent a storm, which put in danger the lives of everyone on board (1:4–6). When the crew cast lots and exposed Jonah as the reason why the tempest was overtaking them, he assured them that casting him overboard would calm the sea (1:11–12). The men hurled Jonah into the waters, and a fish swallowed him (1:15, 2:1 [Eng. 1:17]). After three days and three nights in the belly of the fish, it vomited Jonah onto dry land (2:1 [Eng. 1:17]; 2:11 [Eng. 2:10]).

Jonah's deliverance is a picture of resurrection, for the belly of the deep was "the belly of Sheol" (2:3 [Eng. 2:2]), but the fish rescued him, "and Yahweh my God brought up [וַתַּעַל] my life from the pit" (2:7 [Eng. 2:6]). As argued by Wheaton, "This act of divine intervention when there was no human possibility of escaping death can only be understood as resurrection."[165] Then Jonah emerged when the fish spewed him onto land, a further deliverance.

A confirmation that the belly of the fish was a figurative grave comes from Jesus's words to the scribes and Pharisees when he foretells his own death and resurrection: "For just as Jonah was three days and three

---

164. Psalm 49:16 [Eng. 49:15] will be discussed in the Writings section of this chapter.
165. Wheaton, "As It Is Written," 252.

nights in the belly of the great fish, so will the Son of Man be three days and three nights in the heart of the earth" (Matt 12:40). In Jonah's case the Divine Warrior triumphed over the sea chaos as well as the sea beast. When the fish spewed the prophet onto land, Dempster says Jonah had been raised from the dead, "even if metaphorically understood."[166]

Jonah's individual deliverance had a greater meaning for the Israelites who would soon face destruction. Hamilton discerns the application of Jonah's experiences: "Just as Jonah undergoes a death and resurrection of sorts before obeying and going to Nineveh, so the nation will go through a death and resurrection of sorts when they are exiled to the realm of death and then restored to life in the land of Yahweh's presence."[167]

SUPPORTING EVIDENCE

Additional evidence for resurrection hope in the Prophets can be observed in Judges, 2 Samuel, 2 Kings, Isaiah, and Hosea.

The cycle of rebellion and deliverance (Judg 2:11-19). In the book of Judges, a cycle is discernable and has four steps: the Israelites do what is evil in the sight of the Lord and commit idolatry (Judg 2:11); this idolatry provokes the Lord, who then stirs up an adversary against them (2:14-15); the Israelites cry out to the Lord in their affliction (2:18); and the Lord delivers the Israelites from their adversaries by raising up a judge (2:18). The problem is that when the judge dies, the Israelites turn back to idols and engage in more corruption (2:19). So the cycle repeats itself.

The cycle spanning from rebellion to deliverance is a picture of restoration—*resurrection*. The people become entangled in the foolishness of idolatry. When this foolishness leads to divine judgment, the threat of foreign adversaries puts the Israelites in a position of peril. Following their groaning and oppression, the divine deliverance is their resurrection from peril.

Each judge in the book becomes a resurrection agent. The collective death of the people leads to resurrection because of a mighty warrior whom God raises up. When God powerfully acts upon their national peril, the collective rescue is from further oppression and the gates of destruction.

---

166. Dempster, "The Resurrection of Christ," 19.
167. Hamilton, *God's Glory in Salvation through Judgment*, 247.

The deliverance of David from the snare of death (2 Sam 22:17). On the day David was delivered from the hand of Saul, he sang to Yahweh about his vindication, and the picture looks like resurrection. The conditions of demise are fourfold: waves of death, torrents of destruction, cords of Sheol, and snares of death overwhelmed him (2 Sam 22:5-6). When David called upon God for rescue, "He sent from on high, he took me; he drew me out of many waters" (22:17).

The rescue was like resurrection because of the imminence of death. Like Moses who was drawn out of the water (Exod 2:10), David being drawn out was deliverance from destruction. "David himself is a prime example of the defeat of the forces of death by the resurrecting power of God. It is as if death had wrapped its lethal tentacles around the king and at the last moment Yahweh snatched him from their grasp."[168] Parallel to being "drawn out" is the previous phrase, "he took me." The verb לָקַח describes God delivering his righteous one from death. As Lunn observes, "To be submerged in water according to biblical poetic imagery is an experience associated with death or a near-death encounter."[169]

Also related to future hope is the final verse of David's song: "Great salvation he brings to his king, and shows steadfast love to his anointed, to David and his offspring forever" (2 Sam 22:51). God's deliverance of King David was based on covenant love, which was shown not only to David but also to David's descendant(s). The ultimate deliverance of God's people—bodily resurrection in the future—is connected to covenant love as well. Yahweh's faithfulness would be known in a life beyond the grave.[170] The presence of such confidence is evident: death will not sever the steadfast faithfulness of Yahweh.[171]

Elijah's ascent to heaven apart from death (2 Kgs 2:11). In Genesis 5 readers encountered the unusual story of a man named Enoch, whom God took before death. On another occasion, this time in 2 Kings, God took Elijah apart from death. As Elijah and Elisha talked, "behold, chariots of fire and horses of fire separated the two of them. And Elijah went up by a whirlwind into heaven" (2 Kgs 2:11).

Elisha saw Elijah's ascent and said, "My father, my father! The chariots of Israel and its horsemen!" (2 Kgs 2:12). The power of God was

---

168. Dempster, "The Resurrection of Christ," 13.
169. Lunn, "'Raised on the Third Day According to the Scriptures,'" 526.
170. Wright, *The Resurrection of the Son of God*, 103.
171. This confidence is evident frequently in Psalms, which will be addressed later in this chapter under the main section titled "The Writings."

displayed as this prophet went to heaven without first returning to the dust. This story, like Enoch's translation in Genesis 5, continues to stir the waters of resurrection hope because death is evidently not some insurmountable end to earthly life. Elijah's earthly life did not end in bodily death and showed that God's power is greater than its apparent inevitability. Kidner comments, "As Enochs and Elijahs are rare, this hope did not easily become general; but at least twice the gates of Sheol had not prevailed."[172]

The recovery of Hezekiah (2 Kgs 20:5-6). A king of Judah named Hezekiah became so ill that he was going to die (2 Kgs 20:1; see another record of this account in Isa 38). Illness signaled the power of death at work in the world, and now the shadow of death had fallen upon Judah's king. Even the prophet Isaiah confirmed the king's imminent death (20:1).

King Hezekiah prayed to the Lord for mercy and healing, and the word of the Lord came to Hezekiah with good news. The Lord said, "I have heard your prayer; I have seen your tears. Behold, I will heal you. On the third day you shall go up to the house of the LORD, and I will add fifteen years to your life" (2 Kgs 20:5-6). This healing brought back Hezekiah's life from the threshold of death, and it was a third-day restoration as well.

In the account of Hezekiah's healing in the book of Isaiah, the king wrote about his misery: "In the middle of my days I must depart; I am consigned to the gates of Sheol for the rest of my years. I said, I shall not see the LORD, the LORD in the land of the living; I shall look on man no more among the inhabitants of the world" (Isa 38:10-11). And then the king wrote a prayer about his healing: "Oh restore me to health and make me live! Behold, it was for my welfare that I had great bitterness; but in love you have delivered my life from the pit of destruction" (38:16-17).

Hezekiah had been at the gates of Sheol and in the pit of destruction. But by mighty power that overcomes the forces of death, the Lord healed him. This physical healing was a figurative resurrection, a resurrection of a son of David on the third day.

Divine power over infirmities and desolation (Isa 35:5-7). The power of the Divine Warrior is seen again in Isaiah 35 with vitality and

---

172. Derek Kidner, *Genesis: An Introduction and Commentary*, TOTC (Downers Grove, IL: InterVarsity Press, 1967), 81.

life granted to physical infirmities and places of desolation.[173] When God comes to display his glory and majesty (35:2), the wilderness will be glad, and the desert will thrive (35:1). God's work will be restorative and rejuvenating. According to Levenson, as the Divine Warrior "marches forth in wrath against the oppressive forces of chaos and death, nature languishes, and when he returns enthroned in victory and justice, nature flourishes and luxuriates."[174]

> Then the eyes of the blind shall be opened, and the ears of the deaf unstopped; then shall the lame man leap like a deer, and the tongue of the mute sing for joy. For waters break forth in the wilderness, and streams in the desert; the burning sand shall become a pool, and the thirsty ground springs of water; in the haunt of jackals, where they lie down, the grass shall become reeds and rushes. (Isa 35:5–7)

In a desert the signs of life may be sparse, so the presence of streams and pools and ground springs gives hope and sustains life.[175] The barren land blooms at last. The miraculous extends to the disabilities common to fallen man, such as blindness, deafness, lameness, and muteness. Levenson says, "These transformations, whether of deserts or mountains or unjust fates or human disabilities, were equally impossible and equally exceptional. ... To those of little faith, they were doubtless mere fantasies and impossibilities."[176]

Obviously missing in Isaiah 35 is a reference to death, but prior verses in Isaiah, like 25:8 and 26:19, teach that God's power will undo that as well. The power displayed in these restorative acts begs the question: if God will give sight to the blind, open the ears of the deaf, strengthen the

---

173. Greenspoon: "Vivid descriptions of nature's joyous re-awakening at God's victory are also not lacking in the Hebrew Bible. ... From Isaiah 35 comes the following depiction of nature's exuberant and vital response, a response which stands in marked contrast to the sombre and stark mood attending the collapse of nature" ("The Origin of the Idea of Resurrection," 271).
174. Levenson, *Resurrection and the Restoration of Israel*, 211.
175. Greenspoon: "At the return of the victorious Divine Warrior, once-dormant nature quickens in reaction: everywhere there is a surge of renewed vigor, evident in joyous activity, fertility, and the blossoming forth of life in a wide range of manifestations. It would hardly be too much to refer to all of this as a re-birth, brought about by the active stimulus of God Himself" ("The Origin of the Idea of Resurrection," 276).
176. Levenson, *Resurrection and the Restoration of Israel*, 212.

limbs of the lame, and loose the tongue of the mute, what will he do for the dead?[177]

The offspring that remain in the new creation (Isa 66:22). The last chapter of Isaiah narrates a new world God will make, continuing the notion from 65:17, where God says, "For behold, I create new heavens and a new earth, and the former things shall not be remembered or come into mind." In Isaiah 66 he asserts the permanence of his new creation and his people: "For as the new heavens and the new earth that I make shall remain before me, says the Lord, so shall your offspring and your name remain" (66:22).

A new world that endures is one void of curse and corruption (Isa 65:19-25). Peace will flow there like a river, and joy and comfort will be the theme (66:12-14). The people's hearts will rejoice, and "your bones shall flourish like the grass" (66:14a), a flourishing that denotes physical vitality. The earth and its dwellers will be made new, having a physical existence possible only because of God's power in new creation. Beale says these people have "an unlimited enduring new-creational life."[178] In 66:22 their offspring remain, and this probably picks up the earlier prophecy of the Suffering Servant who will die yet whose seed will be prolonged.[179] The offspring are God's people raised from the dead to indwell God's new creation forever.[180]

Unending judgment on the bodies of the wicked (Isa 66:24). The book of Isaiah ends on a note of judgment. The final verse depicts unending bodily destruction: "And they shall go out and look on the dead bodies of the men who have rebelled against me. For their worm shall not die, their fire shall not be quenched, and they shall be an abhorrence to all flesh" (Isa 66:24).

Earlier in Isaiah 66 Yahweh comes with fiery judgment (66:15-16) and slays the wicked in his wrath. But 66:24 does not picture an extinguishment of the wicked. Instead, undying worms and unquenchable fire shall be upon them. This is a scene worse than bodily death. In some way God's judgment on their bodies will continue unabated.

---

177. Greenspoon says, "Man, as part of nature, could hardly remain unaffected. ... The resurrection of man can be fit into the overall portrayal of nature's response to the victorious Divine Warrior" ("The Origin of the Idea of Resurrection," 276). See Jesus's words in Matt 11:4-5.
178. Beale, *A New Testament Biblical Theology*, 231.
179. Beale, *A New Testament Biblical Theology*, 231-32.
180. Beale, *A New Testament Biblical Theology*, 232.

God says the wicked "shall be an abhorrence to all flesh" (Isa 66:24). The word for "abhorrence" (דֵּרָאוֹן) occurs once more in the Old Testament, in Daniel 12:2, indicating Daniel's dependence on Isaiah 66:24 for the judgment awaiting the wicked.[181] The final verse in Isaiah provides two truths important for Daniel's purposes: the judgment occurs on bodies, and it does not end. Among those who awake from the sleep of death, some will rise "to shame and everlasting contempt" (Dan 12:2).

The return and blossoming of God's people (Hos 14:6–8 [Eng. 14:5–7]). In the last chapter of Hosea, God promises to heal his people. The description of their restoration is a scene of the Divine Warrior bringing vitality and newness of life to the land:

> I will be like the dew to Israel; he shall blossom like the lily; he shall take root like the trees of Lebanon; his shoots shall spread out; his beauty shall be like the olive, and his fragrance like Lebanon. They shall return and dwell beneath my shadow; they shall flourish like the grain; they shall blossom like the vine; their fame shall be like the wine of Lebanon. (Hos 14:6–8 [Eng. 14:5–7])

The language here in Hosea 14 is probably shaped by the earlier resurrection passage in Hosea 6:2–3, where the people hoped God would come "as the showers, as the spring rains that water the earth" to revive them that they might live (6:2–3).[182] And in 14:8 [Eng. 14:7] the verb "return" (from שׁוב) occurs in other passages of resurrection (e.g., 1 Kgs 17:21–22, which may further seal the notion that Hosea both knew about and drew upon the stories of Elijah and Elisha's resurrection miracles).

With the repentance of the Israelites in view (Hos 14:2–4 [Eng. 14:1–3]), God's anger is assuaged, and he commits to heal them (14:4). His hand of mercy will be as rejuvenating waters bringing beauty and splendor. Hosea 6 holds out a hope for resurrection, and 14:6–8 [Eng. 14:5–7] is God's pledge to accomplish it.[183]

---

181. See Wright, *The Resurrection of the Son of God*, 115n130; Levenson, *Resurrection and the Restoration of Israel*, 190. Nickelsburg is correct: Isa 26, along with Isa 66, provides the background for Daniel's prophecy of a resurrection unto life for some and judgment for others (*Resurrection, Immortality, and Eternal Life*, 21–23, 171).
182. See Levenson, *The Resurrection and Restoration of Israel*, 205; Day, "A Case of Inner Scriptural Interpretation," 119–20.
183. See Dempster, "The Resurrection of Christ," 18.

SUMMARY

The Prophets accelerate the growth of the resurrection seeds sown in the Torah. The Divine Warrior triumphs over chaos, distress, and death. The nation's exile and return will be a corporate death and resurrection, language cohering with beliefs already present that pertain to individual postmortem hopes. In some stories there are saints near death who experience deliverances that picture resurrection. And one day death will be swallowed up in the victory of a glorious awakening, when the earth gives birth to its dead. God's power will reverse corruption and bestow fresh vitality in nature, and the effect on death will be its undoing. The victory God is bringing will mean bodily life for the saints but bodily destruction for the wicked. The latter will not flourish in a renewed state but will languish in the abhorrence that accords with their deserved end. God's blessing and curse will be worked out ultimately in the resurrected states of the righteous and the wicked.

THE WRITINGS

INTRODUCTION

In this final section of the Old Testament—the Writings—the journey of observing resurrection hope prior to Daniel 12:2 will be completed. Once again, this hope is on display through various expressions, pictures, and theological convictions. The following sections will address passages in Psalms, Proverbs, Job, Ruth, Esther, and 2 Chronicles. And as with our exploration of the Law and Prophets, the evidence will be divided into *strong* and *supporting*.

STRONG EVIDENCE

Passages from Psalms and Job comprise strong evidence for finding resurrection hope in the Writings.

The holy one not abandoned to Sheol (Ps 16:9–11). To scholars who discuss resurrection hope in the book of Psalms, three psalms consistently rise to the fore: 16, 49, and 73.[184] I agree with these suggestions, but they do not exhaust the presence of this hope. Bauckham claims

---

184. See Wright, *The Resurrection of the Son of God*, 107; Yamauchi, "Life, Death, and the Afterlife," 46; Geerhardus Vos, *The Eschatology of the Old Testament*, ed. James T. Dennison Jr. (Phillipsburg, NJ: P&R, 2001), 15; Johnston, *Shades of Sheol*, 201–6; Johnston, "Death and Resurrection," 445; G. W. Grogan, "Psalms,"

that a hope for resurrection life beyond death is found "especially in the Psalms,"[185] and his assertion is a needed correction to Mowinckel's denial: "Neither Israel nor early Judaism knew of a faith in any resurrection nor is such a faith represented in the psalms."[186]

David wrote in Psalm 16, "Therefore my heart is glad, and my whole being rejoices; my flesh also dwells secure. For you will not abandon my soul to Sheol, or let your holy one see corruption" (Ps 16:9–10). David's confidence is that God would deliver him from death. He concluded, "You make known to me the path of life; in your presence there is fullness of joy; at your right hand are pleasures forevermore" (16:11).

David may have believed his flesh was secure, but death eventually claimed him. His body saw corruption. The confidence of deliverance, however, need not be extinguished by mortality. "The conviction grew that if God's people had truly enjoyed fellowship with God, even death could not disrupt that relationship."[187] He would vindicate the righteous, showing faithfulness to his own, and if this could be fully attained only after death, then he could be trusted to raise the dead.[188]

The psalmist, therefore, is hoping for something more than postponement from dying, for there is no hint of danger or sickness in the context.[189] Psalm 16 can be read naturally as a hope for rescue after death, and this is the way the New Testament applies it.[190] Peter uses Psalm 16 and says David's words fit someone else's experience better: Jesus. "God raised him up, loosing the pangs of death, because it was not possible for him to be held by it" (Acts 2:24). Then Peter explains his statement by quoting Psalm 16:8–11 in Acts 2:25–28. Therefore, the meaning of Psalm 16 was not exhausted by deliverances *from* death actually happening but applied to One who was delivered *after* death occurred.

---

in *NDBT*, ed. T. Desmond Alexander, Brian S. Rosner, D. A. Carson, and Graeme Goldsworthy (Downers Grove, IL: InterVarsity Press, 2000), 208.

185. Bauckham, "Life, Death, and the Afterlife," 85.
186. Sigmund Mowinckel, *The Psalms in Israel's Worship*, trans. D. R. Ap-Thomas (Nashville: Abingdon, 1962), 1:240.
187. Ladd, *I Believe in the Resurrection of Jesus*, 45. Wright asserts, "It is impossible now to tell when this idea first made its appearance" (*The Resurrection of the Son of God*, 103).
188. Bauckham, "Life, Death, and the Afterlife," 86.
189. Ladd, *I Believe in the Resurrection of Jesus*, 46.
190. Geoffrey W. Grogan, *Psalms*, The Two Horizons Old Testament Commentary (Grand Rapids: Eerdmans, 2008), 63. He says, "Many modern commentators are reluctant to understand these passages this way and, it seems to me, tend to set aside this kind of interpretation of them too easily" (291).

Noteworthy as well is that no typical resurrection verb is used in Psalm 16:10-11.[191] This fact serves as one more instance of resurrection hope being pictured in ways that may not be lexically obvious but are contextually evident.

The confidence of awaking and beholding God's face (Ps 17:15). David is confident of his vindication before God's presence (Ps 17:1-2). He calls God to subdue the lion eager to ambush the righteous (17:13-14). Then he says, "As for me, I shall behold your face in righteousness; when I awake [בְהָקִיץ], I shall be satisfied with your likeness" (17:15). As Mays points out, "In Christian interpretation there is a long tradition that sees a reference to the resurrection in verse 15. ... The verse can be read with a second sense, because it is only the resurrection to be with the LORD that brings the final and full justification of the life of the faithful."[192]

The term for waking is used in passages of resurrection and is so here as well (cf. 2 Kgs 4:31; Job 14:12; Isa 26:19; Jer 51:39, 57; Dan 12:2). Beholding God's face is not something the righteous do before death. David is envisioning a time when he will wake from death to behold God's face and be satisfied in his likeness. Vos says, "The words are unique within the limits of the Old Testament and so striking that we need not hesitate to find here also the thought of the resurrection."[193]

The psalmist is looking beyond this life, so a "reference to resurrection here seems more likely than just the dawning of a new day."[194] According to Dahood, it's the plain sense of the verse.[195] The morning in view is not the kind that follows night but the kind that follows death.

---

191. According to Ratzinger, "Even if this text expresses no explicit faith in the overcoming of death, we hear nevertheless the accents of a ringing certitude that Yahweh is stronger than Sheol. The psalmist is aware that he has found shelter in the hands of God, whose life-giving power endures for ever" (Joseph Ratzinger, *Eschatology: Death and Eternal Life*, 2nd ed., trans. Michael Waldstein [Washington, DC: The Catholic University of America Press, 1988], 87).
192. James L. Mays, *Psalms*, Interpretation (Louisville: John Knox, 1994), 90.
193. Vos, *The Eschatology of the Old Testament*, 16.
194. Grogan, *Psalms*, 64. While Craigie doubts the initial setting of Ps 17:15 spoke about resurrection, he notes that "from the perspective of Christian theology (or later Jewish theology), the history of salvation has assumed deeper and wider proportions. The psalm ... may provide both hope for the immediate crisis, as for the psalmist of old, but beyond that a deeper hope for ultimate deliverance from a more dangerous and insidious enemy, a hope that reaches beyond the sleep of death itself" (Peter C. Craigie, *Psalms 1-50*, WBC, vol. 19 [Waco, TX: Word, 1983], 165).
195. Mitchell Dahood, *Psalms I (1-50)*, AB, vol. 16 (Garden City, NY: Doubleday, 1966), 99.

As Delitzsch puts it, David is looking to "that final morning which brings deliverance to the upright and inaugurates their dominion."[196]

The righteous ransomed from the power of Sheol (Ps 49:16 [Eng. 49:15]). In this psalm by the sons of Korah,[197] they note that both the wise and the fool must die (Ps 49:11 [Eng. 49:10]). Death is the shepherd for fools, and it leads them to Sheol (49:15 [Eng. 49:14]). "But God will ransom my soul from the power of Sheol, for he will receive me" (49:16 [Eng. 49:15]).

The phrase "ransom ... from the power of Sheol" (יִפְדֶּה ... מִיַּד־שְׁאוֹל) appears once more in the Old Testament, in Hosea 13:14, and so Psalm 49 is the probable source for that prophet's language. Parallel to "ransom" is "receive," from the verb לקח. This is the same verb used in reference to Enoch and Elijah's transition to God (cf. Gen 5:24; 2 Kgs 2:3),[198] so some scholars have suggested that those unusual events may lie behind the idea of God taking people to himself as expressed in the Psalms.[199] But unlike Enoch and Elijah, who were taken before death, the psalmist would be taken *after* death, ransomed from the power of Sheol by the power of God. "Glancing at [Enoch and Elijah], the poet, who here speaks in the name of all upright sufferers, gives expression to the hope, that God will wrest him out of the power of Sheol and take him to Himself."[200]

The hope to be received to glory after death (Ps 73:24). In Psalm 73, by Asaph,[201] the psalmist feels envious of the wicked who prosper greatly without consequence (73:3-12), but then he remembers the end coming for them—utter ruin and destruction (73:18-19, 27). He is confident of God's guidance in this life and his reception to glory after this life

---

196. Franz Delitzsch, *Biblical Commentary on the Psalms*, trans. Francis Bolton (Edinburgh: T&T Clark, 1871), 1:244. See also Derek Kidner, *Psalms 1-72*, TOTC, vol. 14a (Downers Grove, IL: InterVarsity Press, 1973), 90.
197. According to 1 Chr 6:31-32, the sons of Korah (see 6:37) are "the men whom David put in charge of the service of song in the house of the LORD after the ark rested there. They ministered with song before the tabernacle of the tent of meeting until Solomon built the house of the LORD in Jerusalem, and they performed their service according to their order."
198. See this observation in Grogan, *Psalms*, 104.
199. See Kaiser, *Preaching and Teaching the Last Things*, 9; Bauckham, "Life, Death, and the Afterlife in Second Temple Judaism," 85; Dahood, *Psalms I*, 301; Bruce Vawter, "Intimations of Immortality in the Old Testament," *JBL* 91 (1972): 162n18.
200. Delitzsch, *Biblical Commentary on the Psalms*, 2:118.
201. According to 1 Chr 6:39, Asaph was one of the people who "ministered with song before the tabernacle of the tent of meeting until Solomon built the house of the LORD in Jerusalem" (6:32).

ends: "You guide me with your counsel, and afterward you will receive me to glory" (73:24).

As was the case in Psalm 49:16 (Eng. 49:15), the word "receive" (or "take") in 73:24 is from לקח and may echo the unique events of Enoch and Elijah's rapture (cf. Gen 5:24; 2 Kgs 2:3).[202] God's mighty arm can take his people. If Psalm 73:24 points to resurrection, Broyles notes that the author's path to that conclusion was not the road of the soul's immortality but God himself and the kind of relationship he establishes with his people.[203]

After guiding them in this life, God does not abandon them but will receive them to himself. According to Wright, the psalmist "discovers that he is grasped by a love that will not let him go, a power that even death, and the dissolution of the body, cannot thwart."[204] His power to take them will overwhelm the grave, and their bodies will not be left behind.

Job's hope to be in the flesh and see God (Job 19:26). Certain words from Job's mouth seem to undermine any hope of bodily resurrection. After acknowledging that God has appointed humanity's days, firming up limits that cannot be passed (Job 14:5), Job says, "As waters fail from a lake and a river wastes away and dries up, so a man lies down and rises not again; till the heavens are no more he will not awake or be roused out of his sleep" (14:11-12). Later, with a question phrased to expect a negative answer, Job asks, "If a man dies shall he live again?" (14:14a). But these are not Job's last words on the subject.

Job's friends have been his accusers, calling into question his integrity and blamelessness before God. But Job is confident his vindication will come. "For I know that my Redeemer lives, and at the last he will stand upon the earth! And after my skin has been thus destroyed, yet in my flesh I shall see God, whom I shall see for myself, and my eyes shall behold, and not another. My heart faints within me!" (Job 19:25-27).

At the beginning of the book Satan struck Job with "loathsome sores from the sole of his foot to the crown of his head" (Job 2:7). As Job's great

---

202. See Kaiser, *Preaching and Teaching the Last Things*, 9; James L. Crenshaw, "Love Is Stronger Than Death: Intimations of Life beyond the Grave," in *Resurrection: The Origin and Future of a Biblical Doctrine*, ed. James H. Charlesworth (New York: T&T Clark, 2006), 60; Bauckham, "Life, Death, and the Afterlife in Second Temple Judaism," 85.
203. Craig C. Broyles, *Psalms*, NIBC, vol. 11 (Peabody, MA: Hendrickson, 1999), 304-5.
204. Wright, *The Resurrection of the Son of God*, 106.

suffering persisted, he narrated his physical turmoil: "My breath is strange to my wife, and I am a stench to the children of my own mother" (19:17); "even young children despise me; when I rise they talk against me" (19:18); and "all my intimate friends abhor me, and those whom I loved have turned against me" (19:19). This physical trial sets up the confidence expressed toward the end of that discourse. His flesh will be destroyed, yet in his flesh he shall see God (19:26).

But scholars do not agree on what is happening and what the character believes in Job 19:25–27, for the passage contains interpretive difficulties.[205] For example, Sutcliffe argues that "after my skin has been thus destroyed" need not imply death but only the worst stage of the horrible disease inflicted on Job's body, so that the next phrase, "yet in my flesh I shall see God," expresses confidence that God will not permit the disease to ravage him completely; instead God will restore his flesh.[206]

Johnston adds that Job later asserts he has seen God with his own eyes (cf. Job 42:5), supporting the argument that ultimate vindication took place on earth, not in the next life.[207] Wright says that a resurrection interpretation of Job 19:26–27 runs against the rest of the book and so is unlikely to form an exception to the oblique view of death offered elsewhere by Job.[208] Clines believes Job's desire is to see God as the respondent in his court case while still alive.[209] While the case may not be resolved until after his death, he prefers his name cleared before his flesh is completely destroyed.[210]

Job's language in 19:26–27, however, is *personal* ("I shall see God," 19:26; "I shall see for myself," 19:27; "my eyes shall behold," 19:27) and *physical* ("my skin," 19:26; "my flesh," 19:26; "my eyes," 19:27). As Andersen says, these references "make it clear that Job expects to have this experience as a man, not just as a disembodied shade, or in his mind's eye."[211] Even

---

205. Vos says, "Now, as to verse 26, the text is so obscure that I prefer not to make any attempt at explaining it. ... The resurrection may be there, but the unusual obscurity of a few words, perhaps due to corruption of the text, hinders us from outright affirming it" (*The Eschatology of the Old Testament*, 24–25).
206. Sutcliffe, *The Old Testament and the Future Life*, 133–34.
207. Johnston, *Shades of Sheol*, 213.
208. Wright, *The Resurrection of the Son of God*, 98.
209. David J. A. Clines, *Job 1–20*, WBC, vol. 17 (Dallas: Word, 1989), 458.
210. Clines, *Job 1–20*, 461.
211. Francis I. Andersen, *Job: An Introduction and Commentary* (Downers Grove, IL: InterVarsity Press, 1976), 193. See Hamilton, *God's Glory in Salvation through Judgment*, 302.

Hartley, who does not believe Job's hope is postmortem, thinks "Job hopes to see God from his own body."[212]

The question is whether "after my skin has been thus destroyed" (וְאַחַר עוֹרִי נִקְּפוּ־זֹאת) refers to death or a pre-death physical demise.[213] The verb נִקְּפוּ is from נקף, which in the Piel means "to cut down or tear to shreds."[214] Job's skin is in the process of being destroyed already, so understanding נִקְּפוּ to spell the end of this destruction (i.e., his death) is a natural reading of the text.

Williams suggests that Job 19:26-27 has been "difficult for commentators *because of theological controversies*, not because of the condition of the text."[215] Compared to the gloomy backdrop of Job's trial, 19:26-27 are like diamonds that glimmer best on black velvet.[216] Most likely, Job "expects the experience which follows to take place after his skin has wasted away in death."[217]

The Redeemer who will stand on the earth is Job's advocate.[218] This Redeemer's action could denote a legal setting where a witness stands up for someone in court.[219] Job's faith is such that this Redeemer will plead his case for him even if he dies (Job 19:25-27).[220] Andersen also incorporates 14:12-14, a passage typically used to negate any resurrection hope from Job's mouth. He notes that 14:13 is a request for an appointed time after Job's death at which God would vindicate the righteous sufferer.[221] Job asks "that you would hide me in Sheol" until that day, and the

---

212. John E. Hartley, *The Book of Job*, NICOT (Grand Rapids: Eerdmans, 1988), 296.
213. Hartley sees the importance of the verb: "Whether [Job] believes that this event will take place before or after his death rests on the meaning of the verb [נִקְּפוּ] in v. 26a" (*The Book of Job*, 297).
214. Ludwig Koehler and Walter Baumgartner, *HALOT*, rev. ed. (Leiden: Brill, 2001), s.v. "נקף."
215. J. G. Williams, "Job and the God of Victims," in *The Voice from the Whirlwind: Interpreting the Book of Job*, ed. Leo G. Perdue and W. Clark Gilpin (Nashville: Abingdon, 1992), 217, emphasis mine.
216. Robert L. Alden, *Job*, NAC, vol. 11 (Nashville: B&H, 1993), 209.
217. Robert S. Fyall, *Now My Eyes Have Seen You: Images of Creation and Evil in the Book of Job*, NSBT, vol. 12 (Downers Grove, IL: InterVarsity Press, 2002), 51.
218. Fyall asserts, "It is plain that the words most naturally suggest that Job's vindicator can be none other than God himself" (*Now My Eyes Have Seen You*, 48).
219. Kaiser, *Preaching and Teaching the Last Things*, 17.
220. Dempster, *Dominion and Dynasty*, 203.
221. Andersen, *Job*, 194.

day of his vindication would be synonymous with resurrection. Only until that day, then, "a man lies down and rises not again" (14:12a).²²²

The LXX of Job 14:14 is ἐὰν γὰρ ἀποθάνῃ ἄνθρωπος ζήσεται ("if a man dies, he shall live"),²²³ and the LXX of 19:26a is ἀναστήσαι τὸ δέρμα μου ("will resurrect my skin"). Wright says, "Whoever drafted the translation of LXX Job had no doubt both of the bodily resurrection and of the propriety of making sure the biblical text affirmed it."²²⁴

When Job expresses that in his flesh he shall see God (cf. Job 19:26), William Green cautiously affirms a hope for resurrection:

> The resurrection of the body was probably not present to Job's thoughts, certainly not in the form of a general and simultaneous rising from the dead. And yet it is so linked, seminally at least, with our continued spiritual existence, and it is so natural and even necessary for us to transfer our ideas of being, drawn from the present state, to the greater hereafter, that it may perhaps be

---

222. Fyall observes, "It is indeed true that Job expresses pessimism and hopelessness about the world beyond the grave (see e.g., 3:11-19; 7:9-10; 10:20-22), but these are dramatic not theological statements and express what Job is feeling at that moment. Similarly, when the writer of Ecclesiastes says, 'All go to the same place; all come from dust, and to dust all return' (3:20), he is reflecting the perspective of life 'under the sun' and not giving a definitive statement about the destiny of the departed" (*Now My Eyes Have Seen You*, 50).
223. Kaiser connects Job 14:7 and 14:14 because of the verb חלף in 14:7 and the noun חֲלִיפָה in 14:14. Job 14:7 says "there is hope for a tree" because "it will sprout (יַחֲלִיף) again," and in 14:14 Job says, "All the days of my service I would wait, till my renewal (חֲלִיפָתִי) should come." Kaiser comments, "For often around the base of a felled tree, one shoot after another will spring up as a continuation of the otherwise dead tree. So it is with man in Job 14:14. ... Job 14:14 stated in terms analogous to what happened to felled trees! Very few commentators will connect the two verses, but the writer intended his audience to do so. He did it by using the same Hebrew root in the same context in Job 14:7, 14" (Walter C. Kaiser Jr., *Toward an Old Testament Theology* [Grand Rapids: Zondervan, 1978], 181). If Kaiser is correct, then Job 14:7, 14 would be further support for resurrection hope on the lips of Job himself.
224. Wright, *The Resurrection of the Son of God*, 148. He adds, "All the indications are that those who translated the Septuagint, and those who read it thereafter (i.e., most Jews, in both Palestine and the Diaspora), would have understood the key Old Testament passages in terms of a more definite 'resurrection' sense than the Hebrew would necessarily warrant, and might very likely have heard overtones of 'resurrection' in many places where the Hebrew would not have suggested it" (150).

truly said that the germs of the doctrine of the resurrection may likewise be detected here.²²⁵

SUPPORTING EVIDENCE

Supporting evidence for the presence of resurrection hope in the Writings can be found in Psalms, Proverbs, Job, Ruth, Esther, and 2 Chronicles.

The righteous that stand at the judgment (Ps 1:5). In the first psalm of the book, a division between the righteous man and the wicked man is noteworthy. The righteous man is blessed (1:1) and fruitful (1:3), whereas the wicked man is neither blessed nor fruitful (1:1, 4). On judgment day this division will be evident, for the wicked will be threshed and blown away like chaff (1:4), which means they "will not stand [לֹא־יָקֻמוּ] in the judgment" (1:5).²²⁶ By implication, then, the righteous *will* stand.

Since standing up can picture the reception of bodily vitality after death, this vindication at the judgment may also indicate a resurrection unto life. The imagery of nature flourishing prepares for this climactic "stand." The tree is in vibrant water and yields fruit (Ps 1:3), but the wicked do not experience this vitality (1:4). Their end is judgment. They will not "stand" like the righteous but will perish.²²⁷

David drawn out of the waters of death (Ps 18:17 [Eng. 18:16]). The superscription of Psalm 18 identifies the composition as David's response to deliverance from all his enemies (18:1). The content parallels 2 Samuel 22, so the explanation here will be minimal since I addressed that passage in the section on the Prophets.

David narrated his ensnared state: "The cords of death encompassed me; the torrents of destruction assailed me; the cords of Sheol entangled me; the snares of death confronted me" (Ps 18:5-6 [Eng. 18:4-5]; cf.

---

225. William Henry Green, *The Argument of the Book of Job Unfolded* (1874; repr., Minneapolis: James & Klock, 1977), 216-17.
226. The same expression is used of the wicked in Isa 26:14, which is about bodily resurrection.
227. According to Cole, "Interpreting v. 5 as referring to eschatological resurrection and judgment is not innovative. Ancient translations such as the Targum, Septuagint and Vulgate all read this as a reference to the final resurrection and judgment" (Robert Luther Cole, *Psalms 1-2: Gateway to the Psalter* [Sheffield: Sheffield Phoenix, 2013], 72).

2 Sam 22:5-6). Then he recalled his divine deliverance: "He sent from on high, he took me; he drew me out of many waters" (18:17 [Eng. 18:16]).

Like Moses (cf. Exod 2:10), David was delivered from waters.[228] According to David's words, being "taken" (לקח) is parallel to being "drawn out" (משׁה). The picture of being taken up from Sheol is resurrection from the dead. Death had ensnared him, but God's power overcame that looming fate.[229] Anderson explains how this was a resurrection:

> Some of Israel's psalms indicate that death is something more than a biological event that occurs when the heart stops beating. ... In the view of Israel's psalmists, death's power is at work in us now, during our historical existence. Death's power is felt in the midst of life to the degree that one experiences any weakening of personal vitality through illness, bodily handicap, imprisonment, attack from enemies, or advancing old age. Any threat to a person's welfare ... that is, one's freedom to be and to participate in the covenant community, is understood as an invasion of Death, regarded as a mythical Power, into "the land of the living." In some of the psalms (especially individual psalms of thanksgiving), one can see how the experience of salvation from the power of death moves toward the experience of "resurrection," that is, being restored from death to life.[230]

Restored to life from among those in the pit (Ps 30:3). David described a personal healing in language about being drawn up and restored. He told the Lord, "I will extol you, O LORD, for you have drawn

---

228. See Delitzsch, *Biblical Commentary on the Psalms*, 1:259-60.
229. As Levenson explains, "The range of conditions that the Hebrew Bible groups under the rubric of 'death' includes many that we designate otherwise. ... Whereas we think of a person who is gravely ill, under lethal assault, or sentenced to capital punishment as still alive, the Israelites were quite capable of seeing such an individual as dead. ... In other words, for us death is radically discontinuous with life, a quantum leap, as it were, lying between the two. For the psalmists, by contrast, the discontinuity lay between a healthy and successful life and one marked by adversity, in physical health or otherwise" (*Resurrection and the Restoration of Israel*, 37-38). For examples of how the psalmists describe "death," see Hans-Joachim Kraus, *Theology of the Psalms*, trans. Keith Crim (Minneapolis: Augsburg, 1986), 165-66.
230. Anderson, *Contours of Old Testament Theology*, 312. According to Barth, "In rescuing people from affliction, healing serious sickness, or saving from enemies, God truly raised them from the dead" (Christoph Barth, *God with Us: A Theological Introduction to the Old Testament* [Grand Rapids: Eerdmans, 1991], 277).

me up and have not let my foes rejoice over me. O LORD my God, I cried to you for help, and you have healed me" (Ps 30:1-2).

Being "drawn up" would be from the depths, as if David had been sinking in a watery grave to the gates of death. In the next verse he frames his rescue in terms of deliverance from Sheol: "O LORD, you have brought up my soul from Sheol; you restored me to life from among those who go down to the pit" (Ps 30:3). Later in that psalm, David is clear that he has his death in view: "What profit is there in my death, if I go down to the pit? Will the dust praise you?" (30:9).

Descending to the pit is an image of death and judgment, so being "restored to life" is resurrection. God delivered David's body from the dust of death. Such figurative resurrection language confirms the way the biblical authors depicted death. They wrote of death not merely as what happens in a clinical sense. An individual's bodily decline—as in an illness—signaled the grip of death on the body. Divine healing was wresting the body from death's grip.

The hope to be brought up from the depths of the earth (Ps 71:20). Psalms 70–71 were written by David,[231] and in Psalm 71 he explains God's uniqueness that is worthy of praise: "Your righteousness, O God, reaches the high heavens. You who have done great things, O God, who is like you?" (71:19). One way God is set apart from everyone else is in his power to raise the dead: "You who have made me see many troubles and calamities will revive me again; from the depths of the earth you will bring me up again" (71:20).

The actions of deliverance, "will revive" (חָיָה) and "will bring up again" (שׁוּב), are typical verbs denoting resurrection, and they serve that function in this passage. David has been delivered on multiple occasions by God, and not even death will bring an end to what God's power can do. The depths of the earth may seem impenetrable from a human perspective, but God will do the impossible and bring David up from them. This verse indicates a confidence in bodily resurrection.[232]

The prayer for restoration to life (Ps 80:19 [Eng. 80:18]). In Psalm 80, by Asaph, he prays for the restoration of Israel: "Restore us, O God; let your face shine, that we may be saved!" (80:4 [Eng. 80:3]). For the

---

231. According to Grogan, "This psalm [71] lacks a heading. The editor may have intended it as a virtual continuation of Psalm 70, for its opening verses have the same general theme and they are combined in some manuscripts" (*Psalms*, 130).
232. Grogan, *Psalms*, 131.

time being, it seems Yahweh is ignoring their prayers and making them a joke among their enemies (80:7 [Eng. 80:6]). The psalmist compares Israel to a vine God rescued from Egypt and planted in Canaan (80:9–10 [Eng. 80:8–9]), a vine now cut down and burning (80:17 [Eng. 80:16]). This destruction means death for the Israelites, so the psalmist prays, "Give us life, and we will call upon your name!" (80:19 [Eng. 80:18]).

Ever since Adam and Eve left the garden, the exile of God's people has denoted death. As Asaph expresses his devastation over the nation's demise, the imagery of natural devastation prepares for his plea that the Divine Warrior act and restore what is broken. Their exile is described in terms of broken walls, fruit ravaged by boars and other beasts, and a vine stock burning and severed (Ps 80:13–17 [Eng. 80:12–16]). For the vine—Israel—to flourish again in the land, God must restore them, and this act will mean giving life to what is dead.[233]

Wisdom as a tree of life (Prov 3:18). A tension pervasive in the Scriptures is especially clear in the book of Proverbs: God promises life to his people though they die.[234] So are his promises of life falling short in a fallen world, or will God keep his promises in a greater way that death cannot nullify? Longman's challenge must be considered: if every instance of "life" in Proverbs means the reward of long quantity and good quality of earthly life, then "such a minimalist reading makes the sages seem incredibly naïve."[235] Some passages from Proverbs demonstrate the tension that resurrection will resolve. Verbs of resurrection may not be present, but as I have demonstrated in previous sections, such hope can be present conceptually even though it is absent lexically.[236]

Solomon says the one who finds wisdom is blessed, for "Her ways are ways of pleasantness, and all her paths are peace. She is a tree of life to those who lay hold of her; those who hold her fast are called blessed" (Prov 3:17–18). "The tree of life" (עֵץ הַחַיִּים) first appeared in Genesis 2:9 (cf. 3:22, 24) in the garden of Eden, and the words עֵץ חַיִּים occur elsewhere in the Old Testament only in Proverbs (cf. 3:18; 11:30; 13:12; 15:4).

---

233. See Hamilton, *God's Glory in Salvation through Judgment*, 286.
234. Levenson, *Resurrection and the Restoration of Israel*, 168–69. Or, as Longman asks it, "What does it mean to promise life to those who are wise and death to those who are foolish when everyone knows that all die?" (Tremper Longman III, *Proverbs*, BCOT [Grand Rapids: Baker Academic, 2006], 87).
235. Longman, *Proverbs*, 87.
236. For an examination of eschatological hope in Proverbs, see Jonathan David Akin, "A Theology of Future Hope in the Book of Proverbs" (Ph.D. diss., The Southern Baptist Theological Seminary, 2012).

In Genesis 2 the tree was in the garden to give life to those who ate it, and 3:24 clarified that this life was immortality. Since Adam and Eve lived as embodied image bearers, their life would have been immortal physicality.

In Proverbs 3:18, getting wisdom is compared to eating fruit from the tree of life. In the garden the image bearers transgressed God's command in lieu of seizing what was forbidden, what belonged only to God. Now, in line with the original purpose of the tree of life, choosing Lady Wisdom results in blessing, and the effects of this blessing will mean immortal life for God's people (though the effects begin in the present as well, thus not excluding an inaugurated sense of what the tree of life means for the righteous).

The "tree of life," according to Waltke, represents "perpetual healing" that ensures eternal life.[237] The life wisdom offers is a living relationship with the Creator, and this life does not end with clinical death.[238] As is clear from Daniel 12:2-3, embracing wisdom leads to resurrection glory. The wise will rise from the dust of the earth and shine like the stars.

No death in the path of righteousness (Prov 12:28). Solomon writes, "In the path of righteousness is life, and in its pathway there is no death" (Prov 12:28). Kidner rightly notes that the second Hebrew phrase poses a translation difficulty because of its disputed original wording, so textual critics tend to opt for one of two possibilities: (1) "and the journey of her pathway is no-death," or (2) "but [there is] a way [which is] a path to death."[239]

The first rendering lacks the antithetical parallelism that is present in other life-death proverbs,[240] but it is still closer to the existing text,[241] and it is the choice of translations like the NASB, ESV, and KJV. The phrase אַל־מָוֶת ("no death") is also found in the great majority of codices in the Masoretic tradition.[242] Other scholars say the MT was probably prejudiced toward the doctrine of immortality, which they say was not yet advocated, so they opt for the second rendering, which supplies an

---

237. Bruce K. Waltke, *The Book of Proverbs*, NICOT (Grand Rapids: Eerdmans, 2004), 1:105. He adds, "We should presume, then, that symbol here also represents the *inseparable notions* of healing and immortality" (1:259, emphasis mine).
238. Waltke, *The Book of Proverbs*, 1:105.
239. Derek Kidner, *Proverbs*, TOTC, vol. 15 (Downers Grove, IL: InterVarsity Press, 1964), 100.
240. Johnston, *Shades of Sheol*, 208.
241. Kidner, *Proverbs*, 100.
242. Waltke, *The Book of Proverbs*, 1:544.

antithetical sense and results in a different meaning than the first option.[243] The phrase אֶל־מָוֶת ("unto death") is in the ancient versions and more than twenty medieval codices.[244]

But if the doctrine of immortality is not considered an innovation in the text, then a rendering such as "in its pathway there is no death" is not as unusual, especially since earlier in Proverbs the phrase "the tree of life" (cf. Prov 3:18) is used to inform the reader what wisdom brings, and the allusion is to that tree in the garden of Eden, which held out hope for immortality to the first mortal couple.

Waltke is right that, text-critically, the phrase אַל־מָוֶת ("no death") is the more difficult reading to explain away because it is a hapax legomena in biblical Hebrew.[245] Philologically, in Ugaritic and post-biblical Hebrew the construction אַל־מָוֶת is the normal way of describing "immortality."[246] As Sawyer observes, there is "a remarkable continuity of the meaning 'immortality' for [אַל־מָוֶת] from second millennium BC Syria to the post-biblical Jewish literature."[247] Commentators on Proverbs often reject the reading אַל־מָוֶת in order to uphold the "modern dogma" that there is no afterlife taught in the book.

Assuming, then, that "in its pathway there is no death" is the right reading, the meaning of the words is not true to daily existence, which is characterized by corruption and the curse of death. How can interpreters address the outrageous claim that on this path of righteousness "there is no death"?

The author is not disputing the truth that everyone, righteous and wicked, will one day die (cf. Eccl 9:2–3, 5). The promise of life for the righteous includes the death of the body, but equally true here is the notion that the path of the righteous is not thereby ruined and ended. The promise that "there is no death" will be the final word spoken over the righteous, which means God will do something about death.[248] God's

---

243. See, e.g., William McKane, *Proverbs: A New Approach*, OTL (Philadelphia: Westminster, 1970), 451–52; Johnston, *Shades of Sheol*, 208.
244. Waltke, *The Book of Proverbs*, 1:544.
245. Waltke, *The Book of Proverbs*, 1:544.
246. Waltke, *The Book of Proverbs*, 1:544.
247. J. F. A. Sawyer, "The Role of Jewish Studies in Biblical Semantics," in *Scripta Signa Vocis: Studies about Scripts, Scriptures, Scribes and Languages in the Near East, Presented to J. H. Hospers by His Pupils, Colleagues, and Friends*, ed. H. Vanstiphout et al. (Groningen: E. Forsten, 1986), 204–5.
248. Wright says Prov 12:28 "might have been later read as referring to a post-mortem future" (*The Resurrection of the Son of God*, 107n100).

promise seems incredible, but with his power it is not impossible. The resurrection of the body is God keeping his promise to give life in such a way that "there is no death."

The path that leads upward from Sheol (Prov 15:24). The life of the righteous ends in death, but their path does not lead to the same place as the unrighteous: "The path of life leads upward for the prudent, that he may turn away from Sheol beneath" (Prov 15:24). Sheol is the place the righteous want to avoid.[249] Going there is downward, but the path of the righteous is upward. The movement pictures deliverance from Sheol, perhaps connoting resurrection. Already present in the Scriptures before Solomon's time was the notion that Yahweh brings down to Sheol and raises up (1 Sam 2:6; cf. Deut 32:39).

Longman believes eschatological overtones are evident in Proverbs 15:24 when it is read canonically.[250] Yet even in its immediate context, Proverbs 15:24 is not ambiguous regarding the fact that the outcome for the prudent is different from what happens to the one not walking the path of life. Kitchen is right: "It would seem that the doctrine of life after death, which we find in full flower in the New Testament, is found in at least seed form here."[251] By implication the path of the imprudent will end in Sheol. Waltke says that for the righteous, "Salvation from the grave is more than being spared an untimely death, for otherwise the path of life is swallowed up by death, an unthinkable thought in Proverbs."[252]

The restoration of Job's family and fortunes (Job 42:10, 13). In the first chapter of Job's story, he experiences the death of his animals, servants, and children (Job 1:13-19). Messengers who escaped the tragedies told him, "The oxen were plowing and the donkeys feeding beside them, and the Sabeans fell upon them and took them and struck down the servants with the edge of the sword" (1:14-15); "the fire of God fell from heaven and burned up the sheep and the servants" (1:16); "the Chaldeans ... struck down the servants with the edge of the sword" (1:17); "your sons and daughters were eating and drinking wine in their oldest brother's house ... and it fell upon the young people, and they are dead" (1:18-19).

---

249. See chap. 1 for my interpretation that Sheol is equivalent to the underworld and thus more than the physical grave.
250. Longman, *Proverbs*, 321.
251. John A. Kitchen, *Proverbs: A Mentor Commentary* (Ross-shire, UK: Mentor, 2006), 340.
252. Waltke, *The Book of Proverbs*, 1:634.

As Levenson explains, "Bereavement of progeny is the functional equivalent of death."[253] Since this tragedy is the death of Job's family line, the restoration of children at the end of the story is like resurrection for the righteous sufferer. Yahweh restored Job's fortunes so that he had twice as much as before his test (Job 42:10-12), and he also gave him seven sons and three daughters (42:13). The family line and fortunes of Job were back from the dead, and the glory of the restoration exceeded what he had before the loss.

At the end of the book of Job, the main character dies "an old man, and full of days" (Job 42:17). Where the MT ends, however, the LXX does not. The LXX adds a postscript to the book: γέγραπται δὲ αὐτὸν πάλιν ἀναστήσεσθαι μεθ' ὧν ὁ κύριος ἀνίστησιν ("and it is written that he will be raised again with those whom the Lord raises up"). Again, whoever translated Job into Greek wanted no doubt that the text affirmed bodily resurrection,[254] even if an unoriginal postscript had to be added to drive home the point.

The restoration of Naomi and her family line (Ruth 4:13). Elimelech was from Bethlehem in Judah, and he went with his wife, Naomi, and their two sons to the country of Moab because there was a famine in their land (Ruth 1:1-2). When Elimelech and his two sons died, Naomi and her daughters-in-law (Ruth and Orpah) became widows (1:3-5). "The obstacles to genealogy now are not barren women but dead males."[255] This was the death of the family line, but it would not stay that way for long. Ruth married Boaz, and God gave them a son (4:13). With this birth Yahweh reversed the present situation and received the praise for it: "Blessed be the LORD, who has not left you this day without a redeemer, and may his name be renowned in Israel!" (4:14).

The role of the newborn was important: "He shall be to you a restorer [לְמֵשִׁיב] of life and a nourisher of your old age, for your daughter-in-law who loves you, who is more to you than seven sons, has given birth to him" (Ruth 4:15). This new child brought life (from the verb שׁוב) to Naomi. He consoled her grief "by assuring that her family line, once tragically

---

253. Levenson, *Resurrection and the Restoration of Israel*, 115. Wright says, "To see one's children die or be killed was perhaps the greatest possible personal disaster" (*The Resurrection of the Son of God*, 99).
254. Wright, *The Resurrection of the Son of God*, 148.
255. Dempster, *Dominion and Dynasty*, 191.

headed for extinction, would continue for at least another generation."[256] The use of שוב here also forms an inclusio with 1:21, where God "brought me back" to Bethlehem empty because of the calamity of the deaths in Moab.[257] Her emptiness was like a death, but now with a newborn from Ruth and Boaz, God has brought life back to her (4:15). God has resurrected the line of Elimelech.[258]

Bush observes, "To the devout Israelite, the continuance of the family line was not simply a matter of keeping a name alive. It was part of the way in which God's promises, for Israel and perhaps even for the whole world, would be fulfilled."[259] The significance of this newborn would be greater than the family could have anticipated: he was the grandfather of King David (Ruth 4:17-22), and from the Davidic line would come the Messiah. Given this hope held out by the genealogy in Ruth 4, the book begins with death and ends with life.[260] As Wheaton sees it, "Out of death and hopelessness, life has sprung up."[261]

Favor from the king on the third day (Esth 5:1-2). Queen Esther knew that to approach the Persian king without first being summoned to the inner court was to risk being put to death (Esth 4:11). Nevertheless, she had been providentially placed in the Persian kingdom to act on behalf of the Israelite people. In order to undermine Haman the Agagite's plan to destroy the Jews, she would need to risk her life. She said, "Then I will go to the king, though it is against the law, and if I perish, I perish" (4:16).

"On the third day," Esther went to the inner court of the king's palace (Esth 5:1). When the king saw her, "she won favor in his sight, and he held out to Esther the golden scepter that was in his hand" (5:2). Face to face with the prospect of death, Esther received favor from the king instead. He extended to her favor and life, and this deliverance was "on the third day" (5:1). Like Isaac, Hezekiah, and Jonah before her, Esther's deliverance was connected to this "third day" pattern.

---

256. Robert L. Hubbard Jr., *The Book of Ruth*, NICOT (Grand Rapids: Eerdmans, 1988), 272.
257. Frederic W. Bush, *Ruth, Esther*, WBC, vol. 9 (Nashville: Thomas Nelson, 1996), 257.
258. Dempster, "The Resurrection of Christ," 20.
259. Bush, *Ruth, Esther*, 99-100.
260. Dempster, "The Resurrection of Christ," 19. See Levenson, *Resurrection and the Restoration of Israel*, 116.
261. Wheaton, "As It Is Written," 251.

Since Esther experienced life and not death in the story, the reader is prepared to see divine favor upon the Israelites as a whole. Esther's deliverance foreshadowed what would happen to the people. She was spared from death, and thus the providential momentum was moving in the direction of deliverance for her people.

The foiled plot to kill the Jews (Esth 8:11). Haman the Agagite devised a deadly plot aiming to destroy the Jews. When God used Esther to save the people, their deliverance from extinction was a national resurrection.[262]

Haman convinced King Ahasuerus to offer a royal decree to destroy a "certain people" whose laws were against the king's interests and edicts (Esth 3:8–9). The king capitulated to Haman's diabolical scheme, and letters were sent to all the provinces "to destroy, to kill, and to annihilate all Jews, young and old, women and children, in one day, the thirteenth day of the twelfth month" (3:13).

Esther came forward to help her Jewish people, and she exposed Haman's plot (Esth 4–7). She asked the king to revoke his earlier decree of destruction on the Jews (8:5), but he explained that the edict could not be revoked (8:8). The king issued a new decree that "allowed the Jews who were in every city to gather and defend their lives, to destroy, to kill, and to annihilate any armed force of any people or province that might attack them, children and women included, and to plunder their goods, on one day throughout all the provinces of King Ahasuerus, on the thirteenth day of the twelfth month" (8:11).

Thanks to Esther, says Schreiner, "the attempt to obliterate [God's] people is frustrated, so that the offspring of the serpent end up being crushed by the offspring of the woman."[263] Dumbrell is right that "reversal seems the most important structural theme in Esther."[264] God displayed his power and reversed the apparent inevitability of the Israelites' demise. This reversal meant their deliverance from the plot of death looming over them.

The last word of the Old Testament (2 Chr 36:23). In the final chapter of the Tanak, Judah has declined, Jerusalem is captured, and the temple is destroyed (2 Chr 36:1–19). The people of Judah are exiled

---

262. See Dempster, "The Resurrection of Christ," 21.
263. Schreiner, *The King in His Beauty*, 220. See Dempster, *Dominion and Dynasty*, 223; Hamilton, *God's Glory in Salvation through Judgment*, 321–22.
264. William J. Dumbrell, *The Faith of Israel: A Theological Survey of the Old Testament*, 2nd ed. (Grand Rapids: Baker Academic, 2002), 300.

to Babylon (36:20). Then, after the prophesied time was completed, God stirred the spirit of Cyrus, king of Persia (36:22), and Israel's death in exile would soon be replaced with resurrection. Cyrus said, "The LORD, the God of heaven, has given me all the kingdoms of the earth, and he has charged me to build him a house at Jerusalem, which is in Judah. Whoever is among you of all his people, may the LORD his God be with him. Let him go up" (36:23).

Hamilton says, "Chronicles closes with the climactic judgment of exile, but not without reference to the salvation that comes through the judgment."[265] Cyrus has been raised up to lead a new exodus, "not because God forced the hand of a reluctant Pharaoh, but because he moved the heart of a Persian king."[266] Exile is not the way Chronicles ends. "The note of promise is a directive from Cyrus for them to return to the land and rebuild the temple. ... The Tanakh ends on a note of hope, pointing to the future."[267]

Not only does the Old Testament conclude with promise, but *the very the last word* is from עלה,[268] which in the Hiphil means "to make someone climb up, to lead up, to cause to rise, or to bring up."[269] The same word is used in 1 Samuel 2:6 to assert God's power to raise up those he brings down to Sheol. While the verb on Cyrus's lips in 2 Chronicles 36:23 does not refer to bodily resurrection in that context, the return of a nation from exile is life from the dead.

SUMMARY

God loves his people, and this love will not be broken by death. Moreover, God's commitment to bless the righteous will not permit forever their disembodied state that occurs at death. His promise of life, the fullness of fruit from the tree of life, will mean immortality that includes physicality. More pictures of resurrection occur in the Writings as God raises family lines from the dead and rescues his people from turmoil. He is his people's advocate, their Redeemer who will vindicate them on the last day. The righteous will stand at the judgment.

---

265. Hamilton, *God's Glory in Salvation through Judgment*, 350.
266. Raymond B. Dillard, *2 Chronicles*, WBC, vol. 15 (Nashville: Thomas Nelson, 1987), 302.
267. Dempster, *Dominion and Dynasty*, 48–49.
268. I am indebted to Dempster for this important observation (see "The Resurrection of Christ," 22).
269. Koehler and Baumgartner, *HALOT*, s.v. "עלה."

CONCLUSION

Daniel 12:2 is the clearest and fullest expression of resurrection hope in the Old Testament, and part of what this project asserts is that Daniel relied on earlier Old Testament texts, pictures, and theological convictions when he expressed the hope of bodily resurrection. The burden of this chapter was to explore the Law, Prophets, and Writings to see instances of this hope, either explicitly or implicitly, prior to the book of Daniel, though some examples (e.g., Esther) occur after Daniel.

After an examination of the Old Testament, Collins's claim that resurrection does not appear even implicitly before the book of Daniel (which he dates to the second century BC) cannot be sustained.[270] A belief in resurrection was advanced through theological convictions, images, and verbs, and this belief is rooted deeply in the biblical narrative and appears earlier than is normally supposed.

While some scholars avoid the pursuit "for a single point of origin and a single cause for the belief in resurrection,"[271] Genesis 2–3 proves to be the place where the hope was sown. The tree of life would give God's people immortal physicality, which is what he made them for, and the defeat of the serpent would mean the end of the curse. Those who returned to the dust at death would later return to life in resurrection.

From the beginning of the Old Testament, the Creator is someone who brings life where it was not, and at the end of the tripartite division, the final word points forward in hope to life restored. Over the course of Israel's theological history, belief in resurrection does not advance in a straight line but slowly and unevenly.[272] "Growing out of the convergence of a number of biblical themes, it drew, most centrally, on the long-standing conviction that God would yet again prove faithful to his promises of life for his people and that he had the stupendous might it would take to do so."[273]

The hope of resurrection is rooted in a theological conviction that God is a Divine Warrior.[274] Misfortune and misery are no match for the power of him who reverses death, conquers chaos, restores from exile, and fills barren wombs and barren lands with life and vitality. The God

---

270. Collins, *Encounters with Biblical Theology*, 32.
271. Levenson, *Resurrection and the Restoration of Israel*, xiii. See also Kaiser, *Preaching and Teaching the Last Things*, 14.
272. Levenson, *Resurrection and the Restoration of Israel*, xiii.
273. Levenson, *Resurrection and the Restoration of Israel*, xiii.
274. Levenson, *Resurrection and the Restoration of Israel*, 216–17.

who kills and makes alive, who brings down and raises up, will triumph over the curse of death. "And many of those who sleep in the dust of the earth shall awake, some to everlasting life, and some to shame and everlasting contempt" (Dan 12:2). This statement is hardly an innovation in the worldview of the biblical authors. As Wright says,

> The vision of YHWH's creation and covenant; his promises and his faithfulness to them; his purposes for Israel, not least his gift of the land; his power over all opposing forces, including finally death itself; his love for the world, for his human creatures, for Israel in particular, and especially for those who served him and followed in his way; his justice, because of which evil would eventually be condemned and righteousness upheld—this vision of the creator and covenant god underlies the ancient belief in the national and territorial hope, the emerging belief that the relationship with YHWH would be unbreakable even by death, and the eventual belief that YHWH would raise the dead.[275]

---

275. Wright, *The Resurrection of the Son of God*, 127.

4

The Influence of Daniel 12:2 on Intertestamental Literature

As Roy Ciampa and Brian Rosner observe, "Jewish intertestamental writings from almost every quarter include resurrection as central to their beliefs."[1] In particular, the language and theology of Daniel 12:2 was believed and appropriated by writers during the intertestamental period. Continuing to demonstrate my thesis, this chapter will show the verse's influence on literature written after the end of Malachi's ministry (in the fifth century BC) and up to the ministry of John the Baptist (in the first century AD). Though these books are not canonical, their authors' use of Daniel 12:2 indicates that it made an impact even before the New Testament.[2]

This chapter will divide and address the relevant literature into two groups: first the Pseudepigrapha, then the Apocrypha. To detect whether an author is engaging Daniel 12:2, more must be evident than just a reference in a text to bodily resurrection. Influence of Daniel 12:2 is probable (or possible) if the passage in view contains at least one or more of the following characteristics: (1) a reference to an awakening of the righteous and/or the wicked, (2) a contrast between (eternal) fates of those groups, (3) an implication of resurrection because the described state reflects the shining or transformed language of Daniel 12:3, (4) a promise that the righteous will rise to eternal life, or (5) a picture of the wicked undergoing bodily destruction forever.

---

1. Roy E. Ciampa and Brian S. Rosner, "1 Corinthians," in *Commentary on the New Testament Use of the Old Testament*, ed. G. K. Beale and D. A. Carson (Grand Rapids: Baker Academic, 2007), 744.
2. See André Lacocque, *The Book of Daniel*, trans. David Pellauer (Atlanta: John Knox, 1979), 243. According to Williamson, "Dan. 12:2 is clearly a seminal OT text from which the subsequent idea of a general or universal resurrection most likely developed" (Williamson, *Death and the Afterlife*, 137n18).

DANIEL 12:2 IN THE PSEUDEPIGRAPHA

The Pseudepigrapha consists of authors who chose the names of ancient worthies under which they presented their books, and everyone knew those ancient figures had not written the material bearing their names. Since there is no consensus as to when many (or most) pseudepigraphal works were written, this chapter will not enter that dispute.

This section will address fifteen passages from these seven works: Jubilees, Psalms of Solomon, the Sibylline Oracles, the Apocalypse of Moses, the Testament of Moses, 1 Enoch, and Testaments of the Twelve Patriarchs.[3]

THE BOOK OF JUBILEES

The book of Jubilees is presented as a record of what God revealed to Moses during a forty-day encounter on Mount Sinai. Among the subjects covered is the future vindication of the righteous and judgment of the wicked.

The servants of Yahweh who rise (Jub. 23:30). Nickelsburg says, "Jubilees 23:16–31 is an apocalypse describing the events of Israelite history that lead up to and comprise the eschaton."[4] Toward the end of that section comes the claim of what God will do for his people and against his/their enemies:

> And then the LORD will heal his servants, and they will rise up and see great peace. And they will drive out their enemies, and the righteous ones will see and give praise, and rejoice forever and ever with joy; and they will see all of their judgments and all of their curses among their enemies. And their bones will rest in the earth and their spirits will increase with joy, and they will know that the LORD is an executor of judgment; but he will show mercy to hundreds and thousands, to all who love him. (Jub. 23:30–31)

---

3. Some pseudepigraphal connections to Dan 12:2 are noted by Steve Delamarter in his book *A Scripture Index*, 35, 89. However, this chapter will propose more connections and influence than Delamarter suggests, since his references and mine will overlap in only three places: T. Jud. 25, T. Benj. 10, and Ps. Sol. 3 (see *A Scripture Index*, 35, 89). All translations of these texts are from the corresponding sections of James H. Charlesworth, ed., *The Old Testament Pseudepigrapha*, 2 vols. (New York: Doubleday, 1983–1985).
4. Nickelsburg, *Resurrection, Immortality, and Eternal Life*, 31.

The vindication of God's servants is found in their resurrection ("and they will rise up," Jub. 23:30), and on their enemies will fall "judgments" and "curses" (23:30). The duration of the servants' joy will be "forever and ever" (23:30), and this unending rejoicing will parallel the unending destruction of their enemies. The righteous will have joy because of what they see (23:30), and since their joy never ends, what they see regarding the wicked may never end either (cf. 36:9–10).[5]

Forestell asserts that Jubilees does not teach bodily resurrection.[6] But when the text says the saints who suffered "will rise up," the verb fits the sense of earlier Old Testament texts like Daniel 12:2 and Isaiah 26:19. And the vindication God grants is eternal ("rejoice forever and ever"). The objection to resurrection probably results from 23:31, which says, "Their bones will rest in the earth and their spirits will increase with joy." But I agree with N. T. Wright, who says this latter phrase "refers to the time in between their death and resurrection."[7] If instead the words speak about a disembodied immortality as the final eschatological state, then "will rise up" is the "only occurrence in the relevant literature of something that looks like resurrection language being used to denote something other than new bodily existence."[8]

The logic of Jubilees 23:30–31 appears to be: (1) God will raise the righteous bodily, (2) the righteous will rejoice forever and see the judgment and curse upon their enemies, and so (3) until that day the bones of the righteous will rest secure in the confidence of future vindication. The most likely Old Testament background encapsulating these notions conceptually is Daniel 12:2.

THE PSALMS OF SOLOMON

The Psalms of Solomon are eighteen in number and are attributed to the Old Testament king whom God endowed with incomparable wisdom. In two of these psalms the author explains the final state of believers and

---

5. See Edward William Fudge, *The Fire That Consumes: A Biblical and Historical Study of the Doctrine of Final Punishment*, 3rd ed. (Eugene, OR: Cascade, 2011), 108–9.
6. J. Terence Forestell, "Christian Revelation and the Resurrection of the Wicked," CBQ 19, no. 2 (1957): 169. See also C. D. Elledge, "Resurrection of the Dead: Exploring Our Earliest Evidence Today," in *Resurrection: The Origin and Future of a Biblical Doctrine*, ed. James H. Charlesworth (New York: T&T Clark, 2006), 40–41; Wilson, *Studies in the Book of Daniel*, 133.
7. Wright, *The Resurrection of the Son of God*, 144.
8. Wright, *The Resurrection of the Son of God*, 144.

unbelievers. Kirk is right that "while resurrection is not a major theme in and of itself, it is assumed by the author to be an integral part of the way in which God will set all things right."[9]

The resurrection of God-fearers and destruction of sinners (Ps. Sol. 3:11-12). In the third Psalm of Solomon, the stumbling righteous wait for the deliverance of the Lord (3:5), but not so the sinner, who heads for destruction (3:10-11). The waiting of the righteous will cease with the divine intervention of resurrection.

> The sinner stumbles and curses his life, the day of his birth, and his mother's pains. He adds sin upon sin in his life; he falls—his fall is serious—and he will not get up. The destruction of the sinner is forever, and he will not be remembered when (God) looks after the righteous. This is the share of sinners forever, but those who fear the Lord shall rise up to eternal life, and their life shall be in the Lord's light, and it shall never end. (Ps. Sol. 3:9-12)

Like Daniel 12:2, this portion of the psalm speaks about two groups who have two contrasting destinies before them: resurrection to eternal life for the believer but everlasting destruction for the sinner.[10] The phrase in the Th of Daniel 12:2 (εἰς ζωὴν αἰώνιον) matches what the author of the psalm uses (Ps. Sol. 3:12, εἰς ζωὴν αἰώνιον). Conceptually, light links the two passages, for those who rise to life will "shine like the brightness of the sky above" (Dan 12:3), and "their life shall be in the Lord's light" (Ps. Sol. 3:12). In Psalm of Solomon 3 "resurrection life is the blessing that comes to those who fear the Lord."[11] This expression of vindication and judgment likely alludes to Daniel 12:2.[12]

The sinners who will inherit destruction and perish forever (Ps. Sol. 15:12-13). In the fifteenth Psalm of Solomon, the destruction of sinners is described graphically and elaborately.

> But they shall pursue sinners and overtake them, for those who act lawlessly shall not escape the Lord's judgment. They shall be overtaken as by those experienced in war, for on their forehead (is) the mark of destruction. And the inheritance of sinners is

---

9. J. R. Daniel Kirk, *Unlocking Romans: Resurrection and the Justification of God* (Grand Rapids: Eerdmans, 2008), 24.
10. See Nickelsburg, *Resurrection, Immortality, and Eternal Life*, 131; Wright, *The Resurrection of the Son of God*, 162.
11. Kirk, *Unlocking Romans*, 24.
12. Beale, *A New Testament Biblical Theology*, 132n4.

destruction and darkness, and their lawless actions shall pursue them below into Hades. Their inheritance shall not be found for their children, for lawless actions shall devastate the homes of sinners. And sinners shall perish forever in the day of the Lord's judgment, when God oversees the earth at his judgment. But those who fear the Lord shall find mercy in it and shall live by their God's mercy; but sinners shall perish for all time. (Ps. Sol. 15:8-13)

This section of Psalm of Solomon 15 is similar to 3:9-12.[13] In both places a lengthy expression of the sinners' downfall (cf. 3:9-11; 15:8-12) precedes a brief statement of the saints' vindication (cf. 3:12; 15:13). Both psalms call the two groups "the righteous" and "the sinners" (cf. 3:3-7, 9-11; 15:6-7, 8, 10-13), both say the sinner will perish forever (cf. 3:11-12a; 15:12), and both say the righteous will live (cf. 3:12b; 15:13). This living is a postmortem promise and so refers to resurrection in both psalms. The righteous in both psalms are called "those who fear the Lord" (φοβούμενοι τὸν κύριον, 3:12b; 15:13a).

These parallels between Psalms of Solomon 3 and 15 imply that the Danielic influence on the former is present also on the latter. When 15:12-13 describe the fate of sinners as perishing forever and yet God-fearers as living again by God's mercy, this reflects the theology of the biblical author in Daniel 12:2. No other Old Testament text is more probable.

THE SIBYLLINE ORACLES

The Sibylline Oracles consist of fourteen books according to the titles in each of the parts, though some books are missing, and in other cases there are only fragments. In the fourth book there is one section that, for the purposes of this study, warrants close attention.

Mortals raised for judgment or life (Sib. Or. 4:181-90). In the future God will execute final judgment, and by his power he will raise everyone from the dead.

> But when everything is already dusty ashes, and God puts to sleep the unspeakable fire, even as he kindled it, God himself will again fashion the bones and ashes of men and he will raise up mortals again as they were before. And then there will be a judgment over which God himself will preside, judging the world again. As many as sinned by impiety, these will a mound of earth cover, and broad

---

13. See confirmation in Nickelsburg, *Resurrection, Immortality, and Eternal Life*, 133.

Tartarus and the repulsive recesses of Gehenna. But as many as are pious, they will live on earth again when God gives spirit and life and favor to these pious ones. Then they will all see themselves beholding the delightful and pleasant light of the sun. Oh most blessed, whatever man will live to that time. (Sib. Or. 4:179–92)

This section of the Sibylline Oracles reflects the teaching of Daniel 12:2, which promised a comprehensive resurrection as well as differing destinies for the righteous and the wicked.[14] In 4:181 the fashioning of bones and ashes implies God acting on dead people.[15] This means the expression "he will raise up mortals again" (4:182) refers to renewed bodily existence after bodily death.[16] For the ungodly "there will be a judgment over which God himself will preside, judging the world again" (4:183–84). In this era "common is the placing of resurrection within a judgment scene."[17] However, for God's people (here called the "pious"), he will grant them bodily life on earth (4:187–90).

The phrase "as they were before" (Sib. Or. 4:182) may seem to undermine a transformed existence after resurrection because of what sounds like mere resuscitation. Bauckham clarifies, however, that "the concern that these texts express ... centers on the preservation of personal identity. For those who rise must be understood to be the same persons, in their distinctive embodied forms, who had died."[18] Texts like this are not denying that future resurrection means more than just bodily resuscitation. For example, the righteous "will all see themselves beholding the delightful and pleasant light of the sun" (4:190–91), a state of glory brought about by resurrection and not experienced beforehand.

---

14. Davies and Allison list Sib. Or. 4:181–92 as a text that refers to the resurrection of believers and unbelievers (W. D. Davies and D. C. Allison, *The Gospel According to Saint Matthew*, ICC [New York: T&T Clark, 1988], 1:525).
15. Bauckham suggests that the phrase "will again fashion the bones and ashes of men and he will raise up mortals again as they were before" (Sib. Or. 4:181–82) is inspired by Ezekiel's vision of the bone-ridden valley (Ezek 37:1–14), a background that shows how in the intertestamental period the prophet's vision was understood as a prophetic picture of God restoring flesh to the dead and bringing them to life at the resurrection ("Life, Death, and the Afterlife," 91).
16. See Robert M. Grant, "The Resurrection of the Body," JR 28, no. 2 (1948): 122; Nickelsburg, *Resurrection, Immortality, and Eternal Life*, 140–41.
17. Wright, *The Resurrection of the Son of God*, 158.
18. Bauckham, "Life, Death, and the Afterlife," 92.

THE APOCALYPSE OF MOSES

As the Greek version of the Life of Adam and Eve, the Apocalypse of Moses tells what happened with Adam and Eve after their exile from Eden and up to their deaths.[19] At least two passages show influence from Daniel 12:2.

The resurrection of all flesh from Adam (Apoc. Mos. 13:3-4). According to an account in the Apocalypse of Moses, Seth and his mother Eve were wanting "oil of mercy," and Seth prayed to God for an angel who would give it to them (Apoc. Mos. 13:1).

> And God sent Michael the archangel, and he said to them, "Seth, man of God, do not labor, praying with this supplication about the tree from which the oil flows, to anoint your father Adam; it shall not come to be yours now (but at the end of times. Then all flesh from Adam up to that great day shall be raised, such as shall be the holy people; then to them shall be given every joy of Paradise and God shall be in their midst, and there shall not be any more sinners before him, for the evil heart shall be removed from them, and they shall be given a heart that understands the good and worships God alone)." (Apoc. Mos. 13:2-6)

Only one Old Testament text explicitly predicts a resurrection of all people: Daniel 12:2. In this chapter from the Apocalypse of Moses, the archangel Michael foretells a future day when "all flesh from Adam up to that great day shall be raised" (13:3), and this act is both (1) universal in scope[20] and (2) unmistakably physical in nature. The prediction of bodily resurrection is clear.[21] The author's words indicate that "the eschatological reopening of paradise is also specifically connected to bodily resurrection, and the hope for future cohabitation with God in paradise."[22]

---

19. As Nickelsburg explains, "Approximately one half of the Life of Adam and Eve overlaps with a similar portion of the Apocalypse of Moses. ... The material found in the Life of Adam and Eve but not in the Apocalypse of Moses occurs in three blocks (1, 3, 7)" (George W. E. Nickelsburg, *Jewish Literature Between the Bible and the Mishnah: A Historical and Literary Introduction* [Philadelphia: Fortress, 1981], 256).
20. Nickelsburg, *Resurrection, Immortality, and Eternal Life*, 143n47. Note that in Apoc. Mos. 13:2-6, the wicked are not mentioned specifically, but they are included by implication in the phrase "all flesh from Adam."
21. See Wright, *The Resurrection of the Son of God*, 157-58.
22. Jonathan Pennington, "Refractions of Daniel in the Gospel of Matthew," in *Early Christian Literature and Intertextuality*, vol. 1, *Thematic Studies*, ed. Craig

The promise to raise Adam and his seed (Apoc. Mos. 41:2-3). Earlier in the Apocalypse of Moses, Seth and Eve were denied the "oil of mercy" with which they wanted to anoint the ailing Adam, but God promised Adam that his day of resurrection would come. "And God called Adam and said, 'Adam, Adam.' And the body answered from the ground and said, 'Here I am, LORD.' And the LORD said to him, 'I told you that *you are dust and to dust you shall return*. Now I promise to you the resurrection; I shall raise you on the last day in the resurrection with every man of your seed'" (Apoc. Mos. 41:1-3).

A resurrection is evident because of the phrase "in the resurrection," it is future because of the words "on the last day," and it is universal because of the promise "I shall raise you ... with every man of your seed" (Apoc. Mos. 41:3). These elements indicate the probable influence of Daniel 12:2 because it speaks of comprehensive resurrection, whereas other Old Testament verses of resurrection affirm that hope for the righteous only.

THE TESTAMENT OF MOSES

The Testament (also known as the Assumption) of Moses is a rewriting of Deuteronomy 31-34.[23] Daniel 12 is reflected at a number of points in the extant form of the document, and a section promising the resurrection of Israel probably bears the mark of 12:2 in particular.

Raised to the heights to see your enemies (T. Mos. 10:9). Israel is told their vindication will come. God will rise from his throne and go forth with wrath "on behalf of his sons" (T. Mos. 10:3), creation will be undone at his arrival for judgment (10:4-6), and he will avenge his people by destroying his/their enemies (10:7). Israel will be glad and mount up on the wings of an eagle (10:8): "And God will raise you to the heights. Yea, he will fix you firmly in the heaven of the stars, in the place of their habitations. And you will behold from on high. Yea, you will see your enemies on the earth. And recognizing them, you will rejoice" (10:9-10). Perhaps Israel is "recognizing" their enemies and rejoicing over them because God is exacting justice.

Being raised "to the heights" for vindication (T. Mos. 10:9) may be influenced by Daniel 12:2 because the next phrase, "he will fix you

---

A. Evans and H. Daniel Zacharias (New York: T&T Clark, 2009), 103.

23. Nickelsburg, *Resurrection, Immortality, and Eternal Life*, 29.

firmly in the heaven of the stars," recalls Daniel 12:3.[24] The writer of the Testament of Moses may be using the language, for in 10:9 Israel is fixed in the heavens like stars, and in Daniel 12:2 God's people are raised and shine like the "brightness of the sky above ... like the stars forever and ever" (12:3). Earlier in the Testament of Moses is the prophecy "And there will come upon them ... punishment and wrath such as has never happened to them from the creation till that time" (8:1), language that reflects Daniel 12: "And there shall be a time of trouble, such as never has been since there was a nation till that time" (12:1).

In view of these similarities, Nickelsburg says, "The [Testament of Moses] appears, then, to draw on a form of the material in Daniel 12:1–3 more primitive than the Danielic form,"[25] but that suggestion is based on his dating of Daniel to the second century BC. If Daniel was written centuries earlier than the Testament of Moses, then a better suggestion is the *dependence* of the latter on the former. Israel being raised to the heights in vindication (T. Mos. 10:9) is a picture of vindication through resurrection.[26]

THE BOOK OF 1 ENOCH

The Bible reports that Enoch ascended from earth to God (Gen 5:24), but it does not tell what happened to him after that. In the intertestamental period the book of 1 Enoch seeks to fill that gap and report things Enoch saw and heard. Part of 1 Enoch's message involves future events like the resurrection of the dead, and some expressions of this teaching evoke Daniel 12:2 directly or indirectly. The order of influence here is important, for scholars who hold a second-century BC dating for Daniel argue that Enoch influenced the author(s). This leads Collins to say, "Daniel

---

24. Nickelsburg says, "The description of Israel's exaltation to the stars (10:9) corresponds to Daniel 12:3" (*Resurrection, Immortality, and Eternal Life*, 30), but I am suggesting more than correspondence. Dependence is likely.
25. Nickelsburg, *Resurrection, Immortality, and Eternal Life*, 30.
26. Nickelsburg's words, therefore, are surprising: "In view of the parallels in Daniel, the failure of the [Testament of Moses] to speak of a resurrection is particularly noticeable" (*Resurrection, Immortality, and Eternal Life*, 30). But it is reasonable to think, in light of the dependence of the T. Mos. on Dan 12:1 and 12:3, that being raised up for vindication denotes resurrection. He does concede that the "exaltation of Israel mentioned in verse 9 may presume a resurrection of the righteous dead or their immediate assumption to heaven" (*Resurrection, Immortality, and Eternal Life*, 31). See Wright, *The Resurrection of the Son of God*, 157.

12 is not, then, the earliest Jewish expression of belief in resurrection, since earlier attestation is found in 1 Enoch."[27]

The return of bodily deposits from Sheol (1 En. 51:1-2). The writer in 1 Enoch 51 promises an ultimate deliverance of the righteous among the risen dead: "In those days, Sheol will return all the deposits which she had received and hell will give back all that which it owes. And he shall choose the righteous and the holy ones from among (the risen dead), for the day when they shall be selected and saved has arrived" (51:1-2).

The "deposits" in Sheol are bodies, and their return from Sheol is resurrection.[28] Since "all the deposits" are returned, the resurrection is universal,[29] and among the risen people the righteous are given extra attention. The resurrection of the dead means that, for the righteous, "the day when they shall be selected and saved has arrived." As in other passages during the intertestamental era, the resurrection of the righteous means their long-awaited vindication by God.

The comprehensive resurrection and the vindication of the righteous suggests that Daniel 12:2 is a source for the theology of 1 Enoch 51:1-2.

The righteous and elect ones who shall rise (1 En. 62:14-15). In 1 Enoch 62 the Lord warned the kings and governors that on the day of judgment they will see his Elect One and be silenced (62:1-3). They will

---

27. John J. Collins, *Daniel, First Maccabees, Second Maccabees*, Old Testament Message, vol. 15 (Wilmington, DE: Michael Glazier, 1981), 111. He also says, "The belief in the resurrection of individuals and the judgment after death was introduced into Judaism in the apocalyptic writings, notably 1 Enoch, some parts of which are older than Daniel and date to the third century BCE" (110). Mahalios, however, counters this thinking and says, "It could very well be that 1 Enoch borrowed from Daniel rather than the other way around" (Stefanos Mihalios, *The Danielic Eschatological Hour in the Johannine Literature*, Library of New Testament Studies [New York: T&T Clark, 2001], 49n144).
28. Bauckham clarifies that "one traditional image of resurrection" is when "the place of the dead will give back the dead" (Richard Bauckham, *The Fate of the Dead: Studies on the Jewish and Christian Apocalypses*, NovTSup 93 [Atlanta: Society of Biblical Literature, 1998], 270-71).
29. Wright says 1 Enoch 51:1-2 foresees the resurrection of both the righteous and the wicked (*The Resurrection of the Son of God*, 442n126). In his footnote he does not provide a basis for this claim. But if Sheol and hell give back their dead (a picture of resurrection), and the righteous are then chosen from among the dead that are raised, then by implication both the unrighteous and the righteous have experienced a resurrection.

plead for mercy (62:9), but God will deliver them over to punishment (62:10-11). The outcome will be different for God's people.

> The righteous and elect ones shall be saved on that day; and from thenceforth they shall never see the faces of the sinners and the oppressors. The Lord of the Spirits will abide over them; they shall eat and rest and rise with that Son of Man forever and ever. The righteous and elect ones shall rise from the earth and shall cease being of downcast face. They shall wear the garments of glory. These garments of yours shall become the garments of life from the Lord of the Spirits. Neither shall your garments wear out, nor your glory come to an end before the Lord of the Spirits. (1 En. 62:13-16)

The promise that the righteous "shall ... rise" (1 En. 62:14) will be fulfilled at the resurrection of the dead. This language probably draws from Daniel 12:2 because 12:3—which talks about the wise shining like the brightness of the sky, like the stars—is echoed in 1 Enoch 62:16, where the writer talks about the glorious appearance and garments of the righteous.[30] Wright says, "This is clearly a glorious bodily resurrection, not a matter of becoming a star."[31]

The waking of the righteous from sleep (1 En. 91:10). Enoch gathers his children and exhorts them to walk in righteousness (1 En. 91:4) because wickedness will increase on the earth (91:5-6). God will execute judgment from heaven (91:7) and overthrow the evildoers (91:8-9).

> Then the righteous one shall arise from his sleep, and the wise one shall arise; and he shall be given unto them (the people). ... Then after that in the ninth week the righteous judgment shall be revealed to the whole world. All the deeds of the sinners shall depart from upon the whole earth, and be written off for eternal destruction; and all people shall direct their sight to the path of uprightness. (1 En. 91:10-11, 14)

---

30. See Wright, *The Resurrection of the Son of God*, 155.
31. Wright, *The Resurrection of the Son of God*, 112n118. Wright explains that "it is impossible to cite the book [of 1 Enoch] as a whole as a representative of the 'astral' view; indeed ... we might suggest that at the very least the multiple authors, and the eventual redactor, were not eager to press such a point. Thus, though several texts play with the idea of 'light' in general, and may refer directly to Daniel, it is hard to make a case that 'astral immortality' had taken root in ancient Judaism as it clearly had in ancient paganism" (112).

At least two aspects of the quoted passage reflect Daniel 12. First, the resurrection is pictured as waking from sleep (cf. 12:2). Second, the righteous one who rises is called the "wise" (cf. 12:3). Third, the wicked will face eternal destruction (cf. 12:2).

The influence of Daniel 12:2 on this passage of 1 Enoch is evident as a father exhorts his children to righteous living by keeping before their minds a future resurrection that will mean life and vindication for the wise but destruction and judgment for the wicked.

The hope to shine like the lights of heaven (1 En. 104:2). Among the closing chapters of 1 Enoch is a promise that the angels will remember God's people (104:1). The righteous have endured evil, "but now you shall shine like the lights of heaven, and you shall be seen; and the windows of heaven shall be opened for you. Your cry shall be heard" (104:2).

This, again, is a promise of vindication for God's people. The language "shine like the lights of heaven" reflects Daniel 12:3,[32] which implies the resurrection of 12:2. No verb of resurrection is present, but the implication of the righteous being raised is reasonable because the righteous "shall be seen." In other words, Daniel 12:2 undergirds and upholds the explicit promise that the righteous will be seen and shine like the lights of heaven.

In apocalyptic literature, "stars" are the angelic host, so when the righteous dead become like the lights in 1 Enoch 104:2, the imagery may mean that the righteous become like the angels.[33] Collins says, "Daniel has a point of affinity with the Enoch tradition when it associates the risen sages with the stars (cf. 1 En. 104). It is very probable that Daniel was influenced by the noncanonical Enoch material as well as by the texts in Isaiah."[34] Contra Collins, the book of Daniel is to be dated in the sixth century BC, and thus earlier than the Enoch material,[35] so the influence was not Enoch on Daniel but the reverse. The author of 1 Enoch 104 was influenced by the book of Daniel, and he employed Danielic imagery as he saw fit, even if that application deviated from what the

---

32. Buchanan calls the writer of 1 Enoch 104:2 one of the "early commentators" on Dan 12:3 (*The Book of Daniel*, 380).
33. Collins, *Encounters with Biblical Theology*, 182.
34. Collins, *Encounters with Biblical Theology*, 32.
35. See chap. 1 for a discussion of the date of the book of Daniel.

biblical author would have said.³⁶ Wright says 1 Enoch 104:1-4 has "clear echoes of Daniel 12."³⁷

The righteous ones brought into the light (1 En. 108:11). In the closing verses of 1 Enoch the writer explains the splendor that the righteous have in store for them.

> So now I shall summon their spirits if they are born of light, and change those who are born in darkness—those whose bodies were not recompensed with honor as they deserved for their faithfulness. I shall bring them out into the bright light, those who have loved my holy name, and seat them each one by one upon the throne of his honor; and they shall be resplendent for ages that cannot be numbered; for the judgment of God is righteousness, because he will give faith—as well as the paths of truth—to the faithful ones in the resting place. Then they shall see those who were born in darkness being taken into darkness, while the righteous ones shall be resplendent. (The sinners) shall cry aloud, and they shall see the righteous ones being resplendent; they shall go to the place which was prescribed for them concerning the days and the seasons. (1 En. 108:11-15)

This final passage speaks about two groups of people, the righteous and the sinners, who will meet different ends: the former will be taken into the light, while the latter will be taken into darkness. Each group will be aware of the other's fate, and the climactic tone of the passage indicates a permanent state that each group enters (cf. 108:13 where "for ages that cannot be numbered" is equivalent to "forever").

---

36. Nickelsburg says, "The passage has a number of significant parallels to Dan 12:1-3, sufficient to indicate a traditional connection between the two passages. The precise relationship, however, is difficult to ascertain. It is clear that the present author has used motifs common to Daniel for his own purposes and integrated them into the broader contours of his writing" (George W. E. Nickelsburg, *1 Enoch 1: A Commentary on the Book of 1 Enoch Chapters 1-36; 81-108*, Hermeneia [Minneapolis: Fortress, 2001], 528). And elsewhere Nickelsburg reasons, "Daniel 12:1-3 most closely parallels Enoch 104, and it is not impossible that the author of Enoch 104 knew the former passage in its Danielic context" (*Resurrection, Immortality, and Eternal Life*, 122).
37. Wright, *The Resurrection of the Son of God*, 156. For example, 1 Enoch 104:2 is "simply a quote from Dan 12.3" (112n118).

The use of the word "spirits" indicates that the righteous are currently dead,[38] so this hope is for postmortem vindication. Emphasis is given to the fact that the righteous had "bodies" that were "not recompensed" before death with the honor that would correspond to their faithfulness, suggesting that the vindication of the righteous will involve their bodies—that is, *resurrection*. Wright says, "The righteous are transformed as well as revivified."[39] This hope has probably been shaped by Daniel 12:2 because the result will be God's people shining with resplendent light for the ages to come, a shining that alludes to Daniel 12:3.

An explicit resurrection statement is not used in 1 Enoch 108, but the belief is assumed nonetheless. Two different groups will meet different destinies, and one outcome is associated with light. The most probable Old Testament text informing that passage is Daniel 12:2-3.

THE TESTAMENTS OF THE TWELVE PATRIARCHS

The Testaments of the Twelve Patriarchs claims to be the last words of Jacob's sons.[40] Most of the testaments have eschatological components, and at least three of them have evident echoes of Daniel 12:2.

Abraham, Isaac, and Jacob raised to life (T. Jud. 25:1). Toward the end of Judah's testament, he prophesied that his father, grandfather, and great-grandfather would be resurrected:

> And after this Abraham, Isaac, and Jacob will be resurrected to life and I and my brothers will be chiefs (wielding) our scepter in Israel. ... And you shall be one people of the Lord, with one language. There shall no more be Beliar's spirit of error, because he will be thrown into eternal fire. And those who died in sorrow shall be raised in joy; and those who died in poverty for the Lord's sake shall be made rich; those who died on account of the Lord shall be wakened to life. (T. Jud. 25:1, 3-4)

The patriarchs will be raised "to life" (T. Jud. 25:1), which reflects what will happen to the righteous according to Daniel 12:2.[41] The verb is "res-

---

38. See Loren T. Stuckenbruck, *1 Enoch 91–108*, CEJL (Berlin: Walter de Gruyter, 2007), 731.
39. Wright, *The Resurrection of the Son of God*, 156.
40. For a new study that argues for the *Testaments* as a set of testimonies to Judaism before Jesus, see David A. DeSilva, "The *Testaments of the Twelve Patriarchs* as Witnesses to Pre-Christian Judaism: A Re-Assessment," *JSP* 23 (2013): 21–68.
41. See Pheme Perkins, *Resurrection: New Testament Witness and Contemporary Reflection* (New York: Doubleday, 1984), 42.

urrected," leaving no doubt that bodily life after death is meant.[42] This resurrection will reverse the misfortunes Judah outlines (i.e., sorrow and poverty).[43]

An eternal judgment of fire awaits Beliar, a fate which may build on the everlasting judgment promised in Daniel 12:2. And the resurrection is broader than only Abraham, Isaac, and Jacob, for those who died in sorrow or poverty shall be "raised," and those who were martyred shall be "wakened to life." That last verb—"wakened to life"—is another connection to Daniel 12:2 because rising from the dead is pictured there as waking from sleep to everlasting life.[44]

The confidence of Zebulun to rise again (T. Zeb. 10:2). On his deathbed Zebulun comforted his children with the hope that his death would one day be undone:

> And now, my children, do not grieve because I am dying, nor be depressed because I am leaving you. I shall rise again in your midst as a leader among your sons, and I shall be glad in the midst of my tribe—as many as keep the Law of the Lord and the commandments of Zebulun, their father. But the Lord shall bring down fire on the impious and will destroy them to all generations. (T. Zeb. 10:1-4)

The verb "I shall rise" is a clear hope of resurrection.[45] In contrast to what is in store for Zebulun, the impious will receive eternal fiery destruction. The hope of resurrection and the judgment on the wicked likely reflects the influence of Daniel 12:2.[46]

Everyone raised and changed for glory or dishonor (T. Benj. 10:6-8). In Benjamin's testament the author conveys his dying words to his children, and these words foretell the future vindication of God's people and the judgment of his enemies:

---

42. See Nickelsburg, *Resurrection, Immortality, and Eternal Life*, 34-35; Wright, *The Resurrection of the Son of God*, 159.
43. C. D. Elledge, "The Resurrection Passages in the *Testaments of the Twelve Patriarchs*: Hope for Israel in Early Judaism and Christianity," in *Resurrection: The Origin and Future of a Biblical Doctrine*, ed. James H. Charlesworth (New York: T&T Clark, 2006), 84.
44. See Wright's words to confirm this connection: "The motif of 'wakening' is probably an allusion to Dan. 12.2" (*The Resurrection of the Son of God*, 159n119).
45. Elledge, "The Resurrection Passages in the *Testaments of the Twelve Patriarchs*," 84-85.
46. See Perkins, *Resurrection*, 42.

> You know then, my children, that I am dying. Do the truth, each of you to his neighbor; keep the Law of the Lord and his commandments, for I leave you these things instead of an inheritance. Give them, then, to your children for an eternal possession; this is what Abraham, Isaac, and Jacob did. They gave us all these things as an inheritance, saying, "Keep God's commandments until the Lord reveals his salvation to all the nations." And then you will see Enoch and Seth and Abraham and Isaac and Jacob being raised up at the right hand in great joy. Then shall we also be raised, each of us over our tribe, and we shall prostrate ourselves before the heavenly king. Then all shall be changed, some destined for glory, others for dishonor, for the Lord first judges Israel for the wrong she has committed and then he shall do the same for all the nations. Then he shall judge Israel by the chosen gentiles as he tested Esau by the Midianites who loved their brothers. You, therefore, my children, may your lot come to be with those who fear the Lord. (T. Benj. 10:2–10)

The author explains that, along with Enoch, Seth, and the patriarchs, the righteous will "also be raised" and "be changed" (T. Benj. 10:7-8). This hope is for resurrection and transformation.[47] Unbelievers among Israel and the nations will face judgment. The resurrection seems to involve more than believers only,[48] for some who are changed will be "destined ... for dishonor" (10:8), while others are raised to glory.[49] Unbelievers will be put to shame, while believers will be vindicated. "More than any other previous example [from the Testaments], the Testament of Benjamin asserts the universalist dimensions of the resurrection, not simply for the patriarchs or even just for Israel, but for all."[50]

---

47. Wilson rightly notes that T. Benj. 10:7-8 is the only one of the references to resurrection in this testament that speaks of some people rising to shame (*Studies in the Book of Daniel*, 149).
48. See Elledge, "The Resurrection Passages in the *Testaments of the Twelve Patriarchs*," 87; Johnston, *Shades of Sheol*, 229.
49. According to Elledge, "some unto glory and some unto shame" is "an almost formulaic statement that may reflect the influence of Dan 12:1-3" ("The Resurrection Passages in the *Testaments of the Twelve Patriarchs*," 91). Wright confirms this, saying, "An allusion to Daniel is again likely, this time because of the double resurrection, both to glory and to shame" (*The Resurrection of the Son of God*, 159).
50. Elledge, "The Resurrection Passages in the *Testaments of the Twelve Patriarchs*," 87.

With these aspects from Benjamin's testament in view, the dependence on Daniel 12:2 is evident: the latter speaks of resurrection to different outcomes for the righteous and the wicked.[51]

SUMMARY

Some authors in the Pseudepigrapha speak about the future vindication of God's people and the judgment of his enemies in language shaped by Daniel 12:2. In the passages cited above, frequently a judgment scene pictures the righteous rising and the wicked facing divine wrath. The death of the martyrs and the suffering of God's people finds its solution and reversal as God grants bodily life to the saints, and the apparent escape of the ungodly from earthly accountability will be rectified as they receive eternal recompense for their wickedness. In the Pseudepigrapha, an end-time resurrection functions as both a warning for unbelievers and a motive for believers to obey Yahweh.

DANIEL 12:2 IN THE APOCRYPHA

Moving to the other group of noncanonical literature relevant to this project, this section will address the Apocrypha, a word that means "secret things." Not as many books as the Pseudepigrapha bear marks of influence from Daniel 12:2. Attention will be given to three passages from two books, the Wisdom of Solomon and 2 Maccabees.

WISDOM OF SOLOMON

Though Wright does not hold the typical assumption about the absence of resurrection hope in the Wisdom of Solomon, he accurately summarizes the scholarly scene: "Wisdom clearly teaches the immortality of the soul; therefore, it has regularly been assumed, it cannot simultaneously teach the resurrection of the body. That assumption remains widespread in current scholarship."[52] And too frequently "scholars have denied the possibility of resurrection in this text because of an unsubstantiated assumption that any mention of an immortal soul means Platonism."[53] Not only can resurrection hope be seen in the Wisdom of Solomon, but the influence of Daniel 12:2 is discernible also.

---

51. See Perkins, *Resurrection*, 42–44; Fudge, *The Fire That Consumes*, 107.
52. Wright, *The Resurrection of the Son of God*, 163.
53. Wright, *The Resurrection of the Son of God*, 163n140.

The vindication of the righteous and the fate of the wicked (Wis 3:7–10). In the opening chapters of the Wisdom of Solomon, a classic problem is narrated about how the righteous are oppressed while the wicked seem to thrive. In Wisdom 3:1–4 the righteous have died bodily (3:1–2), but their souls are immortal, so they are in the hand of God after death (3:3–4).

But a disembodied peaceful existence is not the final state of the faithful. Wright correctly observes a two-stage description of what happens to God's people after death: their present disembodied existence, in God's hand no less, "is merely the prelude to what is about to happen."[54] In the furnace of affliction God found them worthy and accepted the offering of their sacrifice(s), so they will receive good from him (Wis 3:5–6).

At the time of their visitation they will shine forth, and run about like sparks in the stubble. They will judge nations, and rule over peoples, and the Lord will be their king for ever. Those who trust in him will understand truth, and those who are loyal and faithful will remain with him in love; for his grace and mercy are upon his chosen ones. But the ungodly will receive their reward according to their own reasonings, because they disregarded the righteous, and rebelled against the Lord. (Wis 3:7–10)[55]

Already in a disembodied state, the righteous have a future "visitation" that will result in their shining forth like sparks, probably an allusion to Daniel 12:3.[56] In the Wisdom of Solomon, "visitation" is a regular word for the day of judgment on which God will vindicate the righteous and condemn the wicked (cf. 2:20; 3:13; 4:15; 14:11; 19:15).[57] This is a future vindication, for they judge the nations and rule the peoples, an elevated status not yet attained. Since the writer uses the image of "shining forth" from Daniel 12, the resurrection does not need an explicit

---

54. Wright, *The Resurrection of the Son of God*, 167.
55. This is N. T. Wright's translation of Wis 3:1–10, available in his book *The Resurrection of the Son of God*, 167.
56. Wright sees that the verb "will shine forth" (ἀναλάμψουσιν) is very close to the Th version of Dan 12:3 (ἐκλάμψουσιν) (*The Resurrection of the Son of God*, 169). Only the prefix differs. Grant also believes Wis 3:7 refers to Dan 12:3 but adds, "It is by no means certain that a fleshly resurrection is implied" ("The Resurrection of the Body," 121). I will argue it is implied.
57. Wright, *The Resurrection of the Son of God*, 169.

mention; it is implied. The disembodied immortality of the righteous will lead to a transformed existence coherent with bodily resurrection.[58]

As with Daniel 12:2, the vindication of God's people also means the ungodly receiving their due at the judgment. In the phrase "like sparks in the stubble," the stubble refers to the unrighteous who will be judged (Wis 3:7). As Wright says, "The whole point is that this is *not* happening at the moment, i.e. in the time described in 3.1-4; at the moment, the righteous seem to be lost and gone, and the wicked are celebrating their disappearance; but they will return as the masters of the world."[59] The ungodly will get what is coming to them, the wage for their rebellion against God and their treatment of the righteous (3:10). "The present passage does not mention the word 'resurrection'. ... But that it teaches the same as Daniel does about the ultimate fate of God's people there should now be no doubt."[60]

SECOND MACCABEES

According to Wright, 2 Maccabees "provides far and away the clearest picture of the promise of resurrection anywhere in the period."[61] One of the book's most famous chapters is the story of a mother's seven sons martyred before her eyes and before her own death at the hands of the same persecutors (2 Macc 7:1-42). Two verses in this account show influence from Daniel 12:2.

A future resurrection to eternal life (2 Macc 7:9). When the first of the seven brothers perished, the second was brought forward for torture. With his final breath he said to his persecutor, "You, you fiend, are making us depart from our present life, but the King of the universe will resurrect us, who die for the sake of His laws, to a new eternal life" (2 Macc 7:9).[62]

The martyr is confident that his resurrection will be not only to life but "to a new eternal life." The son's words are literally εἰς αἰώνιον ἀναβίωσιν ζωῆς ἡμᾶς ἀναστήσει ("he will raise us to an eternal reviving of

---

58. See Wright, *The Resurrection of the Son of God*, 170.
59. Wright, *The Resurrection of the Son of God*, 170.
60. Wright, *The Resurrection of the Son of God*, 171.
61. Wright, *The Resurrection of the Son of God*, 150.
62. For this section I am following the translation of 2 Macc 7 found in Jonathan Goldstein, *II Maccabees*, AB, vol. 41A (Garden City, NY: Doubleday, 1983), 289-91.

life"). The wording reflects the OG of Daniel 12:2: ἀναστήσονται ... εἰς ζωὴν αἰώνιον.[63]

The author of 2 Maccabees puts the hope of Daniel 12:2 on the lips of the second martyred son, and this hope propels his willingness to suffer torture and finally death. "Resurrection functions as the means by which God will deliver the brothers from the destruction that Antiochus inflicts on them."[64]

The warning of no resurrection unto life for the persecutors (2 Macc 7:14). With three sons dead, the torturers bring forward the fourth. At the point of death he said to the king, "Better it is to pass away from among men while looking forward in hope to the fulfillment of God's promises that we will be resurrected by Him, for you shall have no resurrection unto life" (2 Macc 7:14).

Like the second son, this fourth one professes a hope to be raised, but the final statement sets the verse apart: σοὶ μὲν γὰρ ἀνάστασις εἰς ζωὴν οὐκ ἔσται. What Daniel 12:2 promises the righteous, this fourth son denies for the king. That wicked ruler will not be raised to life. The value of the son's warning is in the implication: if the king will not be raised to life, it is because his end will be judgment, a resurrection to shame that vindicates the martyrs.

Though Johnston says that in 2 Maccabees "resurrection is envisaged only for the righteous,"[65] what is specifically predicted is that Antiochus will not have a resurrection *to life*, a truth consistent with Daniel 12:2. The hope of the fourth son is probably based on that Danielic expression.[66]

SUMMARY

Though only a few places in the Apocrypha appear to reflect Daniel 12:2 in some way, those passages nevertheless continue to demonstrate the influence of that verse during the intertestamental period. Righteous sufferers found comfort and perseverance in the knowledge of their future resurrection. They could endure all manner of bodily harm because God would one day raise their bodies to life. At this vindication of the saints, the unrighteous—specifically the persecutors—would face judgment. The saints believed the promise of Daniel 12:2, that their cries

---

63. Goldstein, *II Maccabees*, 305. See Beale, *A New Testament Biblical Theology*, 132n4.
64. Nickelsburg, *Resurrection, Immortality, and Eternal Life*, 94.
65. Johnston, "Death and Resurrection," 446.
66. Goldstein, *II Maccabees*, 306.

would be answered with resurrection. That verse informed at least the Wisdom of Solomon and 2 Maccabees.

CONCLUSION

The goal of this chapter was to discern how, if at all, Daniel 12:2 shaped intertestamental literature.[67] If a passage contained a reference to an awakening of both the righteous and the wicked, a contrast between (eternal) fates of those groups, an implication of resurrection because the described state reflects the shining or transformed language of Daniel 12:3, a promise that the righteous will rise to eternal life, a picture of the wicked undergoing bodily destruction forever, or some combination of the preceding characteristics, then the passage's use of Daniel 12:2 was considered possible (or even probable).

By the time of Jesus, surviving Jewish texts indicate a prevailing belief in bodily resurrection, and for many Jews it seemed to be standard doctrine.[68] Daniel 12 stands behind much of this development.[69]

---

67. For insightful studies on how the book of Daniel influenced intertestamental literature, see G. K. Beale, *The Use of Daniel in Jewish Apocalyptic Literature and in the Revelation of St. John* (Eugene, OR: Wipf and Stock, 1984); Hamilton, *With the Clouds of Heaven.*
68. Wright, *The Resurrection of the Son of God,* 129.
69. See Wright, *The Resurrection of the Son of God,* 130; G. R. Osborne, "Resurrection," in *DGJ* (Downers Grove, IL: InterVarsity Press, 1992), 675.

5

The Use of Daniel 12:2 in the New Testament

Daniel 12:2 is the fullest expression of resurrection hope in the Old Testament, so readers might expect that the resurrection statements in the New Testament would (frequently) quote it.[1] Yet the entire verse is not quoted verbatim anywhere. Wright says that early Christians drew on many obvious texts to express what had happened to Jesus and what would happen to God's people, but they "virtually had no use of Daniel 12.1–3."[2] If the only way the New Testament could use an Old Testament text was with a full quotation, then the question of whether the New Testament authors used Daniel 12:2 would be an open-and-shut case, for there is no such use. But Daniel 12:2 is present in the New Testament in other ways, such as allusion, partial quotation, echo, and implication.[3] This fifth chapter is the final step in the argument for the thesis of this project: Daniel relied on earlier Old Testament texts and theological convictions when he expressed the hope of bodily resurrection, and his expression informed and shaped subsequent nonbiblical and biblical authors.

I will show that Daniel 12:2 was incorporated into all four Gospels, the book of Acts, over half of the Epistles, and the Apocalypse. This canonical order will be what the subsequent sections follow. I am not attempting to address all New Testament passages that speak about the resurrection. I want to show that Daniel 12:2 was central to how the New

---

1. For a concise treatment of the ways that resurrection hope appears in the Old and New Testaments, see Chase, *Resurrection Hope and the Death of Death*.
2. Wright, *The Resurrection of the Son of God*, 478.
3. In Appendix IV of the Nestle-Aland *Novum Testamentum Graece* 28 (NA[28]), titled "Loci Citati Vel Allegati," the list of references suggests that Daniel 12:2 is quoted or alluded to in four NT passages: Matt 27:52; John 5:24, 29; Acts 24:15 (866). The NA[27] also posited four verses, but some were different: Matt 25:46; 27:52; John 5:29; Acts 24:15 (NA[27], 800).

Testament authors conceived of and expressed their eschatological hope (pertaining both to believers and unbelievers). The criteria used to discern the influence of Daniel 12:2 on intertestamental literature will be applied once more to recognize its influence on the New Testament authors. If a passage contains a reference to an awakening of both the righteous and the wicked, a contrast between (eternal) fates of those groups, an implication of resurrection because the described state reflects the shining or transformed language of Daniel 12:3, a promise that the righteous will rise to eternal life, a picture of the wicked undergoing bodily destruction forever, or some combination of the preceding characteristics, then the passage's use of Daniel 12:2 will be considered possible (even probable). And if the information is discernible, it will be helpful to note in each case whether the biblical author is using the MT, Th, or OG of Daniel 12:2.[4]

THE GOSPELS AND ACTS

Since some stories are paralleled in two or more of the Gospels, the parallels will be noted, and the reader will be referred to the section where the material was addressed for a fuller explanation.

MATTHEW

Among the Gospels, the implicit or explicit presence of Daniel 12:2 is discerned the most in the first. "This eschatological hope informed most of the early Jesus movements and Matthew's community was no exception."[5] At least eight passages reflect Daniel 12:2 in some way.[6]

The danger of the whole body being thrown into hell (Matt 5:29-30). In the Sermon on the Mount (Matt 5–7) Jesus graphically

---

4. Wesselius notes that the Th of Daniel is the translation typically cited in the NT (Jan-Wim Wesselius, "The Writing of Daniel," in *The Book of Daniel: Composition and Reception*, ed. John J. Collins and Peter W. Flint, with Cameron VanEpps, VTSup 83 [Leiden: Brill, 2001], 2:593).
5. J. Andrew Overman, *Church and Community in Crisis: The Gospel According to Matthew*, The New Testament in Context (Valley Forge, PA: Trinity Press International, 1996), 396.
6. For a wider examination of the use of Daniel in the Gospel of Matthew, see Pennington, "Refractions of Daniel in the Gospel of Matthew," 65–86. For our purposes, Pennington says in his essay that "Daniel 12 plays an important role in several NT texts, including ... the great resurrection promise that 'many of those who sleep in the dust of the earth shall awake, some to everlasting life, and some to shame and everlasting contempt'" (78).

depicts the danger awaiting those who live for lust (5:27-30). If people do not subdue their bodily impulses now, God will judge their bodies in the future. "If your right eye causes you to sin, tear it out and throw it away. For it is better that you lose one of your members than that your whole body be thrown into hell. And if your right hand causes you to sin, cut it off and throw it away. For it is better that you lose one of your members than that your whole body go into hell" (5:29-30).

Relevant to a discussion of resurrection is the bodily destruction Jesus threatens: the body is thrown into hell. "The possibility that the 'whole body' may be thrown into Gehenna ... certainly suggests a resurrection to condemnation."[7] Since disembodiment occurs at death, Jesus must be assuming that the dead will have bodies once more in order for the threat to be legitimate.[8]

The group to receive bodily judgment in hell is the wicked, so the implication is that they will be resurrected for this judgment to take place. The verse that teaches the resurrection of unbelievers for everlasting judgment is Daniel 12:2, so it is the primary verse informing the warning in Matthew 5:29-30.[9] Knowing that there will be a resurrection of the wicked, Matthew's readers should pursue purity with utter seriousness, or at their resurrection they will be cast, body and all, into hell.

The girl not dead but sleeping (Matt 9:24-25). One miracle of Jesus was the restoration of life to a dead girl. Her father, a ruler, came to him and said, "My daughter has just died, but come and lay your hand on her, and she will live" (Matt 9:18). When Jesus arrived at the ruler's home, he told the flute players and the crowd, "Go away, for the girl is not dead but sleeping" (9:24). Jesus went in and took the girl by the hand, "and the girl arose" (9:25).

---

7. Murray J. Harris, *Raised Immortal: Resurrection and Immortality in the New Testament* (London: Marshall, Morgan & Scott, 1983; Repr. Grand Rapids: Eerdmans, 1985), 174. Davies and Allison comment, "The phrase, 'your whole body,' apparently refers to the resurrection of the just and unjust" (W. D. Davies and D. C. Allison, *The Gospel According to Saint Matthew*, ICC [New York: T&T Clark, 1988], 1:525).
8. R. T. France cautions against an overreading: this passage should not be used to suggest that amputees will be raised in an imperfect body. R. T. France, *The Gospel of Matthew*, NICNT (Grand Rapids: Eerdmans, 2007), 206.
9. See Craig S. Keener, *Revelation*, NIVAC (Grand Rapids: Zondervan, 2000), 467.

There are immediate similarities to the Old Testament resuscitations Elijah and Elisha performed (cf. 1 Kgs 17; 2 Kgs 4).[10] Jesus, like those prophets, is informed of a child's death, goes to the home of the deceased, and restores life to the child. But the language Jesus uses to describe the girl's status is important because at first it sounds as if her father had been mistaken.[11] "Go away, for the girl is not dead but sleeping," Jesus says. In light of the Old Testament, however, it is better to understand Jesus's words metaphorically, with sleep meaning death, but with the sense that rising from death is like waking from sleep.[12]

When Jesus says that "the girl is not dead but sleeping," he is preparing the listeners (and readers) for what is about to happen. Death is no match for his power. "Death is not the end, and in the case of this girl it will prove to be only a temporary experience. Her death is real, but it is not final."[13] Matthew probably reflects Daniel 12:2 in the way he records both Jesus's metaphor and the event of the girl rising.

Seen in parallel, the matching verbs in Matthew 9:24–25 and the Th of Daniel 12:2 likely mean a dependence of the former on the latter:

Matt 9:24–25: τὸ κοράσιον ἀλλὰ καθεύδει ... καὶ ἠγέρθη

Daniel 12:2 Th: πολλοὶ τῶν καθευδόντων ... ἐξεγερθήσονται

Forms of the verbs καθεύδω and ἐγείρω appear in each passage. The first verb, in both cases, is a metaphor for death, and also in both verses the sleep of death ends by an action of waking or rising up. Like the resuscitations in 1 Kings 17 and 2 Kings 4, and unlike the promise in Daniel 12, the girl's rising in Matthew 9 is not to a final state, so her body will die again. Jesus echoed the hope of Daniel 12:2 to demonstrate his power to

---

10. See Craig L. Blomberg, "Matthew," in *Commentary on the New Testament Use of the Old Testament*, ed. G. K. Beale and D. A. Carson (Grand Rapids: Baker Academic, 2007), 35.
11. "But if that was what he meant, and the girl really wasn't dead, why was this story singled out for preservation among many other healings of gravely ill people, and where is the basis for the pronouncement of 11:5 that 'the dead are being raised'? And, in any case, Matthew has not allowed even a hint of doubt about the girl's death from v. 18 on. So it seems that he, unlike the mourners, understood Jesus' words in a nonliteral sense" (France, *The Gospel of Matthew*, 364).
12. Wright says, "This hardly indicates a language-system in which 'sleep' is a regular and obvious metaphor for death, but it may well indicate, at least in the minds of those who told or heard the story, a hint of Daniel 12.2, where those who 'sleep' will be woken up" (*The Resurrection of the Son of God*, 404).
13. France, *The Gospel of Matthew*, 364.

rouse sleepers from death. What he did for the girl he will do for everyone in a lesser to greater sense.[14]

The destruction of both soul and body in hell (Matt 10:28). Jesus does not want his disciples to fear when persecution comes upon them. Knowing that they may incline toward the fear of man, he redirects their hearts to the fear of God: "And do not fear those who kill the body but cannot kill the soul. Rather fear him who can destroy both soul and body in hell" (Matt 10:28).

While bodily death may be terrible, Jesus says that something worse awaits those who do not fear God: the judgment of their bodies in hell. "Mortals can destroy only one's body, but God can resurrect the body for damnation and destroy the whole person."[15] If persecution leads to death—and thus the separation of soul from body occurs—then God's judgment on "soul and body in hell" implies a rejoining of soul and body, a reunion that happens at resurrection. France is right: "The 'one' who has the power to destroy in hell is of course God himself; there is no suggestion in biblical literature that the devil has the power of judgment, nor that God's people should fear him, nor is the devil referred to at all in this context."[16]

If the outcome for those who do not fear God is judgment on their bodies, then a resurrection of the wicked is implied.[17] "Matthew will have understood that one comes to this situation of judgment via resurrection."[18] Daniel 12:2 is the only Old Testament passage that predicts the resurrection of unbelievers unto judgment, so it is likely the background that facilitates the bodily judgment Jesus warns about.[19]

If unbelievers will not be raised, how could Jesus genuinely warn that bodies—as well as souls—will face God's wrath? According to Osborne,

---

14. As Turner puts it, "In light of Matthew's already/not-yet conception of the kingdom, the raising of the little girl points to the ultimate resurrection of the dead by Jesus' power" (David L. Turner, *Matthew*, BECNT [Grand Rapids: Baker Academic, 2008], 260).
15. Craig S. Keener, *A Commentary on the Gospel of Matthew* (Grand Rapids: Eerdmans, 1999), 326.
16. France, *The Gospel of Matthew*, 403.
17. See Harris, *Raised Immortal*, 174.
18. John Nolland, *The Gospel of Matthew*, NIGTC (Grand Rapids: Eerdmans, 2005), 437.
19. See Keener, *Revelation*, 467.

here in Matthew 10:28, "Jesus followed Daniel 12:2 regarding the resurrection of good and evil alike."[20]

The repentant rising to condemn the unrepentant (Matt 12:41-42). Some scribes and Pharisees asked Jesus for a sign, but he answered by calling them an evil and adulterous generation (Matt 12:38-39). He told them no sign would be given except the sign of Jonah, which meant—in Jesus's case—a descent into the earth and resurrection on the third day (12:39-40). Jesus did give the scribes and Pharisees a strong warning if they failed to repent of their wickedness.

> The men of Nineveh will rise up at the judgment with this generation and condemn it, for they repented at the preaching of Jonah, and behold, something greater than Jonah is here. The queen of the South will rise up at the judgment with this generation and condemn it, for she came from the ends of the earth to hear the wisdom of Solomon, and behold, something greater than Solomon is here. (Matt 12:41-42)

These verses from Matthew 12 envision the final judgment. A double resurrection is probably meant because the "men of Nineveh" (the repentant in this illustration) ἀναστήσονται ... μετὰ τῆς γενεᾶς ταύτης (the unrepentant).[21] The saints are vindicated in their condemnation of the wicked (Matt 12:41). Jesus is greater than Jonah and Solomon, so if people who hear him refuse to repent, then they will rise up to face judgment.

Daniel 12:2 says that at the resurrection, some will rise to life and others to shame, and this promise is the background to the event foretold in Matthew 12:41-42. Consistent with Daniel 12:2, Jesus says the repentant will *rise with* the unrepentant and be vindicated while the others are condemned. The verbs of resurrection are ἀνίστημι (Matt 12:41) and ἐγείρω (12:42). A form of the first verb appears in the OG of Daniel 12:2, and a form of the second appears in the Th. The Matthean verses probably reflect the Th rendering because two groups are in view, whereas the OG has three groups.[22]

The righteous who will shine like the sun (Matt 13:43). Matthew 13 is a chapter full of kingdom parables. As Jesus explains the parable of the weeds to his disciples, he said,

---

20. Osborne, "Resurrection," 676.
21. See Harris, *Raised Immortal*, 174; Nolland, *The Gospel of Matthew*, 512.
22. For a detailed analysis and comparison of the OG and Th against the MT, see chap. 2.

> Just as the weeds are gathered and burned with fire, so will it be at the end of the age. The Son of Man will send his angels, and they will gather out of his kingdom all causes of sin and all law-breakers, and throw them into the fiery furnace. In that place there will be weeping and gnashing of teeth. Then the righteous will shine like the sun in the kingdom of their Father. He who has ears, let him hear. (Matt 13:40-43)

Daniel 12:2 described a separation through resurrection, where some are raised for life, and others are raised for shame and contempt. Jesus's words in Matthew 13:40-43 also picture a separation. Unbelievers are gathered for judgment, and the righteous will shine in vindication. This state is the result of the event promised in Daniel 12:2 because the next verse—12:3—is alluded to in Jesus's words "the righteous will shine like the sun."[23] Daniel is told that "those who are wise will shine like the brightness of the sky above; and those who turn many to righteousness, like the stars forever and ever" (Dan 12:3). Jesus's use of that image is clear, and the righteous can only shine in this way after the resurrection of 12:2 has occurred. "It is not an exact reference, since in Daniel the reference is to stars, not to the sun. But it may form a hint, within the complex world of intertextual echo which Matthew certainly knew how to exploit, that the kingdom spoken of in the parables would fulfill, among other promises, that of resurrection."[24]

Since the wicked are gathered for burning with fire, their resurrection—also prophesied in Daniel 12:2—will have happened too. The image of destruction by fire (Matt 13:40, 42a) occurred earlier in Matthew (see 10:28 and 5:29-30, two passages that arguably allude to Dan 12:2 as well), so the bodily punishment of unbelievers is in view.

Jesus's phrase "the fiery furnace" (Matt 13:42) draws on the furnace of judgment in Daniel 3, the furnace that the prophet's three Hebrew friends escaped without the smell of smoke on them (Dan 3:26-27).[25]

---

23. See Wright, *The Resurrection of the Son of God*, 435; Steinmann, *Daniel*, 47; Schreiner, *The King in His Beauty*, 444; Fudge, *The Fire That Consumes*, 134; France, *The Gospel of Matthew*, 537; Grant R. Osborne, *Matthew*, ZECNT (Grand Rapids: Zondervan, 2010), 535; Turner, *Matthew*, 351.
24. Wright, *The Resurrection of the Son of God*, 435. See also Seow, *Daniel*, 189.
25. Greidanus says, "'The furnace of fire' ... seems to be a reference to Daniel 3:6" (Greidanus, *Preaching Christ from Daniel*, 95). See Nolland, *The Gospel of Matthew*, 561; Pennington, "Refractions of Daniel in the Gospel of Matthew," 69; Craig Evans, "Daniel in the New Testament: Visions of God's Kingdom," in *The Book of Daniel: Composition and Reception*, ed. John J. Collins and Peter

The furnace reference increases the probability that a Danielic background lies behind the punishment of the wicked and the shining of the righteous. The Th of Daniel 12:2-3 is the likely source, for the verb ἐκλάμψουσιν is common to both passages,[26] whereas the OG has φανοῦσιν. Both Daniel 12:3 and Matthew 13:43 use a plural of δίκαιος.[27]

The wicked thrown into eternal fire (Matt 18:8-9). Jesus warns of temptation. His followers should do what they can to mortify their impulses and weak links, no matter what part of the body the sin would involve. "And if your hand or your foot causes you to sin, cut it off and throw it away. It is better for you to enter life crippled or lame than with two hands or two feet to be thrown into the eternal fire. And if your eye causes you to sin, tear it out and throw it away. It is better for you to enter life with one eye than with two eyes to be thrown into the hell of fire" (Matt 18:8-9).

With language reminiscent of Matthew 5:29-30 (cf. also 10:28 for a threat of punishment in hell), Jesus explains the physical torment awaiting the wicked, so sin must be taken seriously. For the threat of eternal fire to be genuine, the implication is of a resurrection that will make unbelievers physically susceptible to its judgment,[28] and a resurrection for the unrighteous is promised in the Old Testament only in Daniel 12:2. Thus a Danielic background for Jesus's words is likely.[29]

The heavenly messenger tells Daniel that the wicked will face everlasting shame and contempt, and Jesus speaks about "eternal" fire (Matt 18:8). Jesus also talks about the righteous entering "life" (Matt 18:8-9), which is another way of saying what Daniel heard would come: there would be a resurrection of the righteous unto eternal life.

The destinies of eternal punishment or eternal life (Matt 25:46). During the Olivet Discourse Jesus describes the last judgment with words that reflect Daniel 12:2.[30]

W. Flint, with Cameron VanEpps, VTSup 83 (Leiden: Brill, 2001), 2:522; Jan Willem Van Henten, "Daniel 3 and 6 in Early Christian Literature," *The Book of Daniel*, ed. John J. Collins and Peter W. Flint, with Cameron VanEpps, VTSup 83 (Leiden: Brill, 2001), 1:154.

26. See France, *The Gospel of Matthew*, 537; Pennington, "Refractions of Daniel in the Gospel of Matthew," 78-79.
27. Nolland, *The Gospel of Matthew*, 561n119.
28. See Osborne, "Resurrection," 675; Osborne, *Matthew*, 939.
29. Rightly Nolland, Matt 18:8-9 also reflects Isa 66:24 (*The Gospel of Matthew*, 738).
30. See Steinmann, *Daniel*, 47; Nolland, *The Gospel of Matthew*, 1034; Michael J. Wilkins, *Matthew*, NIVAC (Grand Rapids: Zondervan, 2004), 812.

When the Son of Man comes in his glory, and all the angels with him, then he will sit on his glorious throne. Before him will be gathered all the nations, and he will separate people one from another as a shepherd separates the sheep from the goats. And he will place the sheep on his right, but the goats on the left. ... Then he will say to those on his left, "Depart from me, you cursed, into the eternal fire prepared for the devil and his angels." ... And these will go away into eternal punishment, but the righteous into eternal life. (Matt 25:31–33, 41, 46)

Two groups of people are in view, the righteous and the unrighteous. The former go into eternal life (εἰς ζωὴν αἰώνιον), the same phrase in the Th and OG of Daniel 12:2, and it accurately reflects the MT of the verse as well (לְחַיֵּי עוֹלָם). Since Daniel 12:2 is the first place to use the expression לְחַיֵּי עוֹלָם, it is most certainly the background to Matthew 25:46. Furthermore, the fate of the wicked is eternal in nature, though in contrast to the righteous they are punished in the "fire prepared for the devil and his angels" (25:41).

A resurrection of the wicked is also implied in Matthew 25:46. If the righteous, based on Daniel 12:2, are raised for "eternal life," then the gathering of the nations in Matthew 25:32 must be a picture of bodily resurrection. "Of course the details of the picture cannot be pressed, but the phrases ... more easily comport with the idea of judgment on resurrected persons than with judgment on disembodied spirits."[31]

The raised wicked then enter everlasting punishment, and the raised righteous enter everlasting life. Blomberg's words sum up the matter: "The departure of the people of the nations at the final judgment into eternal punishment or eternal life (25:46) builds on the conceptual background of the resurrection of just and unjust to everlasting life and everlasting contempt, respectively, in Dan. 12:2."[32]

Sleeping saints raised at the death of Jesus (Matt 27:52–53). Jesus breathed his last, and the curtain of the temple split in two (Matt 27:50–51). Accompanying this display of divine work was something unusual and

---

31. Harris, *Raised Immortal*, 174–75.
32. Blomberg, "Matthew," 90. See also Jonathan T. Pennington, *Heaven and Earth in the Gospel of Matthew* (Grand Rapids: Baker Academic, 2009), 288n38; Adela Yarbro Collins, "The Influence of Daniel on the NT," in John J. Collins, *Daniel: A Commentary on the Book of Daniel*, Hermeneia (Minneapolis: Fortress, 1993), 111; Keener, *Revelation*, 467; Pennington, "Refractions of Daniel in the Gospel of Matthew," 78, 85; Evans, "Daniel in the New Testament," 522–23.

that Matthew's Gospel alone reports: "The tombs also were opened. And many bodies of the saints who had fallen asleep were raised, and coming out of the tombs after his resurrection they went into the holy city and appeared to many" (27:52-53).[33]

Parallels between this passage and Daniel 12:2 are at least threefold. First, in both places a form of πολύς is used (cf. Matt 27:52b).[34] Second, the image of the dead as sleepers is present (cf. 27:52b), "and though Matthew uses a different word for 'sleep' from either the LXX or Theodotion, his description of 'many bodies of the saints that slept' is probably a deliberate allusion to the passage."[35] Third, a form of ἐγείρω appears (cf. 27:52b; Dan 12:2 Th).[36]

Though the saints raised in Matthew 27 did not have glorified bodies as they would at their future resurrection, their resuscitation relied on words and images found in Daniel 12:2 in order to bolster, partially fulfill, and advance that hope.[37] Matthew knows "that the church is still awaiting the final, complete general resurrection. ... In other words, he is not saying that this really was the great general resurrection; it was a strange semi-anticipation of it."[38]

---

33. For an exploration of Matthew 27:51-53 in terms of intertextuality and history of reception, see Charles L. Quarles, "Matthew 27:51-53: Meaning, Genre, Intertextuality, Theology, and Reception History," *JETS* 59, no. 2 (2016): 271-86.
34. Nolland rightly observes that "Dn. 12:2 is also likely to be responsible for Matthew's inclusion of 'many'" (*The Gospel of Matthew*, 1214-15).
35. Wright, *The Resurrection of the Son of God*, 633. See also Nolland, *The Gospel of Matthew*, 1214.
36. Pennington is right that "The reference in Matthew to many saints being raised and entering the holy city does relate in general to the resurrection promise of Dan. 12, but the lexical connections are minimal" ("Refractions of Daniel in the Gospel of Matthew," 85n56).
37. See Blomberg, "Matthew," 98; Quarles, "Matthew 27:51-53," 281. Some scholars, like Nolland, suggest that we should "imagine them translated to heaven as were Enoch and Elijah" (*The Gospel of Matthew*, 1217). However, the biblical text never reports such translation.
38. Wright, *The Resurrection of the Son of God*, 635. This is contra Licona's argument that the event reported in Matt 27:52-53 is not even historical but "'special effects' with eschatological Jewish texts and thought in mind" and that it is most plausibly "a poetic device added to communicate that the Son of God had died and that impending judgment awaited Israel" (Michael R. Licona, *The Resurrection of Jesus: A New Historiographical Approach* [Downers Grove, IL: IVP Academic, 2010], 552-53). Hagner is of the same view as Licona, arguing that "the rising of the saints from the tombs in this passage is a piece of theology set forth as history. ... We must thus regard the passage as a piece of realized and

MARK

In the Second Gospel, the two passages I will address have Matthean parallels that were analyzed above, but the Markan verses will be treated here in order to note anything unique about them and to discern if further Danielic echoes come through.

The girl not dead but sleeping (Mark 5:39-41). Reflecting the ideas in Daniel 12:2 about dead people "sleeping" and waking up as "resurrection," Jesus's healing of a dead girl is a foretaste of what awaits everyone.

> They came to the house of the ruler of the synagogue, and Jesus saw a commotion, people weeping and wailing loudly. And when he had entered, he said to them, "Why are you making a commotion and weeping? The child is not dead but sleeping.". ... Taking her by the hand he said to her, "Talitha cumi," which means, "Little girl, I say to you, arise." And immediately the girl got up and began walking. (Mark 5:38-39, 41-42)

Jesus refers to the child as only sleeping, not because she was merely unconscious but because her death was temporary, like a brief rest followed by waking up. Matthew does not record Jesus's words to the girl as Mark does: "Little girl, I say to you, arise [ἔγειρε]" (Mark 5:41). This episode shows how Daniel 12:2 will be accomplished: God will command those who sleep in the dust to arise. The dead girl's body obeys the voice of Jesus and gets up (ἀνέστη τὸ κοράσιον, Mark 5:42). This girl was a sleeper who woke from the dead by the power of God, and one day all sleepers will rise up in obedience as well.

The wicked thrown into eternal fire (Mark 9:43-48). Parallel to the Matthean account, Mark records Jesus's words about fighting against sin with radical determination so as to avoid eternal judgment.

> And if your hand causes you to sin, cut it off. It is better for you to enter life crippled than with two hands to go to hell, to the unquenchable fire. And if your foot causes you to sin, cut it off. It is better for you to enter life lame than with two feet to be thrown into hell. And if your eye causes you to sin, tear it out. It is better for you to enter the kingdom of God with one eye than with two eyes to be thrown into hell, where their worm does not die and the fire is not quenched. (Mark 9:43-48)

---

historicized apocalyptic depending on OT motifs found in such passages as Isa 26:19; Dan 12:2; and especially Ezek 37:12-14" (Hagner, *Matthew 14-28*, 851).

According to Jesus, people will enter into either life or judgment, which is consistent with Daniel 12:2. Eternal states are meant: the fire for the wicked is unquenchable and eternal, and by implication the life for the righteous is everlasting. Daniel 12:2 is likely the background for the bodily destruction promised by Jesus in Mark 9:43-47 (the wicked enter hell hands, feet, eyes, and all), a kind of destruction only possible if the bodies of the unrighteous dead have been raised.[39]

LUKE

In the Third Gospel we can discern the (implicit) presence of Daniel 12:2 in at least three passages, two of which have parallels in Matthew and/or Mark.

The girl not dead but sleeping (Luke 8:52-55). As in the Matthean and Markan parallels (see the corresponding sections above), Jesus enters the home of a ruler whose daughter has died. The presence of weeping and mourning at the home confirms that the child was not merely unconscious. Jesus said to them, "Do not weep, for she is not dead but sleeping" (Luke 8:52). They laughed at him, knowing she was dead, but he took her by the hand and said, "Child, arise" (8:53-54). Her spirit returned, and she got up immediately (8:55).

In Daniel 12:2 the dead are described metaphorically as sleeping, and that is how Jesus describes the girl in Luke 8:52. The verb in both verses is from καθεύδω. The girl "woke" by resuscitation, and the dead will wake up by resurrection. As in the Markan account, Jesus commands the girl to rise, and in the original language, both Luke 8:54 and Mark 5:41 use the imperative ἔγειρε.

The first two Gospels note her instant recovery, but only Luke includes the statement καὶ ἐπέστρεψεν τὸ πνεῦμα αὐτῆς (8:55a). Disembodiment occurs at death, so the return of the girl's spirit confirms her restoration to life.

The repentant rising to condemn the unrepentant (Luke 11:31-32). Luke 11 reports the same event as Matthew 12—the repentant will rise with the unrepentant to condemn them at the final judgment. The Matthean account has the "men of Nineveh" before the "queen of the South" (Matt 12:41-42), while Luke's order is the reverse.

---

39. See Osborne, "Resurrection," 675.

> The queen of the South will rise up at the judgment with the men of this generation and condemn them, for she came from the ends of the earth to hear the wisdom of Solomon, and behold, something greater than Solomon is here. The men of Nineveh will rise up at the judgment with this generation and condemn it, for they repented at the preaching of Jonah, and behold, something greater than Jonah is here. (Luke 11:31-32)

Like the Th of Daniel 12:2, Luke 11:31-32 concerns two groups (not three, as the LXX has), the righteous and the wicked, who will be raised from the dead, the former for vindication and the latter for judgment. Jesus's words are about the resurrection and judgment of all.[40] "For the New Testament the fact of a 'last judgment' presupposes a resurrection of saved and lost."[41]

The resurrection of the just (Luke 14:14). At a dinner Jesus encouraged the guests to not throw a banquet with their own family or wealthy friends in mind (Luke 14:12). Instead, "when you give a feast, invite the poor, the crippled, the lame, the blind, and you will be blessed, because they cannot repay you. For you will be repaid at the resurrection of the just" (14:13-14).

Daniel 12:2 is probably the source for the notion of the "just" being raised for reward. The prophet hears that the righteous will receive "life" (12:2), will shine like the bright sky and like the stars (12:3), and—at least for him in particular—will receive an inheritance (12:13). Cumulatively these notions comprise the "reward" that the just can anticipate at their resurrection. Jesus hopes a belief in resurrection will compel his listeners to be lavish and generous without the thought of earthly recompense, and if they will intentionally bless those who could never repay them, then they will be content to receive their reward when they are raised.

JOHN

The Fourth Gospel in at least three places shows an influence of Daniel 12:2. Wright's words should be heeded: "Resurrection in John continues

---

40. Darrell L. Bock, *Luke 9:51-24:53*, BECNT (Grand Rapids: Baker Books, 1996), 1267n14.
41. E. Earle Ellis, *The Gospel of Luke* (Grand Rapids: Eerdmans, 1983; Repr. Eugene, OR: Wipf and Stock, 2003), 194. See also I. Howard Marshall, *The Gospel of Luke*, NIGTC (Grand Rapids: Eerdmans, 1978), 486; Robert H. Stein, *Luke*, NAC, vol. 24 (Nashville: Broadman, 1992), 335.

to be both present and future, and we should resist attempts to flatten this out by marginalizing the 'future' emphasis or overemphasizing the 'realized eschatology.'"[42]

The one who passes from death to eternal life (John 5:24). After Jesus healed a man on the Sabbath (John 5:9), he explained to the Jews his divine prerogative to do so (5:17-18). He told them that the Father shows him everything and will show even greater works. In the present, the Son gives life to whomever he will: "Truly, truly, I say to you, whoever hears my word and believes him who sent me has eternal life. He does not come into judgment, but has passed from death to life" (5:24).

Those who believe in Jesus are raised in an inaugurated sense *spiritually* ("has passed from death to life"). Eternal life (foretold in Dan 12:2) belongs to the sinner who "hears my word and believes him who sent me" (John 5:24). It is likely that Daniel 12:2 lies in the background here,[43] with the "eternal life" belonging to believers who now will not meet "judgment" on the Last Day. They have awakened from sleep spiritually, though this does not exhaust the meaning of Daniel 12:2 (which promised bodily resurrection).

The resurrection of some to life and others to judgment (John 5:29). One of the greater works the Son will perform (cf. John 5:20) will be the resurrection of the dead, for all dead bodies will respond to the voice of the Son.

> Truly, truly, I say to you, an hour is coming, and is now here, when the dead will hear the voice of the Son of God, and those who hear will live. For as the Father has life in himself, so he has granted the Son also to have life in himself. And he has given him authority to execute judgment, because he is the Son of Man. Do not marvel at this, for an hour is coming when all who are in the tombs will hear his voice and come out, those who have done good to the resurrection of life, and those who have done evil to the resurrection of judgment. (John 5:25-29)

The final two verses, John 5:28-29, allude to Daniel 12:2 in at least five ways. First, two groups are referred to ("those ... and those"). Second, these groups are dead ("all who are in the tombs"). Third, the identities of the groups contrast like day and night ("those who have done

---

42. Wright, *The Resurrection of the Son of God*, 441.
43. The NA[28], in contrast to the NA[27], lists John 5:24 as a verse that alludes to Dan 12:2.

good" and "those who have done evil"). Fourth, the event of resurrection is mentioned for both groups.[44] Fifth, the fates of both groups are consistent with Daniel 12:2 ("to the resurrection of life" and "to the resurrection of judgment"). An allusion to Daniel 12:2 is certain.[45] In fact, "So close is the resemblance with Dan. 12.1-2, that one could even argue the plausibility of a quotation."[46]

When Jesus says that an hour "is now here, when the dead will hear the voice of the Son of God, and those who hear will live" (John 5:25), he means the promise of resurrection is being, in part, realized *spiritually*. Those in Christ are alive now since they have been raised from deadness of their sin, and they will know life to the fullest at their bodily resurrection from the dead. In an important sense, Daniel 12:2 is beginning to come true by the power of Jesus.[47]

The resurrection on the last day (John 11:24). Lazarus died, just as Jesus intended (John 11:6, 14-15). Lazarus's sister Martha told Jesus, "Lord, if you had been here, my brother would not have died. But even now I know that whatever you ask from God, God will give you" (11:21-22). The next piece of dialogue between Jesus and Martha recalls Daniel 12:2. Jesus told her, "Your brother will rise again" (11:23), and she agreed, saying, "I know that he will rise again in the resurrection on the last day" (11:24).

Martha's words denote the end-time resurrection in which Lazarus would participate. She refers to "the resurrection on the last day,"

---

44. Aune says John 5:29 teaches the resurrection of the righteous and the wicked (David E. Aune, *Revelation 17-22*, WBC, vol. 52C [Nashville: Thomas Nelson, 1998], 1091).
45. See Andreas J. Köstenberger, "John," in *Commentary on the New Testament Use of the Old Testament*, ed. G. K. Beale and D. A. Carson (Grand Rapids: Baker Academic, 2007), 442; Forestell, "Christian Revelation and the Resurrection of the Wicked," 183; Greidanus, *Preaching Christ from Daniel*, 389; Steinmann, *Daniel*, 47; Mihalios, *The Danielic Eschatological Hour*, 119-22; Fudge, *The Fire That Consumes*, 165; Beale, *A New Testament Biblical Theology*, 132-33; Andrew T. Lincoln, *The Gospel According to Saint John*, BNTC, vol. 4 (Peabody, MA: Hendrickson, 2005), 205; J. Ramsey Michaels, *The Gospel of John*, NICNT (Grand Rapids: Eerdmans, 2010), 322n74; Philip Edgcumbe Hughes, "The First Resurrection: Another Interpretation," *WTJ* 39, no. 2 (1977): 316.
46. Mihalios, *The Danielic Eschatological Hour*, 120.
47. Beale, *A New Testament Biblical Theology*, 235. As he says elsewhere, "John 5:24-29 sees the resurrection of the saints predicted in Dan. 12:2 as being inaugurated in Jesus' ministry" (*The Book of Revelation*, NIGTC [Grand Rapids: Eerdmans, 1998], 434).

something anticipated in Daniel 12:2.[48] Her faith has been shaped by that verse because she expressed confidence that Lazarus, though dead, would not remain so. And like his words in John 5, Jesus's power is already raising people from the dead spiritually. Those in Christ live now, *and* they will live later, which is why Jesus can claim this title: "I am the resurrection and the life. Whoever believes in me, though he die, yet shall he live, and everyone who lives and believes in me shall never die" (John 11:25-26). And when Jesus called Lazarus from the tomb, it was a "narrative embodiment" of his words earlier in 5:28-29—in other words, this sign anticipates the final resurrection.[49]

ACTS

The apostles in Acts announced that Jesus rose bodily from the dead (cf., e.g., Acts 2:24; 3:15; 4:10; 5:30; 10:41; 13:30; 17:31). Jesus inaugurated the new-creation existence in store for God's people. On at least four occasions someone talked about the future judgment and/or resurrection in ways consistent with and reflecting Daniel 12:2. In the house of Cornelius, in the city of Athens, before the Sanhedrin, and before Felix in Caesarea, Peter and Paul promised the deliverance of God's people and the judgment of the wicked. Their statements show dependence on Daniel 12:2.

The one appointed to judge the living and the dead (Acts 10:42). After God gave Peter a vision, Peter went to the house of Cornelius and heard that man's vision from God as well (Acts 10:23-33). This prompted Peter to announce God's impartiality: "In every nation anyone who fears him and does what is right is acceptable to him" (10:35). And what Jesus did, he did for the nations (10:36-38). Peter added,

> And we are witnesses of all that he did both in the country of the Jews and in Jerusalem. They put him to death by hanging him on a tree, but God raised him on the third day and made him to appear. ... And he commanded us to preach to the people and to

---

48. Schreiner says, "The resurrection, as Martha clearly understands, is an eschatological event (11:24). Martha's understanding accords with the OT, for Daniel locates the resurrection (12:2) at 'the time of the end' (12:9)" (*The King in His Beauty*, 518).
49. Andrew T. Lincoln, "'I Am the Resurrection and the Life': The Resurrection Message of the Fourth Gospel," in *Life in the Face of Death: The Resurrection Message of the New Testament*, ed. Richard N. Longenecker (Grand Rapids: Eerdmans, 1998), 141.

testify that he is the one appointed by God to be judge of the living and the dead. (Acts 10:39-40, 42)

Jesus is the judge, and he is the judge of everyone ("the living and the dead") (cf. John 5:22 where the Father "has given all judgment to the Son"). The notion that dead people will be judged with the living implies bodily resurrection, and since "the living and the dead" is a general statement not specifying the righteous or the wicked, the resurrection of unbelievers is included.

As the one already raised and thus Lord of all, Jesus will judge both believers and unbelievers (cf. John 5:28-29). An implied resurrection of the righteous and wicked, and their comprehensive judgment, reflects chiefly the Old Testament expression of resurrection and judgment in Daniel 12:2. Peter believed that passage, proclaimed in the house of Cornelius that God would accomplish it, and explained that the risen Jesus was God's appointed judge for those activities.

A day for judgment of the world (Acts 17:31). Paul walked the streets of Athens and was outraged at the pervasive idolatry (Acts 17:16). At the Areopagus he confronted his listeners with the message of the true Creator who made everything (17:24-28). He then explained that they are accountable to the one and only God. God overlooked the times of ignorance, "but now he commands all people everywhere to repent, because he has fixed a day on which he will judge the world in righteousness by a man whom he has appointed; and of this he has given assurance to all by raising him from the dead" (17:30-31).

As the man God appointed and as the one God raised from the dead, Jesus is the world's judge. If the whole world will be judged "in righteousness" (Acts 17:31), then final judgment does not occur even when someone dies. Paul is referring to a future judgment when everyone will be called to account before the God-appointed Judge of Righteousness, the risen Jesus. By implication, then, the righteous and the wicked will be raised to meet the world's true Lord.

With the one whom God appointed as the end-time judge—Jesus—the resurrection has already begun because God raised him from the dead (Acts 17:31). This "man" who will be the world's judge is from the book of Daniel—the "one like a son of man" (Dan 7:13).[50] And one day the living and the dead will face him, themselves raised by his power.

---

50. F. F. Bruce, *The Book of Acts*, rev. ed., NICNT (Grand Rapids: Eerdmans, 1988), 341.

An appointed time for judgment, with implied states of resurrection for the righteous and wicked, is likely based on Daniel 12:2. Paul preached his message of repentance (cf. Acts 17:30) because no one will escape that Day or the Man whom God appointed as judge. Peterson says,

> The resurrection of the dead was no more believable in that context than it is for many in our so-called scientific age. The very idea made some of his audience sneer (v. 32)! Yet, if the resurrection of Jesus took place, it challenges human scepticism about the possibility of encountering God and being judged by him. It is the best proof we have of a general resurrection and makes Jesus the key figure in God's plans for humanity.[51]

The hope and resurrection of the dead (Acts 23:6). After Paul travels to Jerusalem in Acts 21, subsequent chapters narrate his hearings before different rulers. In Acts 23, Paul stands before the Sanhedrin in Jerusalem, in the presence of both Sadducees and Pharisees, so he knows how to divide the room. "Brothers, I am a Pharisee, a son of Pharisees. It is with respect to the hope and the resurrection of the dead that I am on trial" (Acts 23:6). His plan to divide the listeners succeeds (23:7), for Sadducees denied a future bodily resurrection (23:8).

Where was this "hope and the resurrection of the dead" based? Paul does not specify a resurrection of the righteous, so likely his statement ("hope and the resurrection of the dead") includes both righteous and unrighteous—which reflects the teaching of Daniel 12:2. The "resurrection of the dead" is probably epexegetical, explaining what the "hope" is.

Based on Daniel 12:2, believers have a hope that they will be raised to life and for vindication, while unbelievers will be condemned and shamed at the final judgment. As will shortly be discovered, Paul is on trial for preaching that God raised Jesus from the dead (cf. Acts 25:19; 26:8, 22–23), which is another way of saying the promise of Daniel 12:2 has been brought into human history and fulfilled by Jesus in the same way first fruits guarantee a future ingathering.

A resurrection of both the just and unjust (Acts 24:15). Paul stood before Felix at Caesarea and in his defense made clearer what he meant by "hope and the resurrection of the dead," spoken earlier to the Sanhedrin in Acts 23:6. After Governor Felix motioned for Paul to speak, the apostle insisted on his blameless activity in the temple and

---

51. David G. Peterson, *The Acts of the Apostles*, PNTC (Grand Rapids: Eerdmans, 2009), 503.

synagogues (23:11-12), asserting that the witnesses speaking against him could not prove their accusations (24:13). "But this I confess to you, that according to the Way, which they call a sect, I worship the God of our fathers, believing everything laid down by the Law and written in the Prophets, having a hope in God, which these men themselves accept, that there will be a resurrection of both the just and the unjust" (24:14-15).

The "hope and the resurrection of the dead" (Acts 23:6) is the "hope in God ... that there will be a resurrection of both the just and the unjust" (24:15). This confirms the influence of Daniel 12:2 on Luke's presentation of Paul's thoughts.[52] His words to Felix reflect a resurrection of two different and opposite groups. Such resurrection is a "hope" even if it involves the unjust being raised for judgment, because the righteous will be vindicated as God keeps his promises to his people. Paul's words may be based on the Th of Daniel 12:2-3 in particular, for after the resurrection in 12:2 is a mention of δικαίων, which Paul uses in Acts 24:15.[53]

SUMMARY

Daniel 12:2 influenced the authors of the four Gospels and the book of Acts. Each one contains passages that allude to or echo the fullest Old Testament expression of bodily resurrection. In some cases only the righteous or the wicked are in view, but in other places both groups are mentioned. When their respective fates are described, they are permanent and physical. The raised righteous will be vindicated, and the raised wicked will be condemned. The future resurrection of the dead should cause disciples to reject sinful pursuits and to walk in holiness. Most interesting is the fact that Jesus's power is already raising sinners from the dead spiritually, a miraculous work that indicates the partial fulfillment of Daniel 12:2. As the apostles proclaimed the risen Jesus around Jerusalem and beyond, Peter and Paul both warned of God's future worldwide judgment, a day on which Jesus would preside in righteousness over believers and unbelievers. This day would bring the living and the dead to account, which implied the resurrection of their

---

52. See Steinmann, *Daniel*, 47; Joseph A. Fitzmyer, *The Acts of the Apostles*, AB, vol. 31 (New Haven, CT: Yale University Press, 1998), 736.
53. I. Howard Marshall, "Acts," in *Commentary on the New Testament Use of the Old Testament*, ed. G. K. Beale and D. A. Carson (Grand Rapids: Baker Academic, 2007), 598.

bodies. Paul, in at least a couple places, expressed the "hope" of resurrection, a hope he said included the just *and* the unjust being raised.

THE EPISTLES AND REVELATION

Having discerned the influence of Daniel 12:2 in the four Gospels and the book of Acts, we now come to the Epistles and the book of Revelation. Out of twenty-one New Testament letters, the following sections will argue that seventeen passages from eleven letters (Romans, 1 Corinthians, 2 Corinthians, Galatians, Ephesians, Philippians, 1 Thessalonians, 2 Thessalonians, 2 Timothy, Hebrews, and 1 Peter) have a subtle or overt dependence on Daniel 12:2. The book of Revelation alludes constantly to the Old Testament, especially to the book of Daniel. Our New Testament study will conclude by discussing one place where Revelation uses Daniel 12:2.

ROMANS

In Paul's magisterial letter to the Romans, he expounds the glory of the gospel against the backdrop of human depravity, exalting God's power to justify sinners and deliver them from unrighteousness. He also discusses the past resurrection of Jesus and the future resurrection of believers. At least two passages bear the marks of Daniel 12:2.

The judgment according to works (Rom 2:5–10). In Romans 1:18–3:20 Paul is indicting Jews and gentiles with lawlessness and idolatry. On judgment day God will not show partiality to anyone based on ethnicity or background. Rather, to those who do evil God will show unrestrained wrath, and to those who obey him he will confirm the verdict of "no condemnation" announced at their initial justification. No one will escape the judgment of God, so those who presume on God's grace should instead let his kindness lead them to repentance (2:3–4).

> But because of your hard and impenitent heart you are storing up wrath for yourself on the day of wrath when God's righteous judgment will be revealed. He will render to each one according to his works: to those who by patience in well-doing seek for glory and honor and immortality, he will give eternal life; but for those who are self-seeking and do not obey the truth, but obey unrighteousness, there will be wrath and fury. There will be tribulation and distress for every human being who does evil, the Jew first

and also the Greek, but glory and honor and peace for everyone who does good, the Jew first and also the Greek. (Rom 2:5-10)

Paul envisions two categories of people who meet contrasting outcomes. The righteous will receive "eternal life" (ζωὴν αἰώνιον, Rom 2:7), a phrase that appears in the Old Testament only in Daniel 12:2 (both OG and Th). But for the unrighteous there will be wrath (Rom 2:8).[54] Then, moving chiastically, Paul addresses the unrighteous again and then the righteous: evildoers will have tribulation and distress (2:9), but those who do good will have glory, honor, and peace (2:10).

The judgment according to works spoken about in Romans 2:5-10 is consistent with and rooted in the theology expressed in Daniel 12:2. In Romans 2, Paul is promising a future event ("the day of wrath when God's righteous judgment will be revealed," 2:5) that is universal in scope (for doers of good and doers of evil, together, are comprehensive categories), takes into account whether one obeys God or not (2:7-8), and results in a permanent state (2:7-8). More so than any other Old Testament verse, Daniel 12:2 is behind Paul's teaching here.

Paul's words in Romans 2:5-10 are reminiscent of Jesus's words in John 5:29, when he told his disciples that everyone would be raised: "those who have done good to the resurrection of life, and those who have done evil to the resurrection of judgment." These statements about a double resurrection to contrasting destinies depended on Daniel 12:2.

Jesus and Paul, therefore, spoke about a final judgment according to works. Jesus talked about "those who have done good" (John 5:29), while Paul described them as "those who by patience in well-doing seek for glory and honor and immortality" and as "everyone who does good" (Rom 2:7, 10). Jesus spoke about "those who have done evil" (John 5:29), while Paul described them as "those who are self-seeking and do not obey the truth" and as "every human being who does evil" (Rom 2:8-9).

When Paul says that God renders all of this "to each one according to his works," the implication is that this recompense follows the resurrection of those who do good and those who do evil. Before God on the last day, the righteous will rise for life, and the unrighteous will rise for

---

54. Harris says that Rom 2:8 is an example of Paul's belief in a resurrection resulting in condemnation (Murray J. Harris, "Resurrection and Immortality in the Pauline Corpus," in *Life in the Face of Death: The Resurrection Message of the New Testament*, ed. Richard N. Longenecker [Grand Rapids: Eerdmans, 1998], 151).

judgment. These notions are grounded in the hope held out in Daniel 12:2.

Everyone to stand before the judgment seat (Rom 14:10). Paul instructs his readers that they should not pass judgment on each other in matters of eating (Rom 14:3-4) or in ascribing importance to certain days (14:5-6). Everyone should seek to honor the Lord because believers live not to themselves but to him anyway (14:7-9). So two pointed rhetorical questions must be asked: "Why do you pass judgment on your brother? Or you, why do you despise your brother?" (14:10). Paul explains the serious tenor of those questions: "For we will all stand before the judgment seat of God; for it is written, 'As I live, says the Lord, every knee shall bow to me, and every tongue shall confess to God.' So then each of us will give an account of himself to God" (14:10-12).

To "stand" may picture resurrection.[55] In Romans 14:10 *all* will stand before God's judgment seat, which indicates a universal resurrection. The scope is comprehensive because Paul cites Isaiah 45:23 to ground his claim that all will stand before God's judgment seat and that Isaianic hope extended to unbelievers: one day everyone would confess God as God, and every knee would bend in allegiance. This promise of a universal gathering at God's judgment seat—a gathering that implies resurrection no less—is a mighty stream flowing from the river of Daniel 12:2. Jesus is "Lord both of the dead and of the living" (Rom 14:9), and all will appear before his judgment seat.

1 CORINTHIANS

In Paul's first (canonical) letter to the Corinthians, he covers a myriad of subjects, and the penultimate one is the future resurrection. In at least three places Paul's words are shaped by the ideas and words of Daniel 12:2.

The greater glory belonging to raised bodies (1 Cor 15:40-41). To the questions, "How are the dead raised? With what kind of body do they come?" the apostle Paul speaks about how God gives a body to what is sown, and each kind of seed has its own body (1 Cor 15:37-38). Humans

---

55. Wright reasons, "The language of 'standing,' cognate with 'standing up,' *anastasis*, and the emphasis that the master/lord has the *power* to 'make him stand,' should almost certainly be taken as at least a sidelong reference to resurrection. At the last judgment, all must give an account of themselves, and the lord will 'make to stand,' in other words, raise from the dead" (*The Resurrection of the Son of God*, 265).

have one kind of flesh, animals another, birds another, and fish another still (15:39). Furthermore,

> There are heavenly bodies and earthly bodies, but the glory of the heavenly is of one kind, and the glory of the earthly is of another. There is one glory of the sun, and another glory of the moon, and another glory of the stars; for star differs from star in glory. So is it with the resurrection of the dead. What is sown is perishable; what is raised is imperishable. It is sown in dishonor; it is raised in glory. It is sown in weakness; it is raised in power. (1 Cor 15:40-43)

According to Paul, the heavenly bodily dwelling is more glorious than the earthly dwelling that dies. The death of the body is like a seed sown, and the resurrection brings forth an imperishable physicality. Daniel 12 is behind the theology of the resurrection here,[56] for Paul is talking about bodies being raised to a state of glory, and Daniel is told that the righteous will be raised "to everlasting life" and "shall shine like the brightness of the sky above" and "the stars forever and ever" (12:2-3). Hays observes, "In Daniel, as in Paul's teaching, there is no thought that the risen righteous ones actually *become* stars; rather, the metaphor is used to suggest something about the glorious state they will enjoy when they rise from the dead."[57]

Since Paul is talking about the glorious existence of the future bodies in store for the righteous, he is not referring to the wicked being raised as well. This does not mean Paul denies a future resurrection of unbelievers (cf. Acts 24:15). Instead, he is answering the questions he posed in 1 Corinthians 15:35, and his answer pertains only to the righteous in this case.

Sown in dishonor, raised in glory (1 Cor 15:43a). When Paul uses the phrase "sown in dishonor ... raised in glory" (1 Cor 15:43a), he is probably appropriating language from the pseudepigraphal Testament of Benjamin, which says at one point, "Then all shall be changed, some destined for glory, others for dishonor" (10:8).[58]

In the intertestamental text, the "some destined for glory" are believers, and the "others for dishonor" are unbelievers. Paul, though, uses

---

56. Richard B. Hays, *First Corinthians*, Interpretation (Louisville: John Knox, 1997), 271. See Wright, *The Resurrection of the Son of God*, 344.
57. Hays, *First Corinthians*, 271. See David E. Garland, *1 Corinthians*, BECNT (Grand Rapids: Baker Academic, 2003), 731-32.
58. See chap. 4 for analysis of T. Benj. 10:8.

both phrases for believers in order to put on display the discontinuity between the body that is sown at death and raised at resurrection. The "dishonor" in that case denotes the body's natural and perishable state (1 Cor 15:43b–44), in contrast to its glorious and powerful existence that resurrection brings to pass. Paul's use of language from the Testament of Benjamin 10:8 is significant because that text depended on Daniel 12:2.[59] Put plainly, Daniel 12:2 influenced 1 Corinthians 15:43a via the Testament of Benjamin 10:8. Thus the connection is more indirect than direct.

Not everyone a sleeper (1 Cor 15:51b). When the perishable puts on the imperishable, not everyone will be already dead. "Behold! I tell you a mystery. We shall not all sleep, but we shall all be changed, in a moment, in the twinkling of an eye, at the last trumpet. For the trumpet will sound, and the dead will be raised imperishable, and we shall be changed" (1 Cor 15:51–52).

The verb "sleep" in 1 Corinthians 15:51b is from κοιμάω. Even though the OG and Th of Daniel 12:2 use καθεύδω, it is still the case that both verses use sleep as a metaphor for death. And the only Old Testament text that explicitly says sleepers will wake up from death is Daniel 12:2.[60] The context of Paul's words also emphasizes that Adam was "from the earth" and "a man of dust," phrases that recall Genesis 2:7 and 3:19 but may also take Daniel 12:2 into account, for it too speaks of "dust" and "earth."

SECOND CORINTHIANS

In Paul's second (canonical) letter to the Corinthians, he once again talks about the future bodily resurrection. In 2 Corinthians 4–5 there are two passages which may be based on what Daniel 12:2 teaches.

The weight of glory beyond comparison (2 Cor 4:17–18). Paul is realistic about the suffering he and other believers face. They are afflicted but not crushed, perplexed but not in despair, persecuted but not abandoned, struck down but not destroyed (2 Cor 4:8–9). Suffering may lead to their death, but God has planned something better: a weight of glory that more than compensates for their earthly distresses.

---

59. Elledge argues that the words "some unto glory and some unto shame" in T. Benj. 10:8 are "an almost formulaic statement that may reflect the influence of Dan 12:1–3" ("The Resurrection Passages in the *Testaments of the Twelve Patriarchs*," 91).

60. Isaiah 26:19 says, "You who dwell in the dust, awake and sing for joy!" But a metaphor for "sleep = death" is implied, not explicitly stated.

> So we do not lose heart. Though our outer self is wasting away, our inner self is being renewed day by day. For this light momentary affliction is preparing for us an eternal weight of glory beyond all comparison, as we look not to the things that are seen but to the things that are unseen. For the things that are seen are transient, but the things that are unseen are eternal. (2 Cor 4:16–18)

The outer self—the body—is wasting away and will die. Compared to eternity, the affliction is "momentary," and compared to the weight of the glory that lies ahead, the affliction is "light." The next passage, 2 Corinthians 5:1–10, elaborates on the weight of glory in store for the saints: a resurrected body, a "building from God, a house not made with hands" (5:1), a "heavenly dwelling" (5:2).

Resurrection hope spurs Paul's faithfulness (2 Cor 4:16). God's inward work continues daily, and at the resurrection the bodily renewal will happen as well (4:16–18). This hope is "eternal" (4:17, 18). Daniel 12:2 was also meant to stir the devotion and capture the allegiance of its readers. The promise was for "eternal" life, a glory that outweighed the suffering that was endured, for the righteous will shine like the stars forever (12:3). The resurrection hope in 2 Corinthians 4:17–18 is probably based on the Old Testament promise expressed in Daniel 12:2.

Receiving what is due for deeds in the body (2 Cor 5:10). After extolling the glory of the saints' bodily resurrection (2 Cor 5:1–4), Paul says that in the meantime Christians have the Spirit as a guarantee of this hope, they are at home in the body for now, they walk by faith, and they aim to please the Lord (5:5–9). How people live in the body matters. "For we must all appear before the judgment seat of Christ, so that each one may receive what is due for what he has done in the body, whether good or evil" (5:10).

Reiterating the truth of the Old Testament—which was carried forward in intertestamental literature—Paul reminds his readers that a day of judgment is coming. Everyone will appear before Christ. Given the preceding context of 2 Corinthians 5:10, this appearance at the judgment seat is in resurrected bodies. And "we all" probably extends beyond believers, for he ends the verse talking about "evil" done in the body.[61] Furthermore, in 5:11 he says, "Therefore, knowing the fear of

---

61. See Ben Witherington III, *The Acts of the Apostles: A Socio-Rhetorical Commentary* (Grand Rapids: Eerdmans, 1997), 711; Beale, *A New Testament Biblical Theology*, 273.

the Lord, we persuade others." Knowing that everyone—believers and unbelievers—will appear before Christ should fill God's people with a proper reverence of the Lord and with an evangelistic urgency toward the wicked.

Paul's words in 2 Corinthians 5:10 are about the judgment awaiting believers and unbelievers when they will all stand before Christ in resurrected bodies.[62] A universal resurrection reflects Daniel 12:2. What Paul envisions is akin to Jesus's pronouncement that before the Son of Man "will be gathered all the nations, and he will separate people one from another as a shepherd separates the sheep from the goats. And he will place the sheep on his right, but the goats on the left" (Matt 25:32-33). The scene is the final judgment. The sleepers have awakened and will enter their final states.

Reinforcing a connection back to Daniel 12:2 are Paul's words that "each one may receive what is due for what he has done in the body" (2 Cor 5:10). This promise implies a bodily reward or retribution. In Daniel 12:2-3 the dead are raised bodily and receive reward or shame, life or contempt. Paul has two different groups in mind—the righteous and the wicked—because the final phrase is "whether good or evil," referring to the lives people lived in their bodies. "Both must be resurrected to receive their due in bodily form for what they had committed in their physical bodies."[63] This is reminiscent of John 5:29 (also shaped by Daniel 12:2), where Jesus said that all who are in the tombs will come out, "those who have done good to the resurrection of life, and those who have done evil to the resurrection of judgment."

GALATIANS

The book of Galatians may be Paul's earliest letter. He mentions resurrection with regard to what the Father did for Jesus (Gal 1:1), and the life of the believer is crucified and now united to this risen Christ (2:20). There is no overt mention of future resurrection for believers or unbelievers, but the theology of Daniel 12:2 may be at work in at least one verse.

---

62. Aune says 2 Cor 5:10 is a verse foretelling the resurrection of the righteous and the wicked (*Revelation 17-22*, 1091).
63. Beale, *A New Testament Biblical Theology*, 273.

Reaping corruption or eternal life (Gal 6:8). In the last chapter of Galatians Paul does not want his readers to be deceived about the unbreakable spiritual law of sowing and reaping.

> Do not be deceived: God is not mocked, for whatever one sows, that will he also reap. For the one who sows to his own flesh will from the flesh reap corruption, but the one who sows to the Spirit will from the Spirit reap eternal life. And let us not grow weary of doing good, for in due season we will reap, if we do not give up. So then, as we have opportunity, let us do good to everyone, and especially to those who are of the household of faith. (Gal 6:7-10)

In letters Paul wrote after Galatians—such as Romans and 2 Corinthians—we can see a judgment according to works promised for all, and I argued that Romans 2:5-10 and 2 Corinthians 5:10 reflect Daniel 12:2 (see the analysis above). In keeping with that Old Testament expression of resurrection to life or judgment, Paul exhorted the Galatians to remember the day of reaping, the day when what has been sown will become known. He has the eschatological harvest in mind.[64]

The two standard groups—the wicked and the righteous—are conceived by Paul as those who sow to the flesh and those who sow to the Spirit, respectively (Gal 6:8). The outcome for the wicked (corruption) contrasts with that of the righteous (eternal life). In fact, the phrase "eternal life" (ζωὴν αἰώνιον) is used only once in the Old Testament, in Daniel 12:2. So "the contrast indicates that corruption refers to final destruction and final judgment."[65]

Galatians 6:8 appears to be a variation of the kinds of statements Jesus and Paul make elsewhere. Jesus says the wicked go to eternal punishment and the righteous to eternal life (Matt 25:46), and those who do good will be raised to life, while those who do evil will be raised to judgment (John 5:29). Paul taught that those who do good will receive glory, honor, and peace (Rom 2:10), but those who do evil will experience tribulation, distress, wrath, and fury (2:8-9).

In Galatians 6:8 Paul has doers of good and doers of evil in mind, and the "doing" is captured in the metaphor "sowing." Probably the "reaping" of what was sown will ultimately take place through bodily resurrection. And the promise that faithfulness or unfaithfulness will result

---

64. Ronald Y. K. Fung, *The Epistle to the Galatians*, NICNT (Grand Rapids: Eerdmans, 1988), 295.
65. Thomas R. Schreiner, *Galatians*, ZECNT (Grand Rapids: Zondervan, 2010), 369.

in contrasting fates for the righteous and wicked—the former receiving eternal life, the other corruption—was probably influenced by Daniel 12:2. "The harvest of corruption, then, is eternal death, the opposite of resurrection life. Corresponding to the sowing to the Spirit is the harvest of eternal life ... which is attained through resurrection from the dead."[66]

The resurrection is the reaping, so Paul's readers should do good as they have opportunity, and not grow weary in doing so. Their efforts will culminate in final, physical resurrection.[67]

EPHESIANS

In Paul's letter to the Ephesians, he emphasizes our present reign with the risen Christ. God "made us alive together with Christ ... and raised us up with him and seated us with him in the heavenly places in Christ Jesus" (Eph 2:5-6). Out of this identity believers should live lives of holiness. At one point in the letter, as Paul exhorts his readers to obedience, he may have adapted the language of Daniel 12:2 to suit his purposes.

The call for sleepers to wake and rise (Eph 5:14). Paul tells the Ephesians, "Take no part in the unfruitful works of darkness, but instead expose them. For it is shameful even to speak of the things that they do in secret. But when anything is exposed by the light, it becomes visible, for anything that becomes visible is light. Therefore it says, 'Awake, O sleeper, and arise from the dead, and Christ will shine on you'" (Eph 5:11-14).

Paul is calling people into the light, that deeds of darkness may be exposed and rejected. In the last verse it appears Paul is quoting something ("Therefore it says"), but the exact source of his words remains uncertain. Some scholars suggest passages in Isaiah (e.g., Isa 26:19; 51:17; 52:1; 60:1),[68] and this is plausible. O'Brien offers his assessment: "Most recent scholars ... prefer to understand it as a fragment of an early Christian hymn that was originally associated with baptism."[69] Hoehner is right, though, that the context does not support the notion of a baptismal

---

66. Frank J. Matera, *Galatians*, Sacra Pagina, vol. 9 (Collegeville, MN: The Liturgical Press, 1992), 216.
67. Beale, *A New Testament Biblical Theology*, 276.
68. See Peter T. O'Brien, *The Letter to the Ephesians*, PNTC (Grand Rapids: Eerdmans, 1999), 374-75; Beale, *A New Testament Biblical Theology*, 279.
69. O'Brien, *The Letter to the Ephesians*, 374.

liturgy.[70] Most likely it is a hymn composed for congregational meetings, and it was heavily influenced by Old Testament texts.[71]

Even if Ephesians 5:14 is an early Christian hymn, its theology would be scriptural, and thus this brings us back to the question of what passage(s) may be in view. Verses from Isaiah are possible sources for the words, but could not a reference to Daniel 12:2 be just as likely, if not more so? And could it be conflated by Paul with Isaianic verses?

Daniel 12:2 promised that "many of those who sleep in the dust of the earth shall awake," and in Ephesians 5:14 Paul says, "Awake, O sleeper, and arise from the dead." Both verses use forms of the verbs καθεύδω and ἀνίστημι, and both verses use sleep as a metaphor. After the statements about rising from sleep, there is a promise of shining: in Daniel 12:3, the righteous will shine like the stars after being raised, and in Ephesians 5:14 the righteous reflect the light of Christ shining on them.[72] Finally, in Ephesians 5:15 the readers are called to walk as wise people, and in Daniel 12:2 it is the wise who will shine like the stars forever.

Given these comparisons between Daniel 12:2-3 and Ephesians 5:14-15, the former may not be the only passage Paul uses, but it is a likely source for some of his words and images in the latter. One important distinction between the passages is that Daniel 12:2 concerned a future bodily resurrection, whereas Ephesians 5:14 used resurrection language in a more spiritual and metaphorical (and inaugurated) sense. This distinction, however, does not preclude Paul's use of Daniel 12 in the aforementioned ways. He exhorts his readers "to awake and with urgency arise from the path that leads to death."[73]

PHILIPPIANS

In Paul's letter to the Philippians, he encourages his readers with the example of Christ and with his own striving to suffer with Christ in order to know the power of his resurrection (Phil 2:1-11; 3:7-11). In at least two places Paul's words imply the presence of Daniel 12:2-3.

---

70. Harold W. Hoehner, *Ephesians: An Exegetical Commentary* (Grand Rapids: Baker Academic, 2002), 686.
71. Hoehner, *Ephesians*, 687.
72. Wright says, "And, as in Philippians, this echoes the promise of Daniel 12.3, but brings it into the present rather than saving it for the future—without in any way implying an over-realized eschatology. Final resurrection remains in the future ... but those on their way to it must shine like lights even in the present time" (*The Resurrection of the Son of God*, 238).
73. Hoehner, *Ephesians*, 688.

Children of God shining as lights in the world (Phil 2:15). Paul tells his readers, "Do all things without grumbling or questioning, that you may be blameless and innocent, children of God without blemish in the midst of a crooked and twisted generation, among whom you shine as lights in the world, holding fast to the word of life, so that in the day of Christ I may be proud that I did not run in vain or labor in vain" (Phil 2:14-16).

Scholars are generally agreed that the language of "shine as lights in the world" reflects Daniel 12:3 in an inaugurated sense,[74] but most of them do not fully connect Paul's words with Daniel 12 to the degree Fee does. Viewed in parallel, Fee's observation is a clear instance of intertextuality:[75]

Daniel 12:3 (OG): φανοῦσν ὡς φωστῆρες τοῦ οὐρανοῦ

Philippians 2:15: φαίνεσθε ὡς φωστῆρες ἐν κόσμῳ

By altering "of heaven" to "in the world," Paul indicates the present sphere of their shining.[76] Fee believes Paul's use of Daniel 12 is reinforced even more by the subsequent phrases of both verses:

Daniel 12:3 (OG): οἱ κατισχύοντες τοὺς λόγους μου

Philippians 2:16a: λόγον ζωῆς ἐπέχοντες

The OG of Daniel 12:3 does not reflect the Hebrew, which has "those who turn many to righteousness." Paul's dependence on Daniel 12 is undoubtedly on the OG. The "my words" of Daniel 12:3 become the "word of life" in Philippians 2:16. As Fee explains, it is through the "word of life"—the gospel—that "my words" have made their way into the world.[77]

Before the final judgment, the wise and righteous are already shining in the midst of a crooked generation, living blamelessly and holding to the gospel. But if Daniel 12:3 promised a shining that resulted from resurrection (cf. 12:2), then an inaugurated shining must imply

---

74. See, e.g., Gordon D. Fee, *Paul's Letter to the Philippians*, NICNT (Grand Rapids: Eerdmans, 1995), 246-47; Stephen E. Fowl, *Philippians*, The Two Horizons New Testament Commentary (Grand Rapids: Eerdmans, 2005), 124-25; F. F. Bruce, *Philippians*, NIBC, vol. 11 (Peabody, MA: Hendrickson, 1989), 87; Wright, *The Resurrection of the Son of God*, 228; Beale, *A New Testament Biblical Theology*, 283.
75. Fee, *Paul's Letter to the Philippians*, 246n26.
76. Fee, *Paul's Letter to the Philippians*, 247n29.
77. Fee, *Paul's Letter to the Philippians*, 247n33. See Beale, *A New Testament Biblical Theology*, 283.

an inaugurated resurrection. If believers are shining as lights in a dark world, then the resurrection promise of Daniel 12:2 is beginning to come true in Christ, though not yet bodily.

Bruce explains that "those who share in Christ's risen life anticipate the ministry of the resurrection age and bear their shining witness already."[78] Believers are raised with Christ, seated with him and reigning with him. They are inwardly renewed day by day, having been raised from spiritual death. Or as Jesus says, "Truly, truly, I say to you, whoever hears my word and believes him who sent me has eternal life. He does not come into judgment, but has passed from death to life" (John 5:24).

A lowly body transformed like Jesus's glorious body (Phil 3:19–21). Paul not only believes Daniel 12:2 has been inaugurated, but he also believes the fullness of resurrection hope will be achieved when Jesus returns. But until that day of Christ's appearing comes, Paul says,

> Brothers, join in imitating me, and keep your eyes on those who walk according to the example you have in us. For many, of whom I have often told you and now tell you even with tears, walk as enemies of the cross of Christ. Their end is destruction, their god is their belly, and they glory in their shame, with minds set on earthly things. But our citizenship is in heaven, and from it we await a Savior, the Lord Jesus Christ, who will transform our lowly body to be like his glorious body, by the power that enables him even to subject all things to himself. (Phil 3:17–21)

Like Daniel 12:2 Paul envisions two groups of people: those who are enemies of the cross and those who are not. The outcomes for these groups contrast starkly: the unrighteous will face destruction, but believers will be raised in glorified bodies. Both the Th of Daniel 12:2 and Philippians 3:19 use the word $αἰσχύνη$; what unbelievers will be raised to, they glory in even now. The righteous will be raised (Phil 3:21), just like Daniel 12:2 says will happen, and the bodies will be glorious like the body of Jesus, which will fulfill the promise in Daniel 12:3 that "those who are wise shall shine like the brightness of the sky above ... like the stars forever and ever."

---

78. Bruce, *Philippians*, 87. In Wright's words, "This is a deliberate echo of Daniel 12.3, indicating that Paul here as elsewhere, had thought through the *present* life and vocation of Christians in terms of a resurrection life which had already, in one sense, begun, even though it was to be completed in the bodily resurrection itself" (*The Resurrection of the Son of God*, 228).

When Paul hopes "that by any means possible I may attain the resurrection from the dead" (Phil 3:11), he unpacks in Philippians 3:17-21 what that will mean for him and what it will mean for enemies of the cross. The deliverance of God's people will mean destruction for the wicked. Paul's thoughts and words in that passage were shaped in part by Daniel 12:2.

FIRST THESSALONIANS

One of the Thessalonians' concerns was whether their deceased Christian brothers and sisters would miss the resurrection of the dead. So, in one of his earliest letters, Paul wrote a section of comfort to them, and these words bear the marks of Daniel 12:2.

The resurrection of those who sleep in Christ (1 Thess 4:13-16). Dead Christians will not miss their resurrection, though the Thessalonian readers feared they would.

> But we do not want you to be uninformed, brothers, about those who are asleep, that you may not grieve as others do who have no hope. For since we believe that Jesus died and rose again, even so, through Jesus, God will bring with him those who have fallen asleep. For this we declare to you by a word from the Lord, that we who are alive, who are left until the coming of the Lord, will not precede those who have fallen asleep. For the Lord himself will descend from heaven with a cry of command, with the voice of an archangel, and with the sound of the trumpet of God. And the dead in Christ will rise first. (1 Thess 4:13-16)

Paul's first sentence uses sleep as a metaphor, just as Daniel 12:2 does. The verbs differ, for Paul uses κοιμάω instead of καθεύδω, but the sense is the same. "What we find beginning in Dan. 12.2 and continuing in Testament of Judah 25.4 and Testament of Issachar 7.9; 2 Macc. 12.44-45; and 1 Enoch 91.10 and 92.3 however is a connection between sleeping and being awakened by the resurrection, an idea Paul further develops here and in 1 Cor. 15.20-21."[79]

Paul calls confidence in resurrection a "hope" (1 Thess 4:13), as he does later in Acts 23:6 and 24:15 (two verses which draw on Dan 12:2). Witherington suggests the possibility that "Paul combines a saying of

---

79. Ben Witherington III, *1 and 2 Thessalonians: A Socio-Rhetorical Commentary* (Grand Rapids: Eerdmans, 2006), 131.

Jesus ['For we declare to you by a word from the Lord,' 1 Thess 4:15] with his own reflections on Dan. 7.13-14 and 12.2-3."[80] All the sleepers will be accounted for at the resurrection: "God will bring with him those who have fallen asleep" (1 Thess 4:14). At his parousia Jesus will command his followers to rise (4:16). The hope that sleepers will rise bodily is based mainly on Daniel 12:2, where such language is clearly found.[81]

SECOND THESSALONIANS

Paul wrote another letter to the Thessalonians, correcting some of their eschatological confusions. The opening chapter emphasizes the judgment Christ will bring at his parousia. The damning outcome for unbelievers reflects Daniel 12:2.

The punishment of eternal destruction for unbelievers (2 Thess 1:9-10). Paul knows the Thessalonian believers are being opposed, so he explains that their suffering is not the final word. God's enemies will answer to him.

> This is evidence of the righteous judgment of God, that you may be considered worthy of the kingdom of God, for which you are also suffering—since indeed God considers it just to repay with affliction those who afflict you, and to grant relief to you who are afflicted as well as to us, when the Lord Jesus is revealed from heaven with his mighty angels in flaming fire, inflicting vengeance on those who do not know God and on those who do not obey the gospel of our Lord Jesus. They will suffer the punishment of eternal destruction, away from the presence of the Lord and from the glory of his might, when he comes on that day to be glorified in his saints, and to be marveled at among all who have believed, because our testimony to you was believed. (2 Thess 1:5-10)

According to Paul, the day when Jesus is revealed from heaven will bring relief to the saints and judgment on unbelievers. The implication is that relief and judgment come through the resurrection of the saints and unbelievers, respectively. Paul explained in his first letter to them that the arrival of Jesus means the dead will rise (1 Thess 4:16), and for unbelievers this is bad news. God will "repay with affliction" those who afflict the saints, so just as the relief for the saints is accomplished through

---

80. Witherington, *1 and 2 Thessalonians*, 135.
81. See Wright, *The Resurrection of the Son of God*, 216.

their resurrection, the judgment and affliction of the ungodly is accomplished through theirs.[82] The punishment of the ungodly is "eternal" (2 Thess 1:9), just as Daniel 12:2 promises ("some to shame and everlasting contempt"). The word is from αἰώνιος in both verses.

In 2 Thessalonians 1:5–10, because the two groups (the righteous and the wicked) will meet contrasting fates (relief and affliction) that last forever, and since a resurrection is implied once this passage is compared with 1 Thessalonians, then the most likely Old Testament background is Daniel 12:2.

SECOND TIMOTHY

In Paul's second letter to Timothy, he ended his letter with an exhortation to preach the Scripture in season and out of season (2 Tim 4:2). Undergirding that charge to Timothy is a statement growing chiefly out of Daniel 12:2.

The judge of the living and the dead (2 Tim 4:1). Timothy should "preach the word" in light of eschatological realities. "I charge you," Paul said, "in the presence of God and of Christ Jesus, who is to judge the living and the dead, and by his appearing and his kingdom" (2 Tim 4:1).

The phrase "the living and the dead" is a merism: Jesus is the judge of *everyone*. Timothy's charge is given in light of Jesus's future parousia, his "appearing." At this event the judgment will commence. Since most people will not be alive when Jesus returns, he is judge of the living and "the dead." It is understandable that "the living" could be judged because they are still alive, but how is it possible that Jesus will also judge "the dead"?

The answer is in what happens at Jesus's "appearing." Elsewhere in Paul's letters he teaches that Jesus's parousia brings resurrection (cf. 1 Thess 4; 1 Cor 15), and this will result in comprehensive judgment (cf. 2 Cor 5:10; Rom 2:5–10). Jesus will be able to judge "the living" *and* "the dead" because bodily resurrection will mean the gathering of nations before his throne (cf. Matt 25:31–33). "The terms referred to those who were physically alive or dead. The statement emphasized that no one

---

82. Harris says 2 Thess 1:8–9 is a passage suggesting Paul's belief in a resurrection of the wicked unto condemnation ("Resurrection and Immortality in the Pauline Corpus," 151).

would escape divine judgment. The dead would be raised for judgment, and the living would also face the divine tribunal."[83]

Behind the notions of general resurrection and comprehensive judgment is the shadow of Daniel 12:2, which promises that some people will rise to everlasting life, while others rise to shame and everlasting contempt.

HEBREWS

The letter to the Hebrews does not talk much about resurrection. But in two sections of the letter, Daniel 12:2 is probably the foundation that the writer builds upon to express the hope of bodily deliverance from death.

The foundational teaching of future resurrection (Heb 6:2). The author of Hebrews expects his readers to be beyond basic teachings by this point. "For though by this time you ought to be teachers, you need someone to teach you again the basic principles of the oracles of God. You need milk, not solid food, for everyone who lives on milk is unskilled in the word of righteousness, since he is a child" (Heb 5:12-13). Rather than milk, his readers should consume solid food, which is for the mature (5:14). "Therefore let us leave the elementary doctrine of Christ and go on to maturity, not laying again a foundation of repentance from dead works and of faith toward God, and of instruction about washings, the laying on of hands, the resurrection of the dead, and eternal judgment" (Heb 6:1-2).

Significant among the foundational teachings explicated in Hebrews 6:1-2 is instruction about the resurrection of the dead. Such a doctrine was a core piece of orthodox instruction. By "resurrection" the writer probably means it encompasses the righteous and unrighteous, because there is no qualifier limiting resurrection to one group, and there is a reference to "eternal judgment" after "resurrection of the dead." As previous texts have established, everyone will appear at the judgment seat of Christ, and this appearance is after resurrection.

In Hebrews 6:2, therefore, the phrases "resurrection of the dead" and "eternal judgment" probably refer to events both believers and

---

83. Thomas D. Lea and Hayne P. Griffin Jr., *1, 2 Timothy, Titus*, NAC, vol. 34 (Nashville: Broadman, 1992), 242. Fee says the same thing in different words: "Thus he will judge both those who are alive at his appearing and those whose death has preceded it and who will be raised for judgment" (Gordon D. Fee, *1 and 2 Timothy, Titus*, NIBC, vol. 13 [Peabody, MA: Hendrickson, 1984], 284).

unbelievers will participate in.[84] If deSilva is correct that the six basic teachings fall into three pairs (the first being "repentance from dead works" and "faith toward God," the second being "instruction about washings" and "the laying on of hands"), then there is literary reinforcement to keep the notions of "the resurrection of the dead" and "eternal judgment" together.[85]

If the author of Hebrews is speaking about a general resurrection of the dead that leads to eternal states,[86] the probable Old Testament passage informing such a notion is Daniel 12:2.[87] And if Hebrews 6:1-2 is about elementary instructions for believers, then Daniel 12:2 contributes to the mere orthodoxy expected of true believers. Hope for resurrection and judgment is not negotiable or dispensable.

Resurrection to a better life (Heb 11:35). The writer of Hebrews exhorts his readers to be forward looking, just as the saints of old were. The patriarchs died in faith, "not receiving the things promised, but having seen them and greeted them from afar, and having acknowledged that they were strangers and exiles on the earth" (Heb 11:13). Moses, too, "was looking to the reward" (11:26b). Saints endured all manner of travail:

> Women received back their dead by resurrection. Some were tortured, refusing to accept release, so that they might rise again to a better life. Others suffered mocking and flogging, and even chains and imprisonment. They were stoned, they were sawn in

---

84. Paul Ellingworth, *The Epistle to the Hebrews*, NIGTC (Grand Rapids: Eerdmans, 1993), 316.
85. David A. deSilva, *Perseverance in Gratitude: A Socio-Rhetorical Commentary on the Epistle "to the Hebrews"* (Grand Rapids: Eerdmans, 2000), 215-19. For further confirmation see R. T. France, *Hebrews*, in vol. 13 of *The Expositor's Bible Commentary*, ed. Tremper Longman III and David E. Garland, rev. ed. (Grand Rapids: Zondervan, 2006), 81; Gareth Lee Cockerill, *The Epistle to the Hebrews*, NICNT (Grand Rapids: Eerdmans, 2012), 263; Peter T. O'Brien, *The Letter to the Hebrews*, PNTC (Grand Rapids: Eerdmans, 2010), 213.
86. Isaacs says, "What we have in 6:2 is more likely to be a reference to the general resurrection" (Marie E. Isaacs, *Reading Hebrews & James: A Literary and Theological Commentary* [Macon, GA: Smyth & Helwys, 2002], 83). See also O'Brien, *The Letter to the Hebrews*, 215n27; David L. Allen, *Hebrews*, NAC, vol. 35 (Nashville: B&H, 2010), 343.
87. France says, "The 'resurrection' referred to is not that of Jesus but that of dead people more generally. And that resurrection leads to an 'eternal judgment,' which will be mentioned again in 9:27 as something all people must face. These beliefs, *which occur together* in Daniel 12:2, would have been shared by many Jews at that time, so that the readers may have already accepted them before they became Christians" (France, *Hebrews*, 82, italics mine).

two, they were killed with the sword. They went about in skins of sheep and goats, destitute, afflicted, mistreated—of whom the world was not worthy—wandering about in deserts and mountains, and in dens and caves of the earth. (Heb 11:35-38)

When the "women received back their dead," those resurrections were not unto glorified bodies; they were resuscitations, so those bodies would die again.[88] But the reason the saints endured such opposition and persecution was their hope for bodily resurrection. The "some" who "were tortured" may be the famous Maccabean martyrs from 2 Maccabees 7.[89] "Specific reference is made to the hope of the resurrection in the account of the sufferings endured by three of the seven brothers, as well as in the encouragement offered to them by their mother (2 Macc 7:9, 11, 14, 22-23, 29)."[90] One day they would "rise again to a better life" (Heb 11:35), and this hope is anchored to Daniel 12:2 most explicitly.

In that clearest and fullest Old Testament resurrection expression, the sleepers wake to eternal life, which is—without question—a "better life" than the one in which they suffered and resisted conformity to the world. Their light and momentary troubles would achieve a glory that outweighed them all (cf. 2 Cor 4:17). This "better resurrection" is the "foundation and premise that empowers God's people to suffer for their loyalty to Christ."[91] It "has to do with the final defeat of death and being raised to eternal life."[92]

FIRST PETER

Peter's first letter to some believers in Asian provinces aims to strengthen them with hope. Though they do not yet see Jesus, one day they shall,

---

88. David deSilva is right that the author of Hebrews probably has in mind the resurrections in the ministries of Elijah and Elisha (cf. 1 Kgs 17:17-24; 2 Kgs 4:18-37) (*Perseverance in Gratitude*, 418). France also believes the miracles of those OT prophets are in view (*Hebrews*, 164).
89. See F. F. Bruce, *The Epistle to the Hebrews*, rev. ed., NICNT (Grand Rapids: Eerdmans, 1990), 325-26; deSilva, *Perseverance in Gratitude*, 419; Isaacs, *Reading Hebrews & James*, 137; France, *Hebrews*, 164; William L. Lane, "Living a Life of Faith in the Face of Death," in *Life in the Face of Death: The Resurrection Message of the New Testament*, ed. Richard N. Longenecker (Grand Rapids: Eerdmans, 1998), 262; Wright, *The Resurrection of the Son of God*, 458.
90. William L. Lane, *Hebrews 9-13*, WBC, vol. 47B (Nashville: Thomas Nelson, 1991), 389.
91. Cockerill, *The Epistle to the Hebrews*, 591.
92. O'Brien, *The Letter to the Hebrews*, 443.

and their belief and joy will consummate in final salvation, which is the outcome of their faith (1 Pet 1:6–9). Though persecuted, they should resolve to live obediently, for everyone will give an account on the day of judgment.

Him who is ready to judge the living and the dead (1 Pet 4:5). Believers should not follow unbelievers into deeds of unrighteousness, even if that means facing verbal revilement for resistance. Such enemies of the gospel "will give account to him who is ready to judge the living and the dead" (1 Pet 4:5).

A motive for holiness is that persecutors will have their day of reckoning. The phrase "the living and the dead" is all encompassing, so Peter's readers can trust that the vindication of God's people is certain: every enemy of the gospel will answer to God. Decades earlier, in the house of Cornelius, Peter had spoken about Jesus being "the one appointed by God to be judge of the living and the dead" (Acts 10:42), so he no doubt has Jesus in mind—as the judge of the earth—when he writes to the Asian believers (cf. 1 Pet 4:5). And as was the case in Acts 10, Daniel 12:2 undergirds Peter's words in his letter. No other Old Testament expression is more likely behind the promise of comprehensive judgment of the living and the dead, for the final judgment of the already dead must mean they are raised once more to join the living and receive their final verdict from God's hand.

For believers—living and dead—their future will be resurrection unto life (cf. 1 Pet 4:6). "The point of the passage, then, is that the judgment is also the time of the vindication of Christians. ... God will have the final say, and his verdict in the final judgment will be life. Thus they will live in resurrection life."[93]

REVELATION

The last book of the New Testament is saturated with language and imagery from the Old.[94] One Old Testament book particularly prominent

---

93. Peter H. Davids, *The First Epistle of Peter*, NICNT (Grand Rapids: Eerdmans, 1990), 155. See also Thomas R. Schreiner, *1, 2 Peter, Jude*, NAC, vol. 37 (Nashville: Broadman & Holman, 2003), 209–10.
94. G. K. Beale and Sean M. McDonough, "Revelation," in *Commentary on the New Testament Use of the Old Testament*, ed. G. K. Beale and D. A. Carson (Grand Rapids: Baker Academic, 2007), 1081.

in the Apocalypse is Daniel.[95] In this final section of my argument I will explore how Daniel 12:2 influenced the canonical climax of the New Testament. John's use of Daniel 12:2 is clearly seen in Revelation 20.[96]

The dead standing before the throne (Rev 20:11-15). John saw in a vision the future vindication of God's people and the final judgment of the wicked. The description of what he saw both gives hope and induces terror.

> Then I saw thrones, and seated on them were those to whom the authority to judge was committed. Also I saw the souls of those who had been beheaded for the testimony of Jesus and for the word of God, and those who had not worshiped the beast or its image and had not received its mark on their foreheads or their hands. They came to life and reigned with Christ for a thousand years. The rest of the dead did not come to life until the thousand years were ended. This is the first resurrection. Blessed and holy is the one who shares in the first resurrection! Over such the second death has no power, but they will be priests of God and of Christ, and they will reign with him for a thousand years. ... Then I saw a great white throne and him who was seated on it. From his presence earth and sky fled away, and no place was found for them. And I saw the dead, great and small, standing before the throne, and books were opened. Then another book was opened, which is the book of life. And the dead were judged by what was written in the books, according to what they had done. Then Death and Hades were thrown into the lake of fire. This is the second death, the lake of fire. And if anyone's name was not found written in the book of life, he was thrown into the lake of fire. (Rev 20:4-6, 11-15)

Scholars differ on how to understand the reference of "a thousand years" (cf. Rev 20:2, 3, 4, 5, 6, 7), but what is clear is that Revelation 20 narrates the fulfillment of what Daniel 12:2 promised. The righteous are raised to life (20:4-6), just as Daniel heard would happen.[97] The dead, "great and small," appear at God's throne and are judged (cf. 20:12). The sea gives

---

95. For a thorough treatment of the use of Daniel in John's Apocalypse, see Beale, *The Use of Daniel in Jewish Apocalyptic Literature*.
96. Hamilton suggests connections between Dan 12:2 and Rev 20:4, 5, 12-15 (James M. Hamilton Jr., *Revelation: The Spirit Speaks to the Churches*, PTW [Wheaton, IL: Crossway, 2012], 434). See also Beale, *The Book of Revelation*, 1021-38.
97. See Grant R. Osborne, *Revelation*, BECNT (Grand Rapids: Baker Academic, 2002), 721-22.

up its dead (20:13), which is an image of resurrection,[98] and God judges each of them according to their works (20:14). Then he throws into the lake of fire whoever was not written in the book of life (20:15). Smalley observes, "The idea is to some extent anticipated in Dan. 12.2 (cf. John 5:28-29)."[99]

Like Paul taught in 2 Timothy 4:1, God is the judge of the living and the dead. The righteous are vindicated, the wicked are condemned, and eternal states are established. As Daniel 12:2 envisioned (along with the host of passages implying and predicting this hope before that), the dust would not hold the dead forever. Disembodied spirits were rejoined to raised bodies. All the sleepers awakened to their everlasting destinies, either to life or to the second death. What Daniel 12:2 predicted found realization in the events of Revelation 20.[100]

SUMMARY

It is not surprising that Daniel 12:2 influenced the theology of the Pauline letters, for the apostle Paul had been a Pharisee, and Pharisees believed in a general resurrection of the dead, a belief anchored especially to the expression in Daniel 12:2. Most of Paul's letters make use of that verse in some way or another. The writers of Hebrews and 1 Peter also depended on the theology (though not necessarily the exact language) of Daniel 12:2. Because God will raise the dead, people should renounce the sinful deeds of the body and consecrate themselves as instruments of righteousness. The final judgment will dispense either reward or retribution, and the effects will be experienced physically and eternally. Reading the book of Revelation, readers may be struck by the pervasive assurance of God's victory. No foe will be left unconquered. Jesus will reign as every enemy is put under his feet, and the last enemy is death (cf. 1 Cor 15:25-26). Resurrection will mean the defeat of death, and the God of life will dwell forever in uncontested majesty, his righteousness on display through his dispensation of judgment and mercy.

---

98. See Bauckham, *The Fate of the Dead*, 269-89.
99. Stephen S. Smalley, *The Revelation of John: A Commentary on the Greek Text of the Apocalypse* (Downers Grove, IL: InterVarsity Press, 2005), 67.
100. Beale and McDonough, "Revelation," 1150. See Beale, *A New Testament Biblical Theology*, 512-14.

CONCLUSION

The influence of Daniel 12:2 continued beyond the intertestamental period and shaped the way the New Testament authors thought and spoke about resurrection. In all four Gospels, the book of Acts, more than half of the epistles, and the book of Revelation, those corresponding authors appropriated the language, imagery, and/or theology of Daniel 12:2, which was the clearest and fullest Old Testament expression of resurrection hope. More than any other verse in the Old Testament, Daniel 12:2 made the greatest impact on the New Testament authors in terms of their belief in resurrection and their articulation of what that eschatological reality would entail for the righteous and the wicked.[101]

---

101. In the words of Adela Collins, "The influence of Daniel 12 is apparent in the centrality of the notion of resurrection in the New Testament" ("The Influence of Daniel on the NT," 112).

Conclusion

Near the end of the final vision in the book of Daniel, the prophet hears what God will do with those who have died: "And many of those who sleep in the dust of the earth shall awake, some to everlasting life, and some to shame and everlasting contempt" (Dan 12:2). Nowhere else in the Old Testament is there such a promise, such a full and pregnant expression of resurrection hope. But whence came this belief in future bodily life? And did the Danielic formulation impact any authors who came after that postexilic prophet?

The chapters in this project have sought to prove the thesis that Daniel relied on earlier Old Testament texts and theological convictions when he expressed the hope of bodily resurrection, and his expression informed and shaped subsequent nonbiblical and biblical authors. The demonstration of this thesis would be a work of biblical theology, all centering around Daniel 12:2.

Groundwork for the thesis involved several preliminary considerations. In chapter 1, I discussed the notion of afterlife, the meaning of Sheol, the dating of the book of Daniel, and the various positions held by scholars concerning the emergence of resurrection hope in Israel's history. I concluded that the Old Testament authors do teach an afterlife, that Sheol is more than the grave and is where the righteous and unrighteous go upon death, that the composition of the book of Daniel was in the sixth century BC by a real prophet named Daniel who received real visions about future events, and that I would approach the subject of resurrection hope with a maximal perspective—meaning that resurrection hope was not a radical innovation late in Israel's history but was an early and Torah-based hope that developed across the biblical revelation.

In chapter 2, I focused on the meaning and context of Daniel 12:2. Stories of deliverance and judgment throughout the book of Daniel created the kind of momentum that would only be satisfied by the declaration of a future time when God would wake up all who were sleeping in death. A book whose first chapter narrated a people in exile (Dan 1) held out hope in its final vision and chapter (Dan 12) that a return from exile would come—a return by resurrection from the exile of death, the most dreaded captor of all. The image of sleepers waking up was a metaphor for bodily resurrection. Language in Daniel 12:2 was reminiscent of passages in Isaiah and Genesis, though others such as Psalm 69 may also be in the background. A natural reading of Daniel 12:2 would mean that everyone will be raised to one of two contrasting destinies: the righteous will be raised to everlasting life, and the wicked will be raised to shame and everlasting contempt. Alternative interpretations are not compelling.

Chapter 3 explored the roots of resurrection hope because the teaching of Daniel 12:2 did not emerge in a vacuum. By locating instances of resurrection hope in the Law, Prophets, and Writings, we were able to see that Daniel 12:2 was the result of a stream flowing from the earliest books of the Old Testament. I divided the evidence into *strong* and *supporting* categories. More than using just verbal expressions, biblical authors could convey a belief in resurrection through theological convictions and figures/pictures. God is a God of life and renewal, a Divine Warrior, and he has the power to reverse and triumph over forces of chaos and corruption. He keeps his promises to the extent that death will not cause his word to fail, and his covenant love for his people is unbreakable and will outlast death. Of course, readers may not be persuaded by every piece of evidence that I put forth, but the cumulative nature of my case stands for seeing resurrection hope in the Law, Prophets, and Writings. Daniel 12:2 is the culminating expression of a long line of hope that God's love and faithfulness will lead to his people embodying a new kind of life that death cannot defeat.

Having considered the Old Testament precursors to the claim in Daniel 12:2, I wanted chapter 4 to engage the nonbiblical literature this verse may have influenced. This nonbiblical literature was intertestamental books, and I divided the survey into the Pseudepigrapha and then the Apocrypha. Discerning the verse's influence on such nonbiblical material is only feasible if the book of Daniel is indeed a historical work written in the sixth century BC. The hope in Daniel 12:2 shaped many intertestamental authors in the way they promised vindication for the righteous and judgment for the wicked. A coming day of reckoning provided motivation for God's people to endure all manner of persecution. Sometimes an image of resurrection was used, and at other times an explicit verb conveyed this hope. While there were other Old Testament passages whose authors advocated a belief in future bodily life, Daniel 12:2 appeared to be chief among those verses that propelled such hope during the intertestamental years.

Chapter 5 completed the last stage of my thesis by focusing on the influence of Daniel 12:2 on the New Testament authors. By exploring the four Gospels, the book of Acts, the epistles, and the book of Revelation, I sought to show that every literary category in the New Testament had been influenced by Daniel 12:2. By noticing how the New Testament authors alluded to and echoed the concepts and/or wording of Daniel 12:2, I concluded that this verse, more than any other in the Old Testament, exercised the greatest influence on how these authors understood and wrote about the future resurrection of the dead.

With one voice across the two Testaments, the biblical authors declare that Death will die, and this death will happen because of resurrection. The risen Jesus is the first fruits of this great hope, and through our union with Christ we are already made alive spiritually. At the parousia of our Lord, his voice will shout to the tombs, "Let there be life," and there will be life. We will rise to shine, beholding and reflecting the glory of our Redeemer. Clothed immortal, we will have what the tree of life held forth because we will have Christ. Death shall be no more.

Bibliography

Akin, Jonathan David. "A Theology of Future Hope in the Book of Proverbs." Ph.D. diss., The Southern Baptist Theological Seminary, 2012.
Alden, Robert L. *Job*. The New American Commentary, vol. 11. Nashville: B&H, 1993.
Alexander, T. D. *From Eden to the New Jerusalem: An Introduction to Biblical Theology*. Grand Rapids: Kregel, 2008.
———. "The Old Testament View of Life After Death." *Themelios* 11, no. 2 (1986): 41–46.
Alfrink, B. J. "L'Idée de résurrection d'après Dn XII, 1, 2." *Biblica* 40 (1959): 362–71.
Allen, David L. *Hebrews*. The New American Commentary, vol. 35. Nashville: B&H, 2010.
Alter, Robert. *The Art of Biblical Narrative*. New York: Basic Books, 1981.
Andersen, Francis I. *Job: An Introduction and Commentary*. Downers Grove, IL: InterVarsity Press, 1976.
Andersen, Francis I., and David Noel Freedman. *Hosea*. The Anchor Bible, vol. 24. Garden City, NY: Doubleday, 1980.
Anderson, Bernard W., with Steven Bishop. *Contours of Old Testament Theology*. Minneapolis: Fortress, 1999.
Armerding, Carl Edwin. "Asleep in the Dust." *Bibliotheca Sacra* 121 (1964): 153–58.
Aune, David E. *Revelation 17–22*. Word Biblical Commentary, vol. 52C. Nashville: Thomas Nelson, 1998.
Bailey, Daniel P. "The Intertextual Relationship of Daniel 12:2 and Isaiah 26:19: Evidence from Qumran and the Greek Versions." *Tyndale Bulletin* 51, no. 2 (2000): 305–8.
Bailey, Lloyd R. *Biblical Perspectives*. Philadelphia: Fortress, 1979.
Baldwin, Joyce G. *Daniel*. Tyndale Old Testament Commentaries. Downers Grove, IL: IVP Academic, 1978.
———. *1 & 2 Samuel*. Tyndale Old Testament Commentaries. Downers Grove, IL: InterVarsity Press, 1988.
Barth, Christoph. *God with Us: A Theological Introduction to the Old Testament*. Grand Rapids: Eerdmans, 1991.
Bauckham, Richard. *The Fate of the Dead: Studies on the Jewish and Christian Apocalypses*. Supplements to Novum Testamentum 93. Atlanta: Society of Biblical Literature, 1998.
———. "Life, Death, and the Afterlife in Second Temple Judaism." In *Life in the Face of Death: The Resurrection Message of the New Testament*, ed. Richard N. Longenecker, 80–95. Grand Rapids: Eerdmans, 1998.

Bauer, Walter. *A Greek-English Lexicon of the New Testament and Other Early Christian Literature*. Edited and translated by William F. Arndt, F. Wilber Gingrich, and Frederick W. Danker. 3rd ed. Chicago: University of Chicago Press, 2001.

Beale, G. K. *The Book of Revelation*. New International Greek Testament Commentary. Grand Rapids: Eerdmans, 1998.

———. *Handbook on the New Testament Use of the Old Testament: Exegesis and Interpretation*. Grand Rapids: Baker Academic, 2012.

———. *A New Testament Biblical Theology: The Unfolding of the Old Testament in the New*. Grand Rapids: Baker Academic, 2011.

———. *The Temple and the Church's Mission: A Biblical Theology of the Dwelling Place of God*. New Studies in Biblical Theology, vol. 17. Downers Grove, IL: InterVarsity Press, 2004.

———. *The Use of Daniel in Jewish Apocalyptic Literature and in the Revelation of St. John*. Eugene, OR: Wipf and Stock, 1984.

———, ed. *The Right Doctrine from the Wrong Texts? Essays on the Use of the Old Testament in the New*. Grand Rapids: Baker Books, 1994.

Beale, G. K., and D. A. Carson, eds. *Commentary on the New Testament Use of the Old Testament*. Grand Rapids: Baker Academic, 2007.

Beale, G. K., and D. A. Carson. Introduction to *Commentary on the New Testament Use of the Old Testament*, ed. G. K. Beale and D. A. Carson, xxiii–xxviii. Grand Rapids: Baker Academic, 2007.

Beale, G. K., and Sean M. McDonough. "Revelation." In *Commentary on the New Testament Use of the Old Testament*, ed. G. K. Beale and D. A. Carson, 1081–1161. Grand Rapids: Baker Academic, 2007.

Beckwith, Roger. "Early Traces of the Book of Daniel." *Tyndale Bulletin* 53 (2002): 75–82.

Blomberg, Craig L. "Matthew." In *Commentary on the New Testament Use of the Old Testament*, ed. G. K. Beale and D. A. Carson, 1–109. Grand Rapids: Baker Academic, 2007.

———. "The Unity and Diversity of Scripture." In *New Dictionary of Biblical Theology*, edited by T. Desmond Alexander, Brian S. Rosner, D. A. Carson, and Graeme Goldsworthy. Downers Grove, IL: InterVarsity Press, 2000.

Blomberg, Craig L., with Jennifer Foutz Markley. *A Handbook of New Testament Exegesis*. Grand Rapids: Baker Academic, 2010.

Bock, Darrell L. *Luke 9:51–24:53*. Baker Exegetical Commentary on the New Testament. Grand Rapids: Baker Books, 1996.

Boring, M. Eugene. *Mark: A Commentary*. New Testament Library. Louisville: Westminster John Knox, 2006.

Brannon, M. Jeff. *The Hope of Life after Death: A Biblical Theology of Resurrection*. Essential Studies in Biblical Theology. Downers Grove, IL: IVP Academic, 2022.

Bronner, Leila Leah. "The Resurrection Motif in the Hebrew Bible: Allusions or Illusions?" *Jewish Bible Quarterly* 30, no. 3 (2002): 143–54.

Broyles, Craig C. *Psalms*. New International Biblical Commentary, vol. 11. Peabody, MA: Hendrickson, 1999.

Bruce, F. F. *The Book of Acts*. Rev. ed. The New International Commentary on the New Testament. Grand Rapids: Eerdmans, 1988.
———. *The Epistle to the Hebrews*. Rev. ed. The New International Commentary on the New Testament. Grand Rapids: Eerdmans, 1990.
———. "The Oldest Greek Version of Daniel." *Oudtestamentische Studiën* 20 (1975): 22–40.
———. *Philippians*. New International Biblical Commentary, vol. 11. Peabody, MA: Hendrickson, 1989.
Brueggemann, Walter. *Reverberations of Faith: A Theological Handbook of Old Testament Themes*. Louisville: Westminster John Knox, 2002.
Buchanan, George Wesley. *The Book of Daniel*. The Mellen Biblical Commentary, vol. 25. Lewiston, NY: Mellen Biblical Press, 1999.
Bush, Frederic W. *Ruth, Esther*. Word Biblical Commentary, vol 9. Nashville: Thomas Nelson, 1996.
Calvin, John. *Commentaries on the Book of the Prophet of Daniel*. Translated by Thomas Myers. 2 vols. Grand Rapids: Eerdmans, 1948.
———. *Genesis*. The Crossway Classic Commentaries. Wheaton, IL: Crossway, 2001.
Carnley, Peter. *The Structure of Resurrection Belief*. Oxford: Clarendon, 1987.
Casey, M. "Porphyry and Syrian Exegesis of the Book of Daniel." *Zeitschrift für die Alttestamentliche Wissenschaft* 81 (1990): 139–42.
Cavallin, H. C. C. *Life after Death: Paul's Argument for the Resurrection of the Dead in 1 Cor 15*. Lund: Gleerup, 1974.
Charlesworth, James H., ed. *The Old Testament Pseudepigrapha*. 2 vols. New York: Doubleday, 1983–1985.
Charlesworth, James H., with C. D. Elledge, J. L. Crenshaw, H. Boers, and W. W. Willis Jr. *Resurrection: The Origin and Future of a Biblical Doctrine*. New York: T&T Clark, 2006.
Chase, Mitchell L. "From Dust You Shall Arise: Resurrection Hope in the Old Testament." *Southern Baptist Journal of Theology* 18, no. 4 (2014): 9–29.
———. "The Genesis of Resurrection Hope: Exploring Its Early Presence and Deep Roots." *Journal of the Evangelical Theological Society* 57, no. 3 (2014): 467–80.
———. *Resurrection Hope and the Death of Death*. Short Studies in Biblical Theology. Wheaton: Crossway, 2022.
Childs, Brevard S. *Old Testament Theology in a Canonical Context*. Minneapolis: Fortress, 1986.
Ciampa, Roy E., and Brian S. Rosner. "1 Corinthians." In *Commentary on the New Testament Use of the Old Testament*, ed. G. K. Beale and D. A. Carson, 695–752. Grand Rapids: Baker Academic, 2007.
Clines, David J. A. *Job 1–20*. Word Biblical Commentary, vol. 17. Dallas: Word, 1989.
Cockerill, Gareth Lee. *The Epistle to the Hebrews*. The New International Commentary on the New Testament. Grand Rapids: Eerdmans, 2012.
Cole, Robert Luther. *Psalms 1–2: Gateway to the Psalter*. Sheffield: Sheffield Phoenix Press, 2013.
Collins, Adela Yarbro. "The Influence of Daniel on the NT." In John J. Collins, *Daniel: A Commentary on the Book of Daniel*, 90–123. Hermeneia. Minneapolis: Fortress, 1993.

Collins, C. John. *Genesis 1–4: A Linguistic, Literary, and Theological Commentary*. Phillipsburg, NJ: P&R, 2006.
Collins, John J. *The Apocalyptic Vision of the Book of Daniel*. Missoula, MT: Scholars Press, 1977.
———. *Daniel: A Commentary on the Book of Daniel*. Hermeneia. Minneapolis: Fortress, 1993.
———. *Daniel, First Maccabees, Second Maccabees*. Old Testament Message, vol. 15. Wilmington, DE: Michael Glazier, 1981.
———. *Encounters with Biblical Theology*. Minneapolis: Fortress, 2005.
Compton, J. M. "Shared Intentions? Reflections on Inspiration and Interpretation in Light of Scripture's Dual Authorship." *Themelios* 33 (2008): 22–33.
Craigie, Peter C. *Psalms 1–50*. Word Biblical Commentary, vol. 19. Waco, TX: Word, 1983.
Crenshaw, James L. "Love Is Stronger Than Death: Intimations of Life beyond the Grave." In *Resurrection: The Origin and Future of a Biblical Doctrine*, edited by James H. Charlesworth, 53–78. New York: T&T Clark, 2006.
Cross, Frank Moore. *Canaanite Myth and Hebrew Epic*. Cambridge, MA: Harvard University Press, 1973.
Dahood, Mitchell. *Psalms I (1–50)*. The Anchor Bible, vol. 16. Garden City, NY: Doubleday, 1966.
Davids, Peter H. *The First Epistle of Peter*. The New International Commentary on the New Testament. Grand Rapids: Eerdmans, 1990.
Davies, W. D., and D. C. Allison. *The Gospel According to Saint Matthew*. 3 vols. International Critical Commentary. New York: T&T Clark, 1988.
Day, John. "A Case of Inner Scriptural Interpretation: The Dependence of Isaiah xxvi.13–xxvii.11 on Hosea xiii.4–xiv.10 (Eng. 9) and Its Relevance to Some Theories of the Redaction of the 'Isaiah Apocalypse.'" *Journal of Theological Studies* 31 (1980): 309–19.
Delamarter, Steve. *A Scripture Index to Charlesworth's* The Old Testament Pseudepigrapha. New York: Sheffield Academic Press, 2002.
Delitzsch, Franz. *Biblical Commentary on the Psalms*. 3 vols. Translated by Francis Bolton. Edinburgh: T&T Clark, 1871.
Dempster, Stephen G. *Dominion and Dynasty: A Theology of the Hebrew Bible*. New Studies in Biblical Theology, vol. 15. Downers Grove, IL: InterVarsity Press, 2003.
———. "An 'Extraordinary Fact': Torah and Temple and the Contours of the Hebrew Canons: Parts 1 and 2." *Tyndale Bulletin* 48 (1997): 23–56, 191–218.
———. "The Resurrection of Christ on 'The Third Day' According to the Scriptures." Paper presented at the annual meeting of the Evangelical Theological Society, Milwaukee, WI, November 14, 2012.
deSilva, David A. *Perseverance in Gratitude: A Socio-Rhetorical Commentary on the Epistle "to the Hebrews."* Grand Rapids: Eerdmans, 2000.
———. "The *Testaments of the Twelve Patriarchs* as Witnesses to Pre-Christian Judaism: A Re-Assessment." *Journal for the Study of the Pseudepigrapha* 23 (2013): 21–68.

Di Lella, Alexander A. "The Textual History of Septuagint-Daniel and Theodotion-Daniel." In *The Book of Daniel: Composition and Reception*, edited by John J. Collins and Peter W. Flint, with Cameron VanEpps, 586–607. 2 vols. Supplements to Vetus Testamentum 83. Leiden: Brill, 2001.

Dillard, Raymond B. *2 Chronicles*. Word Biblical Commentary, vol. 15. Nashville: Thomas Nelson, 1987.

Dreyfus, F. "L'Argument scriptuaire de Jésus en faveur de la résurrection des morts (Marc XII, vv. 26–27)." *Revue biblique* 66 (1959): 213–24.

Dumbrell, William J. *The Faith of Israel: A Theological Survey of the Old Testament*. 2nd ed. Grand Rapids: Baker Academic, 2002.

Edwards, James R. *The Gospel According to Mark*. The Pillar New Testament Commentary. Grand Rapids: Eerdmans, 2002.

Elledge, C. D. "Resurrection of the Dead: Exploring Our Earliest Evidence Today." In *Resurrection: The Origin and Future of a Biblical Doctrine*, edited by James H. Charlesworth, 22–52. New York: T&T Clark, 2006.

———. "The Resurrection Passages in the *Testaments of the Twelve Patriarchs*: Hope for Israel in Early Judaism and Christianity." In *Resurrection: The Origin and Future of a Biblical Doctrine*, edited by James H. Charlesworth, 79–103. New York: T&T Clark, 2006.

Ellingworth, Paul. *The Epistle to the Hebrews*. New International Greek Testament Commentary. Grand Rapids: Eerdmans, 1993.

Ellis, E. Earle. *The Gospel of Luke*. Grand Rapids: Eerdmans, 1983; Eugene, OR: Wipf and Stock, 2003.

Emadi, Samuel. *From Prisoner to Prince: The Joseph Story in Biblical Theology*. New Studies in Biblical Theology. Downers Grove, IL: IVP Academic, 2022.

Emerson, Matthew Y. *"He Descended to the Dead": An Evangelical Theology of Holy Saturday*. Downers Grove, IL: IVP Academic, 2019.

Enns, Peter. *Exodus*. The NIV Application Commentary. Grand Rapids: Zondervan, 2000.

Evans, Craig. "Daniel in the New Testament: Visions of God's Kingdom." In *The Book of Daniel: Composition and Reception*, edited by John J. Collins and Peter W. Flint, with Cameron VanEpps, 490–527. 2 vols. Supplements to Vetus Testamentum 83. Leiden: Brill, 2001.

———. "New Testament Use of the Old Testament." In *New Dictionary of Biblical Theology*, edited by T. Desmond Alexander, Brian S. Rosner, D. A. Carson, and Graeme Goldsworthy. Downers Grove, IL: InterVarsity Press, 2000.

Fee, Gordon D. *1 and 2 Timothy, Titus*. The New International Biblical Commentary, vol. 13. Peabody, MA: Hendrickson, 1984.

———. *Paul's Letter to the Philippians*. The New International Commentary on the New Testament. Grand Rapids: Eerdmans, 1995.

Fitzmyer, Joseph A. *The Acts of the Apostles*. The Anchor Bible, vol. 31. New Haven, CT: Yale University Press, 1998.

Forestell, J. Terence. "Christian Revelation and the Resurrection of the Wicked." *Catholic Biblical Quarterly* 19, no. 2 (1957): 165–89.

Fowl, Stephen E. *Philippians*. The Two Horizons New Testament Commentary. Grand Rapids: Eerdmans, 2005.

France, R. T. *The Gospel of Matthew*. New International Commentary on the New Testament. Grand Rapids: Eerdmans, 2007.

———. *Hebrews*. In *The Expositor's Bible Commentary*, vol 13, edited by Tremper Longman III and David E. Garland, 19–195. Rev. ed. Grand Rapids: Zondervan, 2006.

Freedman, David N. "The Symmetry of the Hebrew Bible." *Studia Theologica* 46 (1992): 83–108.

———. *The Unity of the Hebrew Bible*. Ann Arbor, MI: University of Michigan Press, 1991.

Fudge, Edward William. *The Fire That Consumes: A Biblical and Historical Study of the Doctrine of Final Punishment*. 3rd ed. Eugene, OR: Cascade, 2011.

Fung, Ronald Y. K. *The Epistle to the Galatians*. The New International Commentary on the New Testament. Grand Rapids: Eerdmans, 1988.

Fyall, Robert S. *Now My Eyes Have Seen You: Images of Creation and Evil in the Book of Job*. New Studies in Biblical Theology, vol. 12. Downers Grove, IL: InterVarsity Press, 2002.

Gardner, Anne E. "The Way to Eternal Life in Dan 12:1e–2 or How to Reverse the Death Curse of Genesis 3." *Australian Biblical Review* 40 (1992): 1–19.

Garland, David E. *1 Corinthians*. Baker Exegetical Commentary on the New Testament. Grand Rapids: Baker Academic, 2003.

Gentry, Peter J., and Stephen J. Wellum. *Kingdom through Covenant: A Biblical-Theological Understanding of the Covenants*. 2nd ed. Wheaton, IL: Crossway, 2018.

Goldingay, John E. *Daniel*. Word Biblical Commentary, vol. 30. Nashville: Thomas Nelson, 1989.

Goldstein, Jonathan. *II Maccabees*. The Anchor Bible, vol. 41A. Garden City, NY: Doubleday, 1983.

Gowan, Donald E. *Theology of the Prophetic Books: The Death and Resurrection of Israel*. Louisville: Westminster John Knox, 1998.

Grant, Robert M. "The Resurrection of the Body." *The Journal of Religion* 28, no. 2 (1948): 120–30.

Green, William Henry. *The Argument of the Book of Job Unfolded*. 1874; repr., Minneapolis: James & Klock, 1977.

Greenspoon, Leonard J. "The Origin of the Idea of Resurrection." In *Traditions in Transformation: Turning Points in Biblical Faith*, edited by Baruch Halpern and Jon D. Levenson, 247–321. Winona Lake, IN: Eisenbrauns, 1981.

Greidanus, Sidney. *Preaching Christ from Daniel: Foundations for Expository Sermons*. Grand Rapids: Eerdmans, 2012.

Grogan, G. W. "Psalms." In *New Dictionary of Biblical Theology*, edited by T. Desmond Alexander, Brian S. Rosner, D. A. Carson, and Graeme Goldsworthy. Downers Grove, IL: InterVarsity Press, 2000.

———. *Psalms*. The Two Horizons Old Testament Commentary. Grand Rapids: Eerdmans, 2008.

Hagner, Donald A. *Matthew 14–28*. Word Biblical Commentary, vol. 33B. Nashville: Thomas Nelson, 1995.

Hamilton, James M., Jr. *God's Glory in Salvation through Judgment: A Biblical Theology.* Wheaton, IL: Crossway, 2010.

———. *Revelation: The Spirit Speaks to the Churches.* Preaching the Word. Wheaton, IL: Crossway, 2012.

———. "The Seed of the Woman and the Blessing of Abraham." *Tyndale Bulletin* 58, no. 2 (2007): 253-73.

———. "The Skull Crushing Seed of the Woman: Inner-Biblical Interpretation of Genesis 3:15." *The Southern Baptist Journal of Theology* 10, no. 2 (2006): 30-54.

———. *What Is Biblical Theology? A Guide to the Bible's Story, Symbolism, and Patterns.* Wheaton, IL: Crossway, 2013.

———. *With the Clouds of Heaven: The Book of Daniel in Biblical Theology.* New Studies in Biblical Theology. Downers Grove, IL: InterVarsity Press, 2014.

Harris, Murray J. *Raised Immortal: Resurrection and Immortality in the New Testament.* London: Marshall, Morgan & Scott, 1983; Grand Rapids: Eerdmans, 1985.

———. "Resurrection and Immortality in the Pauline Corpus." In *Life in the Face of Death: The Resurrection Message of the New Testament*, edited by Richard N. Longenecker, 147-70. Grand Rapids: Eerdmans, 1998.

Harris, R. L. "The Meaning of the Word Sheol as Shown by Parallels in Poetic Texts." *Journal of the Evangelical Theological Society* 4 (1961): 129-35.

Hartley, John E. *The Book of Job.* The New International Commentary on the Old Testament. Grand Rapids: Eerdmans, 1988.

Hartman, Louis F., and Alexander A. Di Lella. *The Book of Daniel.* Anchor Bible Commentary, vol. 23. Garden City, NY: Doubleday, 1978.

Hasel, Gerhard F. "Resurrection in the Theology of Old Testament Apocalyptic." *Zeitschrift für die Alttestamentliche Wissenschaft* 92 (1980): 267-84.

Hays, Richard B. *Echoes of Scripture in the Letters of Paul.* New Haven, CT: Yale University Press, 1989.

———. *First Corinthians.* Interpretation. Louisville: John Knox, 1997.

———. *Reading with the Grain of Scripture.* Grand Rapids: Eerdmans, 2020.

———. "Reading Scripture in Light of the Resurrection." In *The Art of Reading Scripture*, edited by Ellen F. Davis and Richard B. Hays, 216-38. Grand Rapids: Eerdmans, 2003.

Hoehner, Harold W. *Ephesians: An Exegetical Commentary.* Grand Rapids: Baker Academic, 2002.

Hollander, John. *The Figure of Echo: A Mode of Allusion in Milton and After.* Berkeley: University of California Press, 1981.

Hubbard, Robert L., Jr. *The Book of Ruth.* The New International Commentary on the Old Testament. Grand Rapids: Eerdmans, 1988.

Hughes, Philip E. *A Commentary on the Epistle to the Hebrews.* Grand Rapids: Eerdmans, 1977.

———. "The First Resurrection: Another Interpretation." *Westminster Theological Journal* 39, no. 2 (1977): 315-18.

Isaacs, Marie E. *Reading Hebrews & James: A Literary and Theological Commentary.* Macon, GA: Smyth & Helwys, 2002.

Janzen, J. Gerald. "Resurrection and Hermeneutics: On Exodus 3.6 in Mark 12.26." *Journal for the Study of the New Testament* 23 (1985): 43-58.

Jeansonne, Sharon Pace. *The Old Greek Translation of Daniel 7–12*. The Catholic Biblical Quarterly Monograph Series, vol. 19. Washington, DC: The Catholic Biblical Association of America, 1988.

Jeremias, J. "πολλοί." In *Theological Dictionary of the New Testament*. Edited by Gerhard Kittel. Translated by Geoffrey W. Bromiley. Grand Rapids: Eerdmans, 1964–1976.

Johnston, Philip S. "Death and Resurrection." In *New Dictionary of Biblical Theology*. Edited by T. Desmond Alexander, Brian S. Rosner, D. A. Carson, and Graeme Goldsworthy. Downers Grove, IL: InterVarsity Press, 2000.

———. "Life, Disease and Death." In *Dictionary of the Old Testament: Pentateuch*. Edited by T. Desmond Alexander and David W. Baker. Downers Grove, IL: InterVarsity Press, 2003.

———. *Shades of Sheol: Death and Afterlife in the Old Testament*. Downers Grove, IL: InterVarsity Press, 2002.

Jordan, James B. *The Handwriting on the Wall: A Commentary on the Book of Daniel*. Powder Springs, GA: American Vision, 2007.

Joüon, Paul. *A Grammar of Biblical Hebrew*. Translated and revised by T. Muraoka. 2 vols. Rome: Editrice Pontificio Istituto Biblico, 2005.

Kaiser, Walter C., Jr. *Preaching and Teaching the Last Things: Old Testament Eschatology for the Life of the Church*. Grand Rapids: Baker Academic, 2011.

———. *Toward an Old Testament Theology*. Grand Rapids: Zondervan, 1978.

———. *Toward Rediscovering the Old Testament*. Grand Rapids: Academie, 1987.

Keel, Othmar. *The Symbolism of the Biblical World: Ancient Near Eastern Iconography and the Book of Psalms*. New York: Seabury, 1978.

Keener, Craig S. *A Commentary on the Gospel of Matthew*. Grand Rapids: Eerdmans, 1999.

———. *Matthew*. The IVP New Testament Commentary Series, vol. 1. Downers Grove, IL: InterVarsity Press, 1997.

———. *Revelation*. The NIV Application Commentary. Grand Rapids: Zondervan, 2000.

Kidner, Derek. *Genesis: An Introduction and Commentary*. Tyndale Old Testament Commentaries. Downers Grove, IL: InterVarsity Press, 1967.

———. *Proverbs*. Tyndale Old Testament Commentaries, vol. 15. Downers Grove, IL: InterVarsity Press, 1964.

———. *Psalms 1–72*. Tyndale Old Testament Commentaries, vol. 14a. Downers Grove, IL: InterVarsity Press, 1973.

Kim, Eun-Jung. "Reconsidering Eternal Life in the Old Testament: The Idea of Resurrection Rooted in the Torah." Ph.D. diss., The Southern Baptist Theological Seminary, 2015.

Kirk, J. R. Daniel. *Unlocking Romans: Resurrection and the Justification of God*. Grand Rapids: Eerdmans, 2008.

Kitchen, John A. *Proverbs: A Mentor Commentary*. Ross-shire, UK: Mentor, 2006.

Kitchen, K. A. "The Aramaic of Daniel." In *Notes on Some Problems in the Book of Daniel*, edited by D. J. Wiseman, 31–79. London: Tyndale, 1965.

Klein, Ralph W. *1 Samuel*. Word Biblical Commentary, vol. 10. Waco, TX: Word, 1983.

Köstenberger, Andreas J. "John." In *Commentary on the New Testament Use of the Old Testament*, edited by G. K. Beale and D. A. Carson, 415-512. Grand Rapids: Baker Academic, 2007.

Kraus, Hans-Joachim. *Theology of the Psalms*. Translated by Keith Crim. Minneapolis: Augsburg, 1986.

Lacocque, André. *The Book of Daniel*. Translated by David Pellauer. Atlanta: John Knox, 1979.

———. *Le Livre de Daniel*. Commentaire de L'Ancien Testament XVb. Paris: Delachaux et Niestlé, 1976.

Ladd, George Eldon. *I Believe in the Resurrection of Jesus*. Grand Rapids: Eerdmans, 1975.

Lane, William L. *Hebrews 9-13*. Word Biblical Commentary, vol. 47B. Nashville: Thomas Nelson, 1991.

———. "Living a Life of Faith in the Face of Death." In *Life in the Face of Death: The Resurrection Message of the New Testament*, edited by Richard N. Longenecker, 247-69. Grand Rapids: Eerdmans, 1998.

Lea, Thomas D., and Hayne P. Griffin Jr. *1, 2 Timothy, Titus*. The New American Commentary, vol. 34. Nashville: Broadman, 1992.

Leithart, Peter. *Deep Exegesis: The Mystery of Reading Scripture*. Waco, TX: Baylor University Press, 2009.

Lenglet, A. "La Structure Litteraire de Daniel 2-7." *Biblica* 53 (1972): 169-90.

Levenson, Jon D. *Resurrection and the Restoration of Israel: The Ultimate Victory of the God of Life*. New Haven, CT: Yale University Press, 2006.

———. "Resurrection in the Torah? A Second Look." Palmer Lecture, Center of Theological Inquiry, Princeton, NJ, March 21, 2002.

———. *Theology of the Program of Restoration of Ezekiel 40-48*. Missoula, MT: Scholars Press, 1976.

Licona, Michael R. *The Resurrection of Jesus: A New Historiographical Approach*. Downers Grove, IL: IVP Academic, 2010.

Lincoln, Andrew T. *The Gospel According to Saint John*. Black's New Testament Commentary, vol. 4. Peabody, MA: Hendrickson, 2005.

———. "'I Am the Resurrection and the Life': The Resurrection Message of the Fourth Gospel." In *Life in the Face of Death: The Resurrection Message of the New Testament*, edited by Richard N. Longenecker, 122-44. Grand Rapids: Eerdmans, 1998.

Lindenberger, James M. "Daniel 12:1-4." *Interpretation* 39 (1985): 181-86.

Longenecker, Richard N., ed. *Life in the Face of Death: The Resurrection Message of the New Testament*. Grand Rapids: Eerdmans, 1998.

Longman, Tremper, III. *Daniel*. The NIV Application Commentary. Grand Rapids: Zondervan, 1999.

———. *Proverbs*. Baker Commentary on the Old Testament. Grand Rapids: Baker Academic, 2006.

Lucas, E. C. "Cosmology." In *Dictionary of the Old Testament: Pentateuch*. Edited by T. Desmond Alexander and David W. Baker. Downers Grove, IL: InterVarsity Press, 2003.

———. *Daniel*. Apollos Old Testament Commentary, vol. 20. Downers Grove, IL: InterVarsity Press, 2002.

Lunn, Nicholas P. "'Raised on the Third Day According to the Scriptures': Resurrection Typology in the Genesis Creation Narrative." *Journal of the Evangelical Theological Society* 57, no. 3 (2014): 523–35.

Marshall, I. Howard. "Acts." In *Commentary on the New Testament Use of the Old Testament*, edited by G. K. Beale and D. A. Carson, 513–606. Grand Rapids: Baker Academic, 2007.

———. *The Gospel of Luke*. The New International Greek Testament Commentary. Grand Rapids: Eerdmans, 1978.

Martin, W. J. "The Hebrew of Daniel." In *Notes on Some Problems in the Book of Daniel*, edited by D. J. Wiseman, 28–30. London: Tyndale, 1965.

Martin-Achard, Robert. *From Death to Life: A Study of the Development of the Doctrine of the Resurrection in the Old Testament*. London: Oliver and Boyd, 1960.

Matera, Frank J. *Galatians*. Sacra Pagina, vol. 9. Collegeville, MN: The Liturgical Press, 1992.

Mays, James L. *Psalms*. Interpretation. Louisville: John Knox, 1994.

McAlpine, Thomas H. *Sleep, Divine and Human in the Old Testament*. Journal for the Study of the Old Testament–Supplement Series 38. Sheffield: JSOT, 1987.

McKane, William. *Proverbs: A New Approach*. Old Testament Library. Philadelphia: Westminster, 1970.

McLay, R. Timothy. *The OG and Th Versions of Daniel*. Septuagint and Cognate Studies 43. Atlanta: Scholars, 1996.

Meitzen, Manfred O. "Some Reflections on the Resurrection and Eternal Life." *Lutheran Quarterly* 24 (1972): 254–60.

Michaels, J. Ramsey. *The Gospel of John*. The New International Commentary on the New Testament. Grand Rapids: Eerdmans, 2010.

Mihalios, Stefanos. *The Danielic Eschatological Hour in the Johannine Literature*. Library of New Testament Studies. New York: T&T Clark, 2001.

Miller, Stephen R. *Daniel*. The New American Commentary, vol. 18. Nashville: B&H, 1994.

Morales, L. Michael. *Who Shall Ascend the Mountain of the Lord? A Biblical Theology of the Book of Leviticus*. New Studies in Biblical Theology. Downers Grove, IL: IVP Academic, 2015.

Morris, Leon. *The Gospel According to Matthew*. Pillar New Testament Commentary. Grand Rapids: Eerdmans, 1992.

Mowinckel, Sigmund. *The Psalms in Israel's Worship*. Translated by D. R. Ap-Thomas. 2 vols. Nashville: Abingdon, 1962.

Nickelsburg, George W. E. *1 Enoch 1: A Commentary on the Book of 1 Enoch Chapters 1–36; 81–108*. Hermeneia. Minneapolis: Fortress, 2001.

———. *Jewish Literature Between the Bible and the Mishnah: A Historical and Literary Introduction*. Philadelphia: Fortress, 1981.

———. *Resurrection, Immortality, and Eternal Life in Intertestamental Judaism*. Harvard Theological Studies 26. Cambridge, MA: Harvard University Press; London: Oxford University Press, 1972.

Nolland, John. *The Gospel of Matthew*. The New International Greek Testament Commentary. Grand Rapids: Eerdmans, 2005.
O'Brien, Peter T. *The Letter to the Ephesians*. Pillar New Testament Commentary. Grand Rapids: Eerdmans, 1999.
———. *The Letter to the Hebrews*. Pillar New Testament Commentary. Grand Rapids: Eerdmans, 2010.
Ollenburger, Ben C. "If Mortals Die, Will They Live Again? The Old Testament and Resurrection." *Ex Auditu* 9 (1993): 29-44.
Osborne, Grant R. *Matthew*. Zondervan Exegetical Commentary on the New Testament. Grand Rapids: Zondervan, 2010.
———. "Resurrection." In *Dictionary of Jesus and the Gospels*, edited by Joel B. Green, Scot McKnight, and I. Howard Marshall, 673-88. Downers Grove, IL: InterVarsity Press, 1992.
———. *Revelation*. Baker Exegetical Commentary on the New Testament. Grand Rapids: Baker Academic, 2002.
Overman, J. Andrew. *Church and Community in Crisis: The Gospel According to Matthew*. The New Testament in Context. Valley Forge, PA: Trinity Press International, 1996.
Pennington, Jonathan T. *Heaven and Earth in the Gospel of Matthew*. Grand Rapids: Baker Academic, 2009.
———. "Refractions of Daniel in the Gospel of Matthew." In *Early Christian Literature and Intertextuality*, vol. 1, *Thematic Studies*, edited by Craig A. Evans and H. Daniel Zacharias, 65-86. New York: T&T Clark, 2009.
Perkins, Pheme. *Resurrection: New Testament Witness and Contemporary Reflection*. New York: Doubleday, 1984.
Peterson, David G. *The Acts of the Apostles*. Pillar New Testament Commentary. Grand Rapids: Eerdmans, 2009.
Porter, Stanley E., ed. *Hearing the Old Testament in the New Testament*. Grand Rapids: Eerdmans, 2006.
Pulse, Jeffrey. *Figuring Resurrection: Joseph as a Death and Resurrection Figure in the Old Testament and Second Temple Judaism*. Studies in Scripture & Biblical Theology. Bellingham, WA: Lexham, 2021.
Quarles, Charles L. "Matthew 27:51-53: Meaning, Genre, Intertextuality, Theology, and Reception History." *Journal of the Evangelical Theological Society* 59, no. 2 (2016): 271-86.
Ratzinger, Joseph. *Eschatology: Death and Eternal Life*. 2nd ed. Translated by Michael Waldstein. Washington, DC: The Catholic University of America Press, 1988.
Rendtorff, R. *Canon and Theology: Overtures to an Old Testament Theology*. Translated by M. Kohl. Minneapolis: Fortress, 1993.
Renihan, Samuel D. *Crux, Mors, Inferi: A Primer and Reader on the Descent of Christ*. Kindle Direct Publishing, 2021.
Rosner, B. S. "Biblical Theology." In *New Dictionary of Biblical Theology*, edited by T. Desmond Alexander, Brian S. Rosner, D. A. Carson, and Graeme Goldsworthy. Downers Grove, IL: InterVarsity Press, 2000.
Sawyer, John F. A. "Hebrew Words for the Resurrection of the Dead." *Vetus Testamentum* 23 (1973): 218-34.

———. "The Role of Jewish Studies in Biblical Semantics." In *Scripta Signa Vocis: Studies about Scripts, Scriptures, Scribes and Languages in the Near East, Presented to J. H. Hospers by His Pupils, Colleagues, and Friends*, ed. H. Vanstiphout, 201–8. Groningen: E. Forsten, 1986.

Schmidt, Werner H. *The Faith of the Old Testament: A History*. Translated by John Sturdy. Philadelphia: Westminster, 1983.

Schnittjer, Gary Edward. *Old Testament Use of Old Testament: A Book-by-Book Guide*. Grand Rapids: Zondervan, 2021.

Schreiner, Thomas R. *1, 2 Peter, Jude*. The New American Commentary, vol. 37. Nashville: Broadman & Holman, 2003.

———. *Galatians*. Zondervan Exegetical Commentary on the New Testament. Grand Rapids: Zondervan, 2010.

———. *The King in His Beauty: A Biblical Theology of the Old and New Testaments*. Grand Rapids: Baker Academic, 2013.

———. *New Testament Theology: Magnifying God in Christ*. Grand Rapids: Baker Academic, 2008.

Seow, C. L. *Daniel*. Westminster Bible Companion. Louisville: Westminster John Knox, 2003.

Shepherd, Michael B. *Daniel in the Context of the Hebrew Bible*. Studies in Biblical Literature 123. New York: Peter Lang, 2009.

Smalley, Stephen S. *The Revelation of John: A Commentary on the Greek Text of the Apocalypse*. Downers Grove, IL: InterVarsity Press, 2005.

Smick, Elmer. "The Bearing of New Philological Data on the Subjects of Resurrection and Immortality in the Old Testament." *Westminster Theological Journal* 31 (1969): 12–21.

Smith, Gary V. *Isaiah 1–39*. The New American Commentary, vol. 15A. Nashville: B&H, 2007.

Sprinkle, Joe M. *Daniel*. Evangelical Biblical Theology Commentary. Bellingham, WA: Lexham, 2020.

Stein, Robert H. *Luke*. The New American Commentary, vol. 24. Nashville: Broadman, 1992.

Steinmann, Andrew E. *Daniel*. Concordia Commentary. St. Louis: Concordia, 2008.

Stuart, Douglas. *Old Testament Exegesis: A Handbook for Students and Pastors*. 3rd ed. Louisville: Westminster John Knox, 2001.

Stuckenbruck, Loren T. *1 Enoch 91–108*. Commentaries on Early Jewish Literature. Berlin: Walter de Gruyter, 2007.

Sutcliffe, Edmund F. *The Old Testament and the Future Life*. London: Burns, Oates & Washbourne, 1946.

Talmon, Shemaryahu. "Double Readings in the Massoretic Text." *Textus* 1 (1960): 144–84.

Towner, W. Sibley. *Daniel*. Interpretation. Atlanta: John Knox, 1984.

Tromp, Nicholas J. *Primitive Conceptions of Death and the Nether World in the Old Testament*. Rome: Pontifical Biblical Institute, 1969.

Turner, David L. *Matthew*. Baker Exegetical Commentary on the New Testament. Grand Rapids: Baker Academic, 2008.

Van Deventer, H. J. M. "Struktuur en Boodskap(pe) in die Boek Daniel." *Hervormde Teologiese Studies* 59, no. 1 (2003): 191–223.
Van Henten, J. W. "Daniel 3 and 6 in Early Christian Literature." In *The Book of Daniel: Composition and Reception*, edited by John J. Collins and Peter W. Flint, with Cameron VanEpps, 149–69. 2 vols. Supplements to Vetus Testamentum 83. Leiden: Brill, 2001.
Vanhoozer, K. J. "Exegesis and Hermeneutics." In *New Dictionary of Biblical Theology*, edited by T. Desmond Alexander, Brian S. Rosner, D. A. Carson, and Graeme Goldsworthy. Downers Grove, IL: InterVarsity Press, 2000.
Vawter, Bruce. "Intimations of Immortality in the Old Testament." *Journal of Biblical Literature* 91 (1972): 158–71.
Vos, Geerhardus. *The Eschatology of the Old Testament*. Edited by James T. Dennison Jr. Phillipsburg, NJ: P&R, 2001.
Waltke, Bruce K. *The Book of Proverbs*. 2 vols. The New International Commentary on the Old Testament. Grand Rapids: Eerdmans, 2004.
———. "The Date of the Book of Daniel." *Bibliotheca Sacra* 133, no. 532 (1976): 319–29.
———. *An Old Testament Theology: An Exegetical, Canonical, and Thematic Approach*. Grand Rapids: Zondervan, 2007.
Waltke, Bruce K., with Cathi J. Fredricks. *Genesis: A Commentary*. Grand Rapids: Zondervan, 2001.
Walton, John H. *Ancient Near Eastern Thought and the Old Testament: Introducing the Conceptual World of the Hebrew Bible*. Grand Rapids: Baker Academic, 2006.
———. *Genesis*. The NIV Application Commentary. Grand Rapids: Zondervan, 2001.
Wenham, Gordon J. "Daniel: The Basic Issues." *Themelios* 2, no. 2 (1977): 49–52.
———. *Genesis 16–50*. Word Biblical Commentary, vol. 2. Nashville: Thomas Nelson, 1994.
Wesselius, Jan-Wim. "The Writing of Daniel." In *The Book of Daniel: Composition and Reception*, edited by John J. Collins and Peter W. Flint, with Cameron VanEpps, 291–310. 2 vols. Supplements to Vetus Testamentum 83. Leiden: Brill, 2001.
Wheaton, Byron. "As It Is Written: Old Testament Foundations for Jesus' Expectation of Resurrection." *Westminster Theological Journal* 70 (2008): 245–53.
Wilkins, Michael J. *Matthew*. The NIV Application Commentary. Grand Rapids: Zondervan, 2004.
Williams, J. G. "Job and the God of Victims." In *The Voice from the Whirlwind: Interpreting the Book of Job*, edited by Leo G. Perdue and W. Clark Gilpin, 208–31. Nashville: Abingdon, 1992.
Williamson, Paul R. *Death and the Afterlife: Biblical Perspectives on Ultimate Questions*. New Studies in Biblical Theology. Downers Grove, IL: IVP Academic, 2018.
Wilson, Robert Dick. *Studies in the Book of Daniel*. New York: Fleming H. Revell, 1938.
Witherington, Ben, III. *1 and 2 Thessalonians: A Socio-Rhetorical Commentary*. Grand Rapids: Eerdmans, 2006.
———. *The Acts of the Apostles: A Socio-Rhetorical Commentary*. Grand Rapids: Eerdmans, 1997.

———. *Matthew*. Smyth & Helwys Bible Commentary. Macon, GA: Smyth & Helwys, 2006.
Wright, N. T. *Jesus and the Victory of God*. Christian Origins and the Question of God, vol. 2. Minneapolis: Fortress, 1996.
———. *Mark for Everyone*. Louisville: Westminster John Knox, 2004.
———. *The New Testament and the People of God*. Christian Origins and the Question of God, vol. 1. Minneapolis: Fortress, 1992.
———. *The Resurrection of the Son of God*. Christian Origins and the Question of God, vol. 3. Minneapolis: Fortress, 2003.
Yamauchi, Edwin. "Life, Death, and the Afterlife in the Ancient Near East." In *Life in the Face of Death: The Resurrection Message of the New Testament*, edited by Richard N. Longenecker, 21–50. Grand Rapids: Eerdmans, 1998.
Ziegler, Joseph, and Olivier Munnich, eds. *Susanna, Daniel, Bel et Draco*. 2nd ed. Septuaginta: Vetus Testamentum Graecum 16.2. Göttingen: Vandenhoeck & Ruprecht, 1999.
Zimmerli, Walther. *Man and His Hope in the Old Testament*. Studies in Biblical Theology. Naperville, IL: Alec R. Allenson, 1968.

Subject & Author Index

1 Enoch (intertestamental book), 5, 17n74, 23, 128, 135-40. *See also* the Pseudepigrapha
2 Maccabees (intertestamental book), 5, 143, 145-47, 184. *See also* the Apocrypha

A

Aaron (biblical character), 11, 80
Abaddon. *See* death; Sheol
Abel (biblical character), 70-71, 74
Abraham (biblical character), 10-11, 52, 54-59, 64-67, 74, 140-42. *See also* the patriarchs; seed of Abraham
Acts (biblical book), 51n5, 148-49, 163, 166-67, 188, 191
Adam (biblical character), 10, 19, 30, 42, 46, 60-64, 77, 95, 117-18, 133-34, 171
the afterlife, 10-11, 23, 72, 189. *See also* death; Sheol
Agur (biblical character), 74
Akin, Jonathan David, 117n236
Alexander, T. D., 10, 61n39, 69n63
Allison, D. C., 132n14, 150n7
Alter, Robert, 58
Anderson, Bernard W., 79n87, 115
Anderson, Francis I., 98, 111-12
Antiochus IV Epiphanes, 146
antithetical parallelism, 118-19
the Apocalypse. *See* Revelation (biblical book)
the Apocalypse of Moses (intertestamental book), 5, 128, 133-34. *See also* the Pseudepigrapha
the Apocrypha, 127, 143-46, 190. *See also* 2 Maccabees; the Wisdom of Solomon
the Areopagus, 164
Armerding, Carl Edwin, 45-46
Asaph (biblical character), 20n93, 109, 116-17
Athens, 163-64
Aune, David E., 162n44, 173n62

B

Baal, 97
Babylon. *See also* exile
  the Babylonians, 16, 18, 31, 93
  the Chaldeans, 120
  demise of, 32, 93-94
  the empire of, 18, 32, 94, 124
  the king of, 27-29, 31
  Nebuchadnezzar, 28, 31-32
  wise men of, 28
Bailey, Lloyd, 1n2, 22, 40n63
Baldwin, Joyce G., 25n4, 36, 84n95
baptism, 73
barrenness, 55-59, 65, 71, 74, 83, 121, 125
Barth, Christoph, 115n230
Bauckham, Richard, 7-8, 20, 106, 132, 136n28
Beale, G. K., 3n7, 5, 6n23 19, 61n39, 62, 65, 66n52, 69n60, 92, 98n163, 104, 147n67, 162n47, 186n95
Beckwith, Roger, 17n74
Bethlehem, 121-22
biblical theology, 2, 4, 189
birth, 70-71
Bishop, Steven, 79n87

Blomberg, C. L., 4n15, 33n20, 156
Boaz (biblical character), 121–22
bones
  of the dead, 129, 131
  of the prophet Elisha, 87, 95
  valley of, 94–96
book of life, 187
Boring, Eugene, 57n21
Brannon, M. Jeff, 75n78, 77
Bronner, Leila, 23, 68n57, 91, 94n144
Broyles, Craig C., 110
Bruce, F. F., 34n29, 34n32, 164, 177, 184
Brueggemann, Walter, 44n85
Buchanan, George Wesley, 138n32
Bush, Frederic W., 122

C

Caesarea, 163, 165
Cain (biblical character), 70–71
Calvin, John, 37n45, 63n46
canonical order, 52, 82, 148
Carnley, Peter, 96
Carson, D. A., 3n7, 5
Cavallin, H. C. C., 22n103
Charlesworth, James H., 22, 128n3
Chase, Mitchell L., 50n2, 50n7-8, 148n1
Childs, Brevard, 45n87
Chronicles (biblical book)
  1 Chronicles
  2 Chronicles, 9n31, 106, 114
  the combined book of Chronicles, 9, 124
Ciampa Roy, 127
Clines, David J. A., 111
Cole, Robert Luther, 114n227
Collins, Adela, 188n101
Collins, John J., 1n2, 16n72, 21–23, 25n4; 33n23, 35–36, 38, 40, 45n87, 47n101, 51, 70, 125, 135, 136n27, 138
Corinthians (biblical books). *See also* the epistles
  1 Corinthians, 167, 169
  2 Corinthians, 167, 171, 174
Cornelius (biblical character), 163–64, 185
Craigie, Peter C., 108n194

creation. *See also* Genesis
  the breath of life, 69–70, 95
  de-creation, 73
  the divine act of creation, 4, 69, 73. *See also* God the Creator
  of man, 11, 19, 69–70, 73, 95
  of the tree of life, 61. *See also* the tree of life
  of the world, 7n27, 73
critical scholarship, 10, 15–16, 18, 22, 40n64, 42, 47, 51, 59, 88n114
Cross, Frank Moore, 85n102

D

Dahood, Mitchell, 108
Daniel
  Aramaic section of the book, 26, 33
  the biblical character, 2, 17–19, 27–31, 40, 45n87, 47, 50, 76, 125, 154, 160, 186, 189
  the book of, 1, 4, 17–19, 25–26, 32, 35, 49, 76, 88, 93, 105, 125, 135, 137n31, 138, 147n67, 167, 170, 185–86, 189
  the dating of, 1, 10, 15–19, 22–23, 36–37, 40n64, 47, 125, 135, 136n27, 138, 189–90
  friends of. *See* Shadrach, Meschach, and Abednego
  Hebrew section of the book, 33
  influence on intertestamental literature, 127–48, 189–91. *See also* intertestamental period and literature; intertextuality
  the prophesies and visions of, 1, 15–18, 30, 47, 189–90
  the structure of the book, 24–25
  use in the New Testament, 17, 35, 148–89, 191. *See also* intertextuality
  use of the Old Testament, 6–7, 38, 43–45, 48, 50, 91, 105, 125, 148, 189–90. *See also* intertextuality
Daniel 12:2
  in Acts, 163–66, 188, 191
  alternative interpretations of, 45–48
  in the Apocrypha, 143–46, 179, 190
  in the epistles, 167, 169–85, 187–88, 191

exegesis of, 35-45
in the gospels, 148-63, 188, 191
ideas and images in, 88, 91
in the Pseudepigrapha, 128-143, 171, 179, 190
in Revelation, 167, 185-88, 191
textual versions of, 32-35. *See also* the Masoretic Text; the Old Greek; Theodotion
darkness, 139, 175. *See also* light
David (biblical character), 12, 14, 20, 43-44, 101, 107-8, 109n197, 114-16, 122. *See also* king of Israel
Davies, W. D., 132n14, 150n7
Day, John, 21n96, 91-92
death. *See also* exile; judgment; the resurrection; Sheol
  burial, 67
  as captivity, 78
  chaos, 85, 100, 103, 106, 125, 190
  concept of, 10-14, 72, 83, 115
  dust, 19, 37-40, 46, 48, 70, 88, 90-91, 102, 116, 118, 125-26, 131, 134, 158, 171, 176, 187
  as the end of a family line, 57-59, 71-72, 74, 121-22. *See also* barrenness
  as exile, 61n38, 62, 77, 95, 190
  the final defeat of, 184, 187, 191
  gates of, 116
  as God's enemy, 88
  the grave and the tomb, 11-12, 14, 28-29, 53, 64, 72-73, 77, 80, 116, 120, 157
  as a penalty, 28, 45, 61-64, 68-70, 80
  physical illness and infirmity, 102-3, 115-16. *See also* leprosy
  as a pit, 115-16
  power of, 115
  ransom from, 98
  of the righteous, 13-14, 107, 119
  sleep, 19, 30, 37-40, 42-43, 45-46, 48, 70, 86, 93, 110, 137-38, 141, 150-52, 157-59, 161, 171, 175-76, 179-80, 184, 187, 190

  sown seed imagery, 169-70
  as uncleanness outside the camp, 79-80. *See also* leprosy
  as the wasting away of the outer self, 172
  of the wicked, 13-14, 119
Delamarter, Steve A., 5n18, 128n3
Delitzsch, Franz, 109
Dempster, Stephen G., 3-4, 9, 19, 69n62, 81, 82n92, 93, 95n149, 97n155, 100
deSilva, David A., 140n40, 183, 184n88
Deuteronomy (biblical book), 52, 68-69, 97n155
the devil, 152, 156. *See also* Satan; the serpent
Di Lella, A. Alexander, 15n65, 22n103, 33n24, 42n77
dreams. *See also* the visions of Daniel
  interpretation of, 27, 32
  of the king of Babylon, 27, 32
Dreyfus, F., 55n14
Dumbrell, William J., 123

E

Ecclesiastes
  the author of, 113n222
  the book of, 113n222
Edwards, James R., 54n12
Egypt
  the Egyptians, 52-53, 56, 76
  exodus from. *See* the historical event of the exodus
  land of, 67, 75, 117
  the Nile, 76
  Pharaoh, 56, 75-77, 124
the elect, 136-37
Elijah (biblical character), 11, 20, 84-86, 96, 98, 101-2, 105, 109-10, 151, 157n37, 184n88
Elimelech (biblical character), 121-22
Elisha (biblical character), 41, 84, 86-87, 95-96, 98, 101, 105, 151, 184n88. *See also* bones of the prophet Elisha
Elledge, C. D., 142n49, 171n59
Emadi, Samuel, 75n79

embodiment, 69–70, 118, 159, 169–72. *See also* resurrection as the reembodiment of the soul; disembodiment of the soul at death
Emerson, Matthew Y., 11n46
Enns, Peter, 76
Enoch
  the author of 1 Enoch, 137. *See also* 1 Enoch
  the biblical character, 11, 20, 72, 101–2, 109–10, 135, 142, 157n37
Ephesians (biblical book), 167, 175. *See also* the epistles
the epistles (biblical books), 148, 167, 188, 191. *See also* the books of 1–2 Corinthians; 1 Peter; 1–2 Thessalonians; 2 Timothy; Ephesians; Galatians; Hebrews; Philippians; Romans
Esau (biblical character), 67, 142
Esther
  the biblical character, 122–23
  the book of, 106, 114
eternal life, 14, 28, 35, 41–44, 48, 60–62, 88, 118–19, 124–25, 130, 145, 155–56, 161, 168, 170, 172, 174–75, 178, 184. *See also* the resurrection
Eusebius of Caesarea, 18
Eve (biblical character), 19, 60–63, 70–71, 95, 117–18, 133–34. *See also* the seed of the woman
exile. *See also* death; the resurrection
  as death, 61n38, 62, 106, 190
  from the garden, 10, 42, 60–62, 70, 77, 95, 117, 133. *See also* the garden of Eden; trees
  imagery of, 117
  from the land, 13, 18–20, 22, 26–27, 29, 31–32, 78, 88, 95, 100, 106, 117, 123–24, 190
  return from, 26–27, 29, 61, 77–78, 95, 100, 106, 190
Exodus. *See also* Egypt; return from exile
  the book of, 19, 51–52, 57, 59, 69
  the historical event of, 52–53, 77–78

Mount Sinai, 128
the new exodus, 124
the tenth plague, 76–77
a type of deliverance, 78
the Red Sea, 77–78
Ezekiel
  the biblical character, 90, 94–96, 132n15
  the book of, 19, 22, 82
Ezra-Nehemiah (biblical book), 9

F
faith, 20, 28, 65–67, 70n64, 88, 103, 112, 163, 172, 183, 185
Fee, Gordon D., 177, 182n83
Felix (biblical character), 163, 165–66
the flood, 73. *See also* judgment; waters
Forestell, J. Terence, 129
France, R. T., 150n8, 151n11, 152, 183n87, 184n88
Freedman, David N., 9, 98
Fyall, Robert S., 112n218, 113n222

G
Galatians (biblical book), 167, 173–74. *See also* the epistles
garden. *See also* the land; paradise; trees
  of Eden, 10, 42, 60–64, 70, 77, 95, 117–19, 133
  imagery, 103, 105, 114
Gardner, Anne E., 38n56, 45
genealogy, 72, 121–22
Genesis (biblical book), 9n31, 10–11, 19, 35, 40, 48–49, 52, 69–70, 190
the gentiles, 142, 167–68
Gentry, Peter J., 25n3
glorification, 169–72, 178. *See also* glory after death
God
  as advocate, 112, 124
  the angel of, 29
  anger of, 105, 133
  arm of, 110
  as the avenger, 83, 134
  as the conqueror of death, 88, 187
  children of, 177

as Creator, 118, 125–26, 164. *See also* creation
as Divine Warrior, 85–86, 87n110, 95–98, 100, 102, 106, 117, 125, 190
face of, 108
faithfulness of, 20, 35n35, 57, 101, 107, 125–26, 190
the Father, 161, 164, 173
fear and reverence of, 130–31, 173
fellowship with, 41, 107
glory of, 79, 103
of heaven, 124
holiness of, 79
image bearers of, 11, 61, 63–64, 70, 88, 118. *See also* creation of man
impartiality of, 163, 167
justice of, 20, 68, 126, 134
who kills and makes alive, 67–69, 82–84, 97, 116, 120, 124–26
of life, 79, 187, 190
as a lion, 96, 98
love of, 20, 101, 124, 126, 190
mercy of, 131, 187
people of, 14, 20–21, 26, 28, 41–43, 47–48, 69, 75–79, 88, 101, 104, 107, 110, 118, 137, 173, 186, 190. *See also* Israel; Judah
plan of, 14, 77, 97
presence of, 79
promises of, 52, 56–58, 61, 63–65, 67–68, 71, 74, 80, 117, 119–20, 122, 124–26, 146, 190
the Redeemer, 78, 98, 110–12, 124, 191
righteousness of, 116, 126, 187
as a rock, 83
sovereign power of, 26, 70n64, 72, 74, 77, 82, 84–87, 91, 98, 101–2, 115–16, 120, 124, 126, 158
the Spirit of. *See* the Holy Spirit
throne of, 134, 186
uniqueness of, 116
word of, 102
wrath of, 44, 96, 103–4, 134, 167. *See also* judgment of God
Goldingay, John, 25n5, 39n60, 42n77, 46

Goldstein, Jonathan, 145n62
the gospel
the message of, 167, 177
the Gospel accounts, 53, 148–49, 158–60, 166–67, 188, 191. *See also* the books of Matthew; Mark; Luke; John
the word of life, 177
the Greek. *See* the gentiles
Green, William Henry, 113
Greenspoon, Leonard, 6n22, 7, 8n29, 19–20, 39, 41, 42n77, 44n82, 68, 69n60, 83n94, 84, 85n100, 87, 89, 91n129, 92, 93n140, 95–96, 97n155, 98, 103n173, 103n175, 104n177
Greidanus, Sidney, 25n4–5, 47, 154n25
Grogan, Geoffrey W., 107n190, 116n231

H

Hagner, Donald A., 54n13, 157n38
Haman (biblical character), 122–23
Hamilton, James M., Jr., 4n16, 9, 15n60, 25n4, 29, 52n9, 97n159, 100, 124, 186n96
Hannah (biblical character), 82–84
hapax legomena in biblical Hebrew, 119
Harris, R. L., 12n48
Harris, Murray J., 168n54, 181n82
Hartley, John E., 112
Hartman, Louis F., 15n65, 22n103, 42n77
Hasel, Gerhard F., 36n42, 41, 90n123
Hays, Richard B., 3n7, 6n23, 53n10, 54n11, 56n18, 57, 60, 170
heavenly being, 30, 44, 155. *See also* the angel of God
Hebrews
the author of, 182–83, 184n88, 187
the book of, 66, 72, 76, 167, 182. *See also* the epistles
the Hebrew Bible. *See* the Tanak
Hezekiah (biblical character), 13, 102, 122
Hoehner, Harold W., 175
the Holy Spirit
at creation, 69

as a guarantee of resurrection hope, 172
sowing to, 174–75
Hosea
the biblical character, 97–98, 105
the book of, 20–22, 82, 91–92, 100, 105
Hughes, Philip E., 65

I
inheritance, 37, 52, 80, 83, 160
intertestamental period and literature, 2, 5, 8, 127, 132n15, 136, 147, 170, 188, 190–91. See also the Apocrypha; the Pseudepigrapha
intertextuality
criteria, 6–8, 23
definitions of quotation, allusion, and echo, 6n23
intertestamental use of the Old Testament, 2, 4–5, 8, 127–47, 171–72, 179. See also Daniel's influence on intertestamental literature
Old Testament use of the Old Testament, 63, 91–92, 99, 105, 109. See also Daniel's use of the Old Testament
New Testament use of intertestamental literature, 170–72, 179
New Testament use of the Old Testament, 2–4, 8, 43, 51–60, 66, 81, 107, 151, 154, 177. See also use of Daniel in the New Testament
scriptural use of earlier Scripture, 50n1
Isaac (biblical character), 10, 52, 54–57, 59, 64–67, 76, 122, 140–42. See also the patriarchs; seed of Abraham
Isaacs, Marie E., 183n86
Isaiah
the biblical character, 87–88, 102
the book of, 19, 21n94, 22, 35, 39–40, 48, 82, 87–88, 92, 100, 102, 104–5, 175–76, 190
the Little Apocalypse, 88
the Servant Songs, 92
Ishmael (biblical character), 67

Israel. See also exile; the southern kingdom of Judah; seed of Abraham
camp of, 79–80. See also uncleanness outside the camp
division of, 20n93
history of, 8, 12
the Israelites, 27, 46, 53, 56, 75, 77–81, 100, 105, 117, 122–23
the Jews, 122–23, 147, 161, 167
king of, 31, 102
liberation and restoration from captivity and oppression, 5, 20–22, 52–53, 78, 93, 116–17
nation of, 90, 93–97, 115, 134–35, 142
the northern kingdom of, 98
rebellion of, 100
as a vine, 117

J
Jacob (biblical character), 10–11, 13, 52, 55–59, 67, 75, 140–42. See also the patriarchs; seed of Abraham
Janzen, J. Gerald, 55n16–17, 56n20, 59–60
Jeansonne, Sharon Pace, 42
Jehoiakim (biblical character), 31. See also king of Israel
Jeremiah (biblical book), 19, 82, 93
Jeremias, J., 37
Jerome, 18
Jerusalem, 31, 123, 165–66. See also the temple
Jesus
belief in, 161
the believers' reign with, 175, 178
death of, 156–57, 179
disciples of, 60n36, 152–53, 168
example of, 176
the first fruits of the resurrection, 165, 191
as judge of the living and the dead, 163–64, 166, 169, 172–73, 180–81, 185, 187
as Lord of all, 164, 169
the Messiah, 47, 81, 122
miracles of, 150–52, 158–59, 161

use of the Old Testament, 51–60, 71, 81,
  99–100, 151, 153–54, 156
parables of, 153–54
power of, 151, 163, 166
prophet like Moses, 81
the resurrection of, 81, 107, 148,
  163–67, 176, 178–79
the second coming (parousia), 178–81,
  191
the Son of God, 157n38, 161–62
the Son of Man, 100, 154, 156, 161, 173
teachings of, 60n36, 149–50, 152–53,
  155, 158–63, 168, 173–74, 178
throne of, 156, 181
the time of, 147
the voice of, 161–62
union with, 73, 162–63, 173, 175, 178–79,
  191
Job
  the biblical character, 13, 58, 110–13,
    120–21
  the book of, 19, 106, 111, 113–14, 121
  family and fortune of, 120–21
  friends of, 110
  interpretations of Job 19:25–27, 111–12
John
  the apostle, 61, 186
  the gospel of, 160
  John the Baptist, 127
Johnston, Philip, 12n47, 13–14, 21, 36,
  93n140, 111, 146
Jonah
  the biblical character, 99, 122, 153
  the book of, 82
  the great fish, 99–100
  the sign of, 153
Jordan, James B., 29n15, 30, 47–48
Joseph (biblical character), 67, 75
Joshua (biblical character), 67
Jubilees (intertestamental book), 5,
  128–29. *See also* the Pseudepigrapha
Judah (the land and kingdom of), 31,
  88, 96, 102, 121, 123–24. *See also* exile;
  Israel; the testament of Judah
Judges (biblical book), 100

judgment. *See also* death; exile; the
  resurrection; Sheol; vindication
according to works, 167–68, 172–75,
  187
on Babylon, 93–94. *See also* demise of
  Babylon
believers passing judgment one
  another, 169
as bodily, 104–5, 147, 150, 152, 154–56,
  159
day of, 114, 124, 131, 136, 144, 161,
  164–68, 172, 180, 185, 187
of the dead, 23, 89
destruction of sinners, 89, 130–31,
  137–38, 147, 152, 159, 180–81
as eternal, 104–5, 141, 143, 150, 155–56,
  158–59, 180–82, 183n87, 187
at the fall, 10, 38, 45, 60–62
final judgment, 93–94, 131, 153, 155–56,
  160, 163–66, 168, 173–74, 177, 185–87
of fire, 141, 154–56, 158–59
of God, 5, 7, 13, 26, 31, 44, 63, 68, 73, 77,
  80, 83, 88–89, 93–94, 96, 98, 130–31,
  134, 137, 163–67, 180, 186–87
hell, 149–50, 152, 155, 158
at Jesus's second coming (parousia).
  See the second coming (parousia)
judgment seat, 169, 172, 182
the lake of fire, 187
promise of, 1, 30, 32, 43–44, 63, 73,
  87–88, 96
on rebellious Israel, 96, 98, 100, 142
the second death, 186–87
as a separation of sheep and goats,
  173
of the serpent, 62–63
sowing and reaping, 174–75
stories of, 30–32, 80
type of, 94
as universal, 168–69, 173, 182, 183n87,
  185. *See also* the resurrection as
  universal
justification, 167. *See also* the resurrection as the final justification of the
  faithful

K

Kaiser, Walter C., Jr., 12n48, 65, 72, 113n223
Keener, Craig S., 57n21
Kidner, Derek, 102, 118
Kim, Eun-Jung, 11n44
kingdom
  of God (heavenly), 25, 32, 152n14, 154, 158, 180–81
  of man (earthly), 25, 32, 124
  the parables, 153–54. See also teachings of Jesus
  of Persia. See Persia
Kings (biblical book)
  1 Kings, 82, 84
  2 Kings, 82, 84, 100–101
  the combined book of Kings, 19, 82, 84
Kirk, J. R. Daniel, 130
Kitchen, John A., 120
Kitchen, K. A., 16
Klein, Ralph W., 84n95
Korah (sons of), 20n93, 109
Kraus, Hans-Joachim, 115n229

L

Lacocque, André, 29
Ladd, George Eldon, 21n97, 70n64, 96n153, 97n158
Lamech (biblical character), 62–64
the land. See also exile; the garden of Eden
  Canaan, 67, 80, 117
  conquest of, 18, 20
  division of, 18, 20
  entrance of the righteous, 88–89
  healing of, 97, 103, 105
the Law. See also the Pentateuch; the Torah
  as a literary corpus in the Tanak, 2, 12, 29n13, 48, 50–52, 69, 83, 125, 166, 190
  of the Lord, 142
  of Moses, 81
  strong evidence of resurrection hope in, 52–69, 190
  supporting evidence of resurrection hope in, 69–82, 190
Lazarus (biblical character), 162–63
Leah (biblical character), 74
Leithart, Peter, 24
Lenglet, A., 25n4
leprosy, 79–80
Levenson, Jon D., 45, 57, 58n25, 58n27, 78, 81, 85–86, 90n124, 92, 93n137, 103, 115n229, 121
Leviticus (biblical book), 69
levirate marriage, 53, 57–58
Licona, Michael R., 157n38
light, 130, 139, 175. See also darkness
Lindenberger, James M., 36n36
Longman, Tremper, III, 26n7, 29n15, 117, 120
Lucas, E. C., 22n106
Luke
  the biblical character, 166
  the gospel of, 159
Lunn, Nicholas P., 73n74, 101

M

Malachi (biblical character), 127
Mark (biblical book), 158–59
Markley, Jennifer Foutz, 33n20
Martha (biblical character), 162, 163n48
Martin, W. J., 16
Martin-Achard, Robert, 22n103, 90
martyrdom, 35–37, 47, 141, 143, 145–46, 184. See also suffering of believers
the Masoretic Text (MT), 32–35, 118, 121, 149, 156. See also textual versions of Daniel 12:2
Matthew (biblical book), 149, 152, 157–59. See also the Sermon on the Mount
Mays, James L., 108
McAlpine, Thomas H., 38n49
McLay, Timothy R., 33n23, 33n26
Meitzen, Manfred O., 10
Michael (biblical character), 133
the Midianites, 142
Mihalios, Stefanos, 136n27
Miriam (biblical character), 80
the Mishnah, 51

Moab, 121
Morales, L. Michael, 79
Morris, Leon, 54n11
Moses
    the Apocalypse of. *See* the Apocalypse of Moses
    the biblical character, 11, 52, 56, 67–68, 70–71, 75–77, 80–81, 101, 128, 134, 183
    the song of, 68, 83
    the Testament of. *See* the Testament of Moses
Mowinckel, Sigmund, 107
Munnich, Olivier, 33n23

N

Naomi (biblical character), 121
Nestle-Aland (NA), 148n3, 161n43
the new creation, 73, 104, 163
the New Jerusalem, 61
Nickelsburg, George W., 5n18, 21, 36, 42n77, 105n181, 128, 133n19, 135
Nineveh, 99–100, 153, 159
Noah (biblical character), 62–63, 73
Nolland, John, 157n34, 157n37
noncanonical literature. *See also* the Apocrypha; intertestamental period and literature; the Pseudepigrapha
    4QMMT, 9
    Baba Bathra, 9
    Tobit, 17n74
    Ecclesiasticus, 17n74
    prologue to Sirach, 9
Numbers (biblical book), 69

O

O'Brien, Peter T., 175
the Old Greek (OG), 32–35, 46, 146, 149, 153, 155–56, 168, 171, 177. *See also* textual versions of Daniel 12:2
the Olivet Discourse, 155
oppression
    oppressive forces of death, 103
    oppression of Israel, 5, 21, 27, 77, 83, 89, 100
    oppression of the righteous, 137, 144
Origen, 18
Orpah (biblical character), 121

Osborne, Grant R., 152

P

paradise, 79, 133. *See also* garden; the land; trees
the Passover, 77. *See also* Egypt, Exodus
the patriarchs, 10, 49, 52, 54–57, 58n27, 59, 64, 66–67, 140, 142, 183. *See also* Abraham; Isaac; Jacob; the Testament of the Twelve Patriarchs
Paul
    the apostle, 51, 74, 81–82, 163–81, 187
    the epistles of, 181, 187. *See also* 1–2 Corinthians; 1–2 Thessalonians; 2 Timothy; Ephesians; Galatians; Philippians; Romans
Pennington, Jonathan T., 149n6, 157n36
the Pentateuch, 52, 71. *See also* the Law; the Torah
Persia
    Ahasuerus, 123
    Cyrus, 16n70, 18, 124
    Darius, 28
    the empire of, 122
    the king of, 122–24
    the Persians, 16, 18
    Zoroastrianism, 22, 23n109
Peter
    the apostle, 20, 73, 81, 107, 163–64, 166, 184–85
    the book of 1 Peter, 167, 184, 187. *See also* the epistles
Peterson, David G., 165
the Pharisees, 153, 165, 187. *See also* the Sadducees
Philippians (biblical book), 167, 176. *See also* the epistles
Platonism, 143
Porphyry, 15, 18, 46–47
Porter, Stanley E., 3n7
prayer, 25, 28, 44, 82–84, 102, 116–17
the priests, 79
progressive revelation, 3
the Prophets

as a literary corpus in the Tanak, 2,
4, 7, 9, 12, 29n13, 48, 50–51, 60, 78,
82–83, 100, 106, 125, 166, 190
the Former Prophets, 9
strong evidence of resurrection hope
in, 82–100, 190
supporting evidence of resurrection
hope in, 100–105, 190
the Writing Prophets, 9
Proverbs (biblical book), 106, 114, 117, 119
the prudent, 120. See also wisdom
Psalms
the book of, 9n31, 19–20, 106–7, 114
editor of, 116n231
individual psalms, 20, 99, 106,
108n194, 109, 114–16
the psalmist, 13n55, 14, 20, 107,
108n194, 109, 115, 117
Psalms of Solomon (intertestamental
book), 5, 128–31. See also the Pseudepigrapha
the Pseudepigrapha, 127–28, 143, 190.
See also 1 Enoch; the Apocalypse of
Moses; Jubilees; Psalms of Solomon;
the Sibylline Oracles; the Testament
of Moses; the Testaments of the
Twelve Patriarchs
Pulse, Jeffrey, 75n78

Q

Quarles, Charles L., 157n33
queen of the South (biblical character),
153, 159–60

R

Rachel (biblical character), 84
Ratzinger, Joseph, 108n191
Rebekah (biblical character), 74
Renihan, Samuel D., 11n46
repentance, 96, 97n155–156, 98, 105, 153,
159, 164–65, 167
rest from toil, 63–64. See also the curse
on the ground
the resurrection. See also death; evidence of resurrection hope in the
Law; in the Prophets; in the Writings;
Sheol

as awaking from sleep, 89–91, 93, 108,
138, 141, 147, 150–52, 156–59, 161, 171,
175–76, 179–80, 184, 187, 190
as birth from barrenness, 65, 125. See
also barrenness
as bodily, 1–2, 10, 14, 19–24, 32, 36, 41,
45–48, 50–51, 53–54, 61–62, 69, 87,
89–91, 94–97, 111–112, 114n226, 116,
120, 129, 132–33, 136–37, 140, 143,
145–47, 152, 161, 165–66, 169–76, 178,
180–82, 184, 190
as deliverance, 14, 25–29, 31–32, 35, 43,
66, 101, 107, 108n194, 115, 123, 136,
146, 182
as the final justification of the faithful, 108
glory after death, 109, 118, 184. See
also glorification
as healing, 102–3, 105, 116, 118. See also
physical illness and infirmity; the
healing of the land
intertestamental hope and expectation of, 128, 130–31, 133–34, 136–41,
144–46, 190–91
at Jesus's second coming (parousia).
See the second coming (parousia)
New Testament conception and hope
of, 51–54, 120, 148–50, 152–53, 155–56,
158–65, 167, 169–72, 174–75, 177–83,
185–86, 191
as national (corporate) restoration
of Israel, 46–48, 89–90, 94–97, 100,
123–24, 134. See also alternative
interpretations of Daniel 12:2
as nonphysical rather than bodily,
45–46, 48. See also alternative interpretations of Daniel 12:2
Old Testament hope and promise of,
1–2, 4–10, 18–23, 26–27, 30, 32, 35–37,
40–48, 50, 68–69, 85, 87, 89, 94, 96,
98–99, 101, 105–7, 108n194, 112–13,
117, 119–20, 122, 124–25, 134, 138,
189–90
Old Testament imagery, pictures, and
stories of, 7, 19, 22–23, 26–32, 38–41,
43, 52, 60, 62, 64, 67, 69–70, 72–82,

84, 86–88, 90–94, 96, 98–102, 104–6, 108–10, 114–18, 120–23, 125, 135, 137
  as return from exile, 61n38, 95, 106, 124–25. *See also* exile
  on the last day, 162–63
  as ransom, 98–99, 109
  as restoration from the pit, 115–16
  as the restoration of a family line, 121–22, 124. *See also* death as the end of a family line
  as the reembodiment of the soul, 5, 111, 124, 132, 145, 152, 187. *See also* embodiment; disembodiment of the soul at death
  resuscitation stories (temporary resurrection), 41, 69, 84, 86–87, 132, 151, 157, 159, 184
  as a reversal, 19, 38, 45, 62, 71, 74, 82, 85–86, 106, 121, 123, 125, 143
  of the righteous (to life), 5, 7, 21, 23, 32, 35–36, 40–44, 48, 89, 106–7, 114, 119, 124, 126, 128–32, 136–38, 140–47, 153–56, 159–68, 170, 172–75, 178–82, 186–87, 190
  the sea gives up its dead, 186–87
  as spiritually inaugurated in the present, 161–63, 166, 176–78, 191
  as the triumph of God, 74, 85–86, 88, 103 106. *See* God as the Divine Warrior
  type of, 66, 76
  as universal (or general), 36, 44, 86n105, 127n2, 133–34, 136, 142, 157, 169, 173, 182–83, 187, 190
  verbs of, 6n22, 84–87, 89–91, 92–94, 98, 105, 108, 115–16, 124–25, 129, 138, 141, 151, 153, 159, 169, 171, 176, 191
  as vindication, 1, 20–21, 27–29, 35, 48, 69, 77, 87, 93, 101, 107–8, 110, 112–13, 124, 128–29, 131, 134–36, 138, 140–46, 154, 160, 165–66, 185–87, 190
  of the wicked (to judgment), 5, 7, 23, 32, 35–36, 40–44, 48, 89, 93, 104–6, 114, 126, 129–32, 137–38, 140–47, 150, 152–56, 159–68, 172–75, 178, 180–82, 187, 190. *See also* judgment

Revelation
  the book of, 148, 167, 185, 187, 191
  the thousand years, 186
Romans (biblical book), 167, 174. *See also* the epistles
Rosner, Brian S., 7, 127
Ruth
  the biblical character, 121–22
  the book of, 106, 114, 122

S

the Sabbath, 161
the Sadducees, 51, 53–57, 59–60, 92, 165. *See also* the Pharisees
Samuel
  1 Samuel, 82
  2 Samuel, 100
  the biblical character, 82
  the combined book of Samuel, 19
the Sanhedrin, 163, 165
Sarah (biblical character), 64–65, 74
Satan, 110. *See also* the devil; the serpent
Saul (biblical character), 101
Sawyer, J. F. A., 6n22, 39n59, 84, 92, 119
Schmidt, Werner H., 35n34
Schnittjer, Gary Edward, 39n61
Schreiner, Thomas R., 3n7, 64n47, 92n133, 123, 163n48
the scribes. *See* the Pharisees; the Sadducees
seed
  of Abraham, 64–65, 74
  of Adam, 134
  of David, 102
  of the serpent, 70–71
  of the Suffering Servant, 104
  of the woman, 19, 62–63, 70–71
Seow, C. L., 36n36
the Sermon on the Mount, 149
the Septuagint (LXX), 46, 70–71, 113, 121, 157, 160
Seth (biblical character), 70–71, 74, 133–34, 142
the serpent, 19, 62–63, 70, 125. *See also* the devil; Satan

Shadrach, Meshach, and Abednego, 27–29, 31, 154
Sheol. *See also* the afterlife; death
concept of, 10–14, 23, 74, 83, 98–99, 106–7, 112, 115–16, 120, 189
cords of, 101, 114
gates of, 102
ransom from, 98–99, 109
return of bodily deposits from, 136. *See also* the resurrection
Shepherd, Michael, 9n31, 15–17
Sibylline Oracles (intertestamental book), 5, 128, 131–32. *See also* the Pseudepigrapha
sin. *See also* death; exile; judgment
the curse of, 38, 52n9, 62–63, 73, 104, 125–26
the curse on the ground, 62–63
the sinful flesh, 174
human depravity, 167
transgression of God's command, 118
Smalley, Stephen S., 187
Smick, Elmer, 51
Smith, Gary V., 88
Solomon (biblical character), 109n201, 117–18, 120, 129, 153. *See also* king of Israel
the soul
eternality of, 143–44
disembodiment of the soul at death, 144, 150, 152, 159. *See also* embodiment; resurrection as the reembodiment of the soul
Sprinkle, Joe M., 15n60, 23n110, 37n44
stars. *See also* light
Abraham's offspring, 64, 74. *See also* seed of Abraham
angelic host, 138. *See also* the angel of God; heavenly being
Israel as, 134–35
lights of heaven, 138
to shine, 118, 137–38, 144, 147, 153–55, 160, 172, 175–78, 191. *See also* the resurrection
Steinmann, Andrew E., 15–18, 25n3–4, 28, 33n23, 37n43, 38, 43n80, 44

structure
chiastic structure, 25–26, 168
of Daniel. *See* the structure of the book of Daniel
inclusio, 26
Stuart, Douglas, 33n20
suffering of God's people, 171–72, 180, 183–85, 190–91. *See also* martyrdom
the Suffering Servant, 92–93, 104. *See also* Jesus; the Servant songs in Isaiah
Sutcliffe, Edmund F., 22n106, 111

T

the tabernacle, 78–80, 109n197, 109n201. *See also* the temple
the Tanak, 2, 8–9, 12, 45, 82, 123–24. *See also* the Law; the Prophets; the Writings
the temple, 20n93, 31, 82, 123, 165. *See also* the tabernacle
the Testament of Moses (intertestamental book), 5, 128, 134–35. *See also* the Pseudepigrapha
the Testaments of the Twelve Patriarchs. *See also* the Pseudepigrapha
the intertestamental book, 5, 128, 140–43
the testament of Benjamin (T. Benj.), 141–43, 170–71
the testament of Issachar (T. Iss.), 179
the testament of Judah (T. Jud.), 140–41, 179
the testament of Zebulun (T. Zeb.), 141
Theodotion (Th), 32–35, 46, 130, 149, 151, 153, 155–57, 166, 168, 171, 178. *See also* textual versions of Daniel 12:2
Thessalonians (biblical books). *See also* the epistles
1 Thessalonians, 167, 179, 181
2 Thessalonians, 167, 180
the third day, 96, 99–100, 102, 122, 153
Timothy
the biblical character, 181
2 Timothy, 167, 181. *See also* the epistles

the Torah, 4, 7, 13, 18–19, 51–53, 55, 59–60, 72n72, 81, 82n92, 106, 189. *See also* the Law; the Pentateuch
Towner, W. Sibley, 29n15, 47n102
tree
   of the knowledge of good and evil, 60–61
   of Lebanon, 105
   of life, 42, 60–62, 117–19, 124–25, 191
Tromp, Nicholas J., 12n47
Turner, David L., 152n14

U

the underworld. *See* death; Sheol

V

Van Deventer, H. J. M., 25n5
Vanhoozer, Kevin J., 7
Vos, Geerhardus, 108, 111n205

W

Waltke, Bruce K., 12n48, 15n60, 62, 65n49, 118–20
Walton, John H., 12–13, 63n45
waters. *See also* baptism; the flood
   of judgment and death, 73, 75–77, 99 101, 114–16
   of healing and refreshment, 103, 105
Wellum, Stephen J., 25n3
Wenham, Gordon, 15n62, 64n48
Wesselius, Jan-Wim, 149n4
Wheaton, Byron, 66, 76n80, 99, 122

widowhood in the Bible, 53, 55, 81n90, 84, 121
the wilderness, 80–81, 103
Williams, J. G., 112
Williamson, Paul R., 19n82, 93n139, 127n2
Wilson, Robert Dick, 16–18, 142n47
wisdom, 117–19
the Wisdom of Solomon (intertestamental book), 5, 143–45, 147. *See also* the Apocrypha
Witherington, Ben, III, 56n19, 179
Wright, N. T., 1–2, 10, 21, 24, 41, 45, 47, 51n6, 54n12, 67n56, 70, 72, 84n99, 90, 92, 94, 107n187, 110–111, 113, 119n248, 121n253, 126, 129, 136n29, 137, 139–40, 141n44, 142n49, 143–45, 148, 151n12, 160, 169n55, 176n72, 178n78
the Writings
   as a literary corpus in the Tanak, 2, 7, 9, 12, 29n13, 48, 50, 60, 106, 125, 190
   strong evidence of resurrection hope in, 106–14, 190
   supporting evidence of resurrection hope in, 114–24, 190

Y

Yamauchi, Edwin, 21n97, 23n109

Z

Ziegler, Joseph, 33n23
Zimmerli, Walther, 39

Scripture Index

Old Testament

Genesis
1 .... 19, 69, 73, 79
1–2 70
1–3 .... 19, 62
1:1–2:3 69
1:2 69
1:9 69
1:9–10 73
1:9–13 69
1:11 69
1:20–31 73
2 .... 19, 46, 69, 118
2–3 .... 61, 125
2:4 69
2:5 64
2:7 .... 38, 69–70, 95, 171
2:9 .... 60, 117
2:14 .... 30n17
2:15 64
2:17 .... 10, 61
2:21 .... 30, 46
3 ..... 10, 19, 38, 42, 45, 52n9,
 61n38, 62–63, 88
3:6 62
3:15 .... 19, 62–63, 70–71
3:15 (LXX) 70
3:16–19 62
3:17–19 63
3:17b 63
3:18 63
3:19 .... 38–39, 42, 45, 63, 171
3:19a 63
3:22 .... 42, 60–62, 117
3:23–24 10
3:24 .... 41, 62, 117–18
4 71
4:1 70
4:2 70
4:8 70
4:25 70–71
4:25 (LXX) 71
5 .... 10, 72, 101–102
5:22 72
5:23 72
5:24 .... 11, 20, 72, 109–10,
 135
5:29 62–63
6:13 73
7–8 73
7:17–20 73
8:11 73
8:18–19 73
11:30 .... 58, 74
12 .... 52n9
12:1 10
12:1–7 56
12:2–3 .... 52, 64, 74
12:7 .... 67, 74
13:15 67
15 58
15:1 58
15:2–3 58
15:4 64–65
15:5 .... 64, 74
15:12–21 30
15:15 10
15:18 67
16:2 58
17:8 67
17:17 65
18:11–12 65
18:11–13 58
18:14 64
18:14a 65
21:1–3 65
21:1–2 74
21:1–13 .... 65n49
21:2–3 64
21:12 65
22 .... 64, 66
22:2 64
22:3 64
22:5 64
25:8 .... 10, 54, 67n55
25:8–10 10
25:9 67
25:17 .... 67n55

25:21 74	3:5 52	**Deuteronomy**
28 .... 38n55	3:6 .... 51–55, 57, 59, 71	18:15 81
28:14 .... 38n54	3:6–8 52	18:18 81
29:31 74	3:8 .... 57, 78	25:5 58
30:1 58	12 77	25:5–10 53
30:22 74	12:5 77	31–34 134
35:29 .... 10, 54, 67	12:7 77	32 83
37 75	12:23 76–77	32:1–43 68
37:5–8 75	12:29 77	32:3 68
37:24 75	14 78	32:4 83
37:28 75	14:6–9 77	32:4–9 68
37:33 75	14:11 77	32:10–18 68
37:33–35 58	14:13 78	32:15 83
39:1 75	14:21–22 77	32:18 83
39:3–6 75	14:22 77	32:19–22 68
39:11–20 75	14:30 77	32:22 83
39:22–23 75	14:31 77	32:23–24 83
41 75	15:5 77	32:23–27 68
41:25–36 75	15:10 77	32:28–33 68
41:41 75	15:11–13 77	32:34–35 68
41:41–45 75	15:12 77	32:35 83
45:28 75	15:21 77	32:36 83
48:11 58	40 79	32:36–38 68
49:29–30 67	40:35 78–79	32:39 ...... 19, 67–69, 83, 85,
49:31 67	**Leviticus**	97, 120
49:33 ...... 10–11, 54, 67n55	1–7 79	32:40–43 68
50:12–14 11	13 80	32:41–43 83
50:13 67	13:1–17 79	32:50 11
50:24–25 67	13:8 79	**Judges**
Exodus	13:46 79	2:11 100
1:7–8 56	**Numbers**	2:11–19 100
1:10 .... 56, 76	1 80	2:14–15 100
1:11–14 56	12 80	2:18 100
1:16 56	12:12 80	2:19 100
1:22 .... 56, 76	13 80	**Ruth**
2:1–3 76	13:25–33 80	1:1–2 121
2:3 75	14:31–32 80	1:3–5 121
2:5–6 76	16:30–33 13	1:21 122
2:10 .... 75–76, 101, 115	26 80	4 122
2:24 56	27:13 11	4:13 121
3 .... 52–53, 56, 66, 71	31:2 11	4:14 121
3:4 52		4:15 121

SCRIPTURE INDEX

4:17–22 122

1 Samuel
2:1–10 82
2:2 83
2:5 82
2:5b 83
2:6 .... 82–85, 120, 124
2:6a 83–84
2:6b 83
2:8 83
2:8–10 83
2:9–10 83

2 Samuel
22 114
22:5–6 .... 101, 115
22:17 101
22:51 101

1 Kings
17 .... 85–87, 151
17:2 151
17:17–18 84
17:17–24 ..... 87n111, 184n88
17:20 84
17:20–23 84
17:21 84
17:21–22 105
17:22b 84

2 Kings
2:1–18 11
2:3 .... 20, 109–10
2:6 13
2:11 .... 72n72, 101
2:12 101
4 .... 41, 87, 151
4:18–37 .... 87n111, 184n88
4:20–24 86
4:31 .... 38n49, 86, 108
4:31b 86
4:32–33 86
4:34 86
4:34–35 86

4:35 86
13:20 87
13:20–21 87
13:21 .... 38n49, 87, 95, 98
20:1 102
20:5–6 102

1 Chronicles
6:31–32 ...... 20n93, 109n197
6:32 .... 109n201
6:37 .... 20n93, 109n197
6:39 .... 20n93, 109n201

2 Chronicles
36:1–19 123
36:20 124
36:22 124
36:23 123–24

Esther
3:8–9 123
3:13 123
4–7 123
4:11 122
4:16 122
5:1 122
5:1–2 122
5:2 122
8:5 123
8:8 123
8:11 123

Job
1:13–19 120
1:14–15 120
1:16 120
1:17 120
1:18–19 120
2:7 110
3:11–19 .... 113n222
3:13 .... 38n49, 46
5 .... 38n55
5:6 .... 38n54
7:9–10 .... 113n222
7:21 .... 38n50

10:20–22 .... 113n222
14:5 110
14:7 .... 113n223
14:11–12 110
14:12 .... 38n49, 108
14:12–14 112
14:13 112
14:14 .... 113n223
14:14 (LXX) 113
14:14a 110
17:13–16 12
19:17 111
19:18 111
19:19 111
19:25–27 110–12
19:26 .... 110–11, 113
19:26–27 111–12
19:26a (LXX) 113
19:27 111
21:26 .... 38n50
24:19 14
34:15 .... 38n50
42:5 111
42:10 120
42:10–12 121
42:13 120–21
42:17 121

Psalms
1:1 114
1:3 114
1:4 114
1:5 114
6:5 12
9:17 14
13:3 .... 38n49
13:4 46
16 106–7
16:8–11 107
16:9–11 106
16:9–10 .... 20, 107
16:10–11 108
16:11 .... 41, 107

17:1–2 108	73:18–19 109	5:14 14
17:13–14 108	73:23 41	14:9 13
17:15 .... 41, 108	73:24 ....20, 41, 109–10	24 88
18 114	73:27 109	24–27 88
18:1 114	80:4 (Eng. 80:3) 116	24–25 88
18:4–5 12–13	80:7 (Eng. 80:6) 117	24:1 88
18:5–6 (Eng. 18:4–5) 114	80:9–10 (Eng. 80:8–9) ...117	24:3–6 88
18:17 (Eng. 18:16) 114–15	80:13–17 (Eng. 80:12–16)	24:17 88
21:3 41	 117	24:19–20 88
23:1 14	80:17 (Eng. 80:16) 117	25 ....45, 88
28:9 41	80:19 (Eng. 80:18) 116–17	25:8 .... 43, 87–88, 103
30:1–2 116	87:6 (LXX) 46	25:8a 88
30:3 ....12–13, 115–16	89:48 14	26 .... 21–22, 40, 88–89,
30:9 .... 12, 116	104:29 .... 38n50	91, 105n181
31:17 14	109:30 .... 37n44	26–27 .... 88, 91–92
37:18 41	133:3 41	26:1–2 88
37:27–28 41	139:8 ....12, 14	26:3 89
41:12 41	141:7 14	26:7 88
49 ....20n93, 106, 109	**Proverbs**	26:12 89
49:11 (Eng. 49:10) 109	3:17–18 117	26:13 .... 89, 91
49:14 14	3:18 117–19	26:14 .... 21, 88–91, 93,
49:14–15 13–14	5:5 14	114n226
49:15 (Eng. 49:14) 109	7:27 14	26:17–18 91
49:16 (Eng. 49:15) 20, 99,	9:18 14	26:19 ....21, 38n50, 39–41,
109–10	10:25 41	45, 70, 88n114, 89–92,
55:15 12	10:30 41	103, 108, 129, 157n38,
69 .... 43–45, 190	11:30 117	171n60, 175
69:1–3 43	12:28 .... 118, 119n248	27:2–6 91
69:6 43	13:12 117	27:8 91
69:10 (Eng. 69:9) 43	15:4 117	27:9 91
69:11 (Eng. 69:10) 43	15:11 12	27:11 91
69:14–15 43	15:24 120	28:15 14
69:22 43	19:6 .... 37n44	28:18 14
69:24 43	30:15–16 74	35 102–3
69:27 43	**Ecclesiastes**	35:1 103
70 .... 116n231	3:20 ....113n222	35:2 103
70–71 116	9:2–3 119	35:5–7 102–3
71 116	9:5 119	38 102
71:19 116	9:10 ....12, 14	38:10 13
71:20 116	**Isaiah**	38:10–11 102
73 ....20n93, 106, 109	2:2–3 37	38:16–17 102
73:3–12 109		45:23 169

51:17 175	**Daniel**	3:26–27 154
52:1 175	1 .... 26–29, 31, 35n35, 190	3:28 29
53 93	1–11 24	3:30 29
53:4–9 92	1:1 31	4 31
53:7–9 .... 93n139	1:1–2 33	4–5 26
53:10–12 .... 93n140	1:1–7 26	4:1–37 25
53:10–11 92	1:2 29	4:30 31
53:11–12 .... 37n44	1:2–3 31	4:31–32 31
53:12 .... 93n139	1:5 27	4:32–33 31
60:1 175	1:6–7 29	5 31
65:17 104	1:1–21 25	5:1–31 25
65:19–25 104	1:8 27	5:1–4 31
66 .... 104, 105n181	1:10 27	5:5 31
66:12–14 104	1:12 27	5:25–28 31
66:14a 104	1:13 27	5:30 31
66:15–16 104	1:15 .... 27, 29	6 .... 28–29, 31, 35n35
66:22 104	1:20 .... 27, 29	6:1–28 25
66:24 .... 44–45, 104–5,	1:21 18	6:17 31
155n29	2 .... 25, 27, 29, 35n35	6:22–23 31
	2–7 25	6:24 31
Jeremiah	2:1–49 25	6:28 29
31:15 58	2:4b–7:28 33	6:7 28
51 93	2:5 27	6:9–10 28
51:39 ..... 38n49, 46, 93, 108	2:8–9 27	6:13 28
51:48–49 94	2:12 27	6:16 28
51:57 .... 46, 93	2:13 27	6:19–23 28
51:62–64 94	2:17 27	6:22 29
	2:18 .... 30n17	6:26 28
Ezekiel	2:19 27	6:27 28
31:15–16 13	2:21 .... 30n17, 32	7 .... 25–26, 32
36 95	2:31–45 27	7–12 17
36:35 95	2:37–44 32	7:1 17
37 .... 22, 29n13, 47, 78,	2:48 29	7:1–28 25
90n124, 94–96, 98	3 .... 28–29, 31, 35n35	7:11 32
37:1–14 .... 94n144, 132n15	3:1–30 25	7:12–14 32
37:1–2 94	3:22 31	7:13 164
37:3 95	3:5–12 28	7:13–14 180
37:3–6 94	3:6 .... 154n25	8 .... 25–26, 30, 32
37:7–10 94–95	3:15 28	8–10 17
37:10 94–95	3:17–18 28	8–12 25
37:11–12 94	3:19–23 28	8:1 17
37:12–14 .... 157n38	3:25–26 28	8:1–27 25

Reference	Pages
8:1–12:3	25
8:1–12:13	33
8:18	30
8:18–27	30
8:20–25	32
9	26
9:1–27	25
9:2	17, 93
9:27	37n44
10	30
10:1	17
10:1–12:3	1, 25, 26n6
10–12	25
10:4	30n17
10:5–6	30
10:8	30
10:9	30, 48
10:9–11	30
10:10	30
10:11	30
11:2	26n6
11:2–12:3	30
11:32	35
11:33	35, 47
11:34b	35
11:41	47
12	5, 21, 32, 37–38, 40, 47, 134–36, 138–39, 144, 147, 149n6, 151, 157n36, 170, 176–77, 188n101, 190
12:1	35, 135
12:1–2	162
12:1–3	135, 139n36, 142n49, 148, 171n59
12:2	1–2, 4–8, 15, 19, 21–24, 26, 29–48, 50, 70, 76, 86, 89, 91, 105–6, 108, 125–38, 140–41, 143, 145–69, 171–91
12:2 (LXX)	46
12:2 (OG)	146, 153, 156, 168, 171
12:2 (Th)	151, 153, 156, 157, 160, 168, 171, 178
12:2–3	26, 28, 88, 118, 140, 170, 173, 176, 180
12:2–3 (Th)	155, 166
12:3	26n6, 127, 130, 135, 137–38, 139n37, 140, 144, 147, 149, 154–55, 160, 172, 176–78
12:3 (OG)	177
12:4	26n6
12:4–13	25–26
12:5–8	17
12:8	26n6
12:9–13	26n6
12:13	26, 37, 48, 160

Hosea

Reference	Pages
5:11–14	96
6	22, 78, 98, 105
6:1–3	97n155
6:1	97
6:2	21, 92, 96–98
6:2–3	105
6:3	91, 97
6:4	96
13	98
13–14	91–92
13:4	91
13:7–8	98
13:13	91
13:14	91, 98–99, 109
13:14a–b	98
13:15	91
14	105
14:2–4 (Eng. 14:1–3)	105
14:4	105
14:5–6	91
14:6 (Eng. 14:5)	91
14:6–8 (Eng. 14:5–7)	91, 105
14:8 (Eng. 14:7)	105
14:9 (Eng. 14:8)	91
14:10 (Eng. 14:9)	91

Jonah

Reference	Pages
1:2–3	99
1:4–6	99
1:11–12	99
1:15	99
2:1 (Eng. 1:17)	99
2:2	13
2:3 (Eng. 2:2)	99
2:7 (Eng. 2:6)	99
2:11 (Eng. 2:10)	99

Habakkuk

Reference	Pages
2:5	12

New Testament

Matthew

Reference	Pages
5–7	149
5:27–30	150
5:29–30	149–50, 154–55
9	151
9:18	150, 151n11
9:24	150
9:24–25	150–51
9:25	150
10:28	152–55
11:5	151n11
12	153, 159
12:38–39	153
12:39–40	153
12:40	100
12:41	153
12:41–42	153, 159
12:42	153

13 153
13:40 154
13:40–43 154
13:42 154
13:42a 154
13:43 .... 153, 155
18:8 155
18:8–9 155
22 .... 54n13, 58–60, 66
22:23 .... 51, 53
22:23–28 51
22:24–28 53
22:24–25 55
22:24 58
22:26 55
22:29 .... 55, 60
22:30 53
22:31–32 .... 51, 53
22:32 71
22:32b 53, 55
22:34 51
23:35 9
24:15 17
25:31–33 .... 156, 181
25:32–33 173
25:32 156
25:41 156
25:46 ..... 148n3, 155–56, 174
27 157
27:50–51 156
27:51–53 .... 157n33
27:52 .... 148n3
27:52b 157
27:52–53 156–57

Mark
5:38–39 158
5:39–41 158
5:41 158–59
5:41–42 158
5:42 158
9:43–48 158
9:43–47 159

12:27a 54n12

Luke
8:52 159
8:52–55 159
8:53–54 159
8:55 159
8:55a 159
11 159
11:31–32 159–60
14:12 160
14:13–14 160
14:14 160
15 58
15:32 58
24:44 9

John
5:9 161
5:17–18 161
5:20 161
5:22 164
5:24 .... 148n3, 161, 178
5:24–29 .... 162n47
5:25 162
5:25–29 161
5:28–29 .... 161, 164, 187
5:29 ...... 148n3, 161, 162n44,
168, 173–74
11:6 162
11:14–15 162
11:21–22 162
11:23 162
11:24 162

Acts
2:24 .... 107, 163
2:25–31 20
2:25–28 107
3 81
3:15 .... 81, 163
3:22–23 81
3:26 81
4:10 163

5:30 163
10 185
10:23–33 163
10:35 163
10:36–38 163
10:39–40 164
10:41 163
10:42 .... 163–64, 185
13:30 163
17:16 164
17:24–28 164
17:30 165
17:30–31 164
17:31 163–64
17:32 165
21 165
23 165
23:6 .... 165–66, 179
23:7 165
23:8 .... 51, 53, 165
23:11–12 166
24:13 166
24:14–15 .... 51, 82, 166
24:15 .... 148n3, 165–66,
170, 179
25:19 165
26:8 165
26:22–23 165

Romans
1:18–3:20 167
2 168
2:3–4 167
2:5 168
2:5–10 .... 167–68, 174, 181
2:7 168
2:7–8 168
2:8 168
2:8–9 .... 168, 174
2:9 168
2:10 .... 168, 174
4:17 74
4:19 74

4:21 74	2:20 173	5:14 182
14:3-4 169	6:7-10 174	6:1-2 182-83
14:5-6 169	6:8 174	6:2 .... 182, 183n86
14:7-9 169	**Ephesians**	9:27 .... 183n87
14:9 169	2:5-6 175	11 66
14:10 169	5:11-14 175	11:5a 72
14:10-12 169	5:14 175-76	11:5b 72
1 Corinthians	5:14-15 176	11:11-12 74
15 181	5:15 176	11:13 183
15:20-21 179	**Philippians**	11:17-19 .... 65n49
15:25-26 187	2:1-11 176	11:19 .... 65-66, 76
15:35 170	2:14-16 177	11:22 67
15:37-38 169	2:15 177	11:26b 183
15:39 170	2:16 177	11:35 183-84
15:40-43 170	2:16a 177	11:35-38 184
15:40-41 169	3:7-11 176	**1 Peter**
15:42 88	3:11 179	1:6-9 185
15:43a 170-71	3:17-21 178-79	3:20-21 73
15:43b-44 171	3:19 178	4:5 185
15:51-52 171	3:19-21 178	4:6 185
15:51b 171	3:21 178	**1 John**
15:54-55 88	**1 Thessalonians**	3:12 71
15:54b 43	4 181	**Revelation**
2 Corinthians	4:13 179	20 186-87
4-5 171	4:13-16 179	20:2 186
4:8-9 171	4:14 180	20:3 186
4:16 172	4:15 180	20:4 186
4:16-18 172	4:16 180	20:4-6 186
4:17 .... 172, 184	5:10 46	20:5 186
4:17-18 171-72	**2 Thessalonians**	20:6 186
4:18 172	1:5-10 180-81	20:7 186
5:1 172	1:8-9 .... 181n82	20:11-15 186
5:1-10 172	1:9 181	20:12 186
5:1-4 172	1:9-10 180	20:12-15 .... 186n96
5:2 172	**2 Timothy**	20:13 187
5:5-9 172	4:1 .... 181, 187	20:14 187
5:10 .... 172-74, 181	4:2 181	20:15 187
5:11 172	**Hebrews**	22:2 61
Galatians	5:12-13 182	22:2b 61
1:1 173		

Other Ancient Witnesses

1 Enoch
22 .... 40n64
51 136
51:1-2 136
62 136
62:1-3 136
62:9 137
62:10-11 137
62:13-16 137
62:14 137
62:14-15 136
62:16 137
91:4 137
91:5-6 137
91:7 137
91:8-9 137
91:10 .... 137, 179
91:10-11 137
91:14 137
92:3 179
104 .... 138, 139n36
104:1 138
104:1-4 139
104:2 .... 138, 139n37
108 140
108:11 139
108:11-15 139
108:13 139

2 Maccabees
7 .... 145n62, 184
7:1-42 145
7:9 .... 145, 184
7:11 184
7:14 .... 146, 184
7:22-23 184
7:29 184
12:44-45 179

The Apocalypse of Moses
13:1 133
13:2-6 133
13:3 133
13:3-4 133
41:1-3 134
41:2-3 134
41:3 134

Jubilees
23:16-31 128
23:30 128-29
23:30-31 128-29
23:31 129
36:9-10 129

Mishnah Sanhedrin
10:1 52

Psalms of Solomon
3 131
3:3-7 131
3:5 130
3:9-11 131
3:9-12 130-31
3:10-11 130
3:11-12 130
3:11-12a 131
3:12 130-31
3:12b 131
15 131
15:6-7 131
15:8 131
15:8-12 131
15:8-13 131
15:10-13 131
15:12-13 130
15:12 131
15:13 131
15:13a 131

The Sibylline Oracles
4:179-92 132
4:181-90 131
4:181 132
4:182 132
4:183-84 132
4:187-90 132
4:190-91 132

The Testament of Moses
8:1 135
10:3 134
10:4-6 134
10:7 134
10:8 134
10:9 134-35
10:9-10 134

The Testaments of the Twelve Patriarchs
T. Benj. 10:2-10 142
T. Benj. 10:6-8 141
T. Benj. 10:7-8 142
T. Benj. 10:8 ..... 142, 170-71
T. Iss. 7:9 179
T. Jud. 25:1 140
T. Jud. 25:3-4 140
T. Jud. 25:4 179
T. Zeb. 10:1-4 141
T. Zeb. 10:2 141

The Wisdom of Solomon
2:20 144
3:1-2 144
3:1-4 144-45
3:1-10 .... 144n55
3:3-4 144
3:5-6 144
3:7 .... 144n56, 145
3:7-10 144
3:10 145
3:13 144
4:15 144
14:11 144
19:15 144

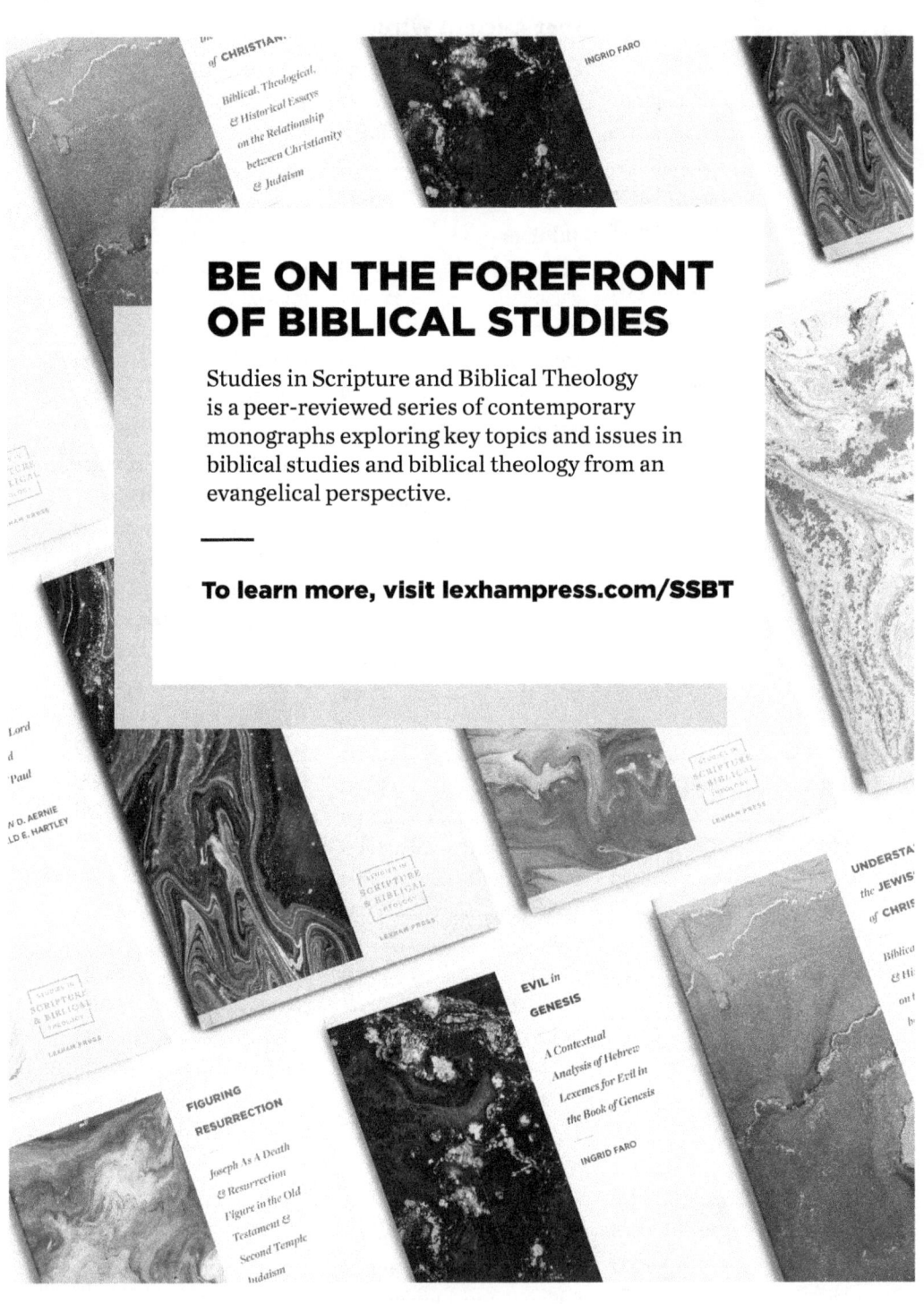